ADIN BALLOU

ADIN BALLOU (1803-1890) grew up on a farm in Cumberland, Rhode Island. When he was 11 his family was converted by the Christian Connexion, under whose auspices he began preaching at age 18. Shortly afterward he converted to Universalism. He served as Universalist minister in New York City and in Milford, Massachusetts, 1824-31. In 1831 he was one of a group of Universalists who seceded to form their own denomination, the Massachusetts Association of Universal Restorationists. While serving a Unitarian church in Mendon, Massachusetts, 1831-1842, he was for nearly a decade a leader of the Restorationist movement.

During the 1830s Ballou became increasingly interested in reform causes, notably temperance and abolitionism. In 1838 he was converted to the cause of peace and Christian non-resistance. His promotion of social causes was a major factor in the breakup of the Restorationists in 1839. In 1842 he organized Fraternal Community No. 1 (later called the Hopedale Community) in Hopedale, Massachusetts. This community, founded on non-resistant principles, repudiated participation in any government that relied upon ultimate recourse to coercive force. The people of Hopedale experimented with various forms of socialism, rejecting pure communism and eventually adopting a joint-stock constitution. The community survived and largely prospered for 14 years before the largest shareholders engineered its sudden collapse in 1856 and converted the community into a company town.

During the Hopedale years Ballou edited the community's newspaper, the *Practical Christian*, and wrote his major works, *Christian Non-Resistance* (1846) and *Practical Christian Socialism* (1854). During the Civil War he was nearly alone among abolitionists in maintaining his pacifist principles. He remained in Hopedale as minister of the Unitarian church, retiring in 1880. Late in life he wrote a number of historical books including the *History of the Hopedale Community*, *History of the Town of Milford*, and his *Autobiography*. In the last year of his life he corresponded with Leo Tolstoy, upon whom Ballou's exposition of Christian non-resistance had a great influence.

ADIN BALLOU

Practical Christianity

An Epitome of *Practical Christian Socialism*

Edited and arranged by Lynn Gordon Hughes

 Blackstone Editions
Providence

Blackstone Editions, Providence, Rhode Island 02906
© 2002 by Lynn Gordon Hughes
All rights reserved. Published 2002
Reprinted 2009
Printed in the United States of America

ISBN 978-0-9725017-0-5

To the Friends of Adin Ballou

Nation shall not lift up sword against nation,
neither shall they learn war any more;
but they shall sit every man under his vine and under his fig tree,
and none shall make them afraid.
Micah 4:3-4

Contents

Adin Ballou and the
Hopedale Community

UTOPIAN EXPERIMENTS have always been part of the American scene, but between 1841 and 1845 experimental communities were founded at a much greater rate than at any time before or since. As Ralph Waldo Emerson famously wrote to Thomas Carlyle, "We are all a little wild here with numerous projects of social reform. Not a reading man but has a draft of a new community in his waistcoat pocket."

Once the United States itself had been a utopian enterprise. By the 1840s, however, it was clear that the great days of nation-building were over. The impulse to draft constitutions for ideal societies was in part an expression of regret for the passing of the Revolutionary era. It was also a response to a reality painfully at odds with the ideals of freedom and equality. Social stratification, rigid gender roles, and, especially, the great contradiction of slavery in the land of the free, fed a widespread perception that something had gone badly wrong. Yet the discontent was balanced by an almost limitless belief in the possibilities for change. Much of the energy that went into social reform derived from the peculiar nature of American religion: no staid state church, but a shifting kaleidoscope of new sects and movements, each stridently proclaiming its version of the true gospel.

Much of the interest in communitarianism was inspired by the ideas of the French utopian socialist Charles Fourier. Between 1841 and 1845, at least forty new experimental communities were founded, including some two dozen Fourierist communities, or "phalanxes." Fourier's work captured the public imagination not so much because of his utopian vision, which was eccentric to say the least, but because of his passionate critique of industrialism. Communities such as Hopedale, Brook Farm, and the Fourierist phalanxes were intended not as a refuge for their members, but as prototypes for a new and better form of social organization.

The Hopedale Community had its genesis in a document called the "Standard of Practical Christianity."* The Standard was composed in 1839 by Adin Ballou and signed by four of his ministerial colleagues and two lay persons. They were members of the Massachusetts Association of Universal Restorationists (MAUR), a small sect that had seceded from the Universalist denomination eight years before. Ballou had been one of the principal organizers of the association, and was deeply committed to its success. He edited its newspaper, lectured in its behalf, championed its cause in debates both written and oral, preached at installations and annual meetings, and supervised the training of ministerial students.

At the same time, Ballou was becoming more and more interested in social reform. He first adopted the temperance reform, a relatively popular cause that was embraced by many of his Restorationist colleagues. In 1837 he declared himself an abolitionist. This was a more controversial stand, for many who disapproved of slavery were nonetheless horrified by the willingness shown by the more radical abolitionists to dissolve the Union over the issue. When Ballou introduced resolutions on Total Abstinence, Anti-Slavery, and Moral Reform at the annual meeting of the MAUR in 1837, he later wrote, "a very unpleasant discussion followed." Eventually the group agreed to allow those members who wished to sign the resolutions to do so, without committing the organization as a whole.[1]

This experience led Ballou to fear the worst when he espoused an even more unpopular cause, a radical form of pacifism called Christian Non-Resistance. As a Non-Resistant, he felt called to withdraw, so far as was possible, from participation in local, state, and national government, on the ground that all government was ultimately based on coercive power. In the Standard of Practical Christianity he wrote, "We can take no part in the politics, the administration, or the defense of those governments, either by voting at their polls, holding their offices, aiding in the execution of their legal vengeance, fighting under their banners, claiming their protection against violence, seeking redress in their courts, petitioning their legislatures to enact laws, or obeying their unrighteous requirements."

---

* Appendix A

The Standard was presented at the annual meeting of the MAUR in 1839, and met the expected response. The more conservative members, Ballou wrote, "gave us up as impracticable fanatics, with whom they could go no further."

> I knew that I was largely responsible for what so disaffected and disappointed them. It was strange almost to myself that it was so – that I, who had devoted myself so ardently to the cause represented by that association ... should have come to be so transcendentally interested in moral reform, even to the extreme of social reorganization, that I was ready to give that body up or let it cease to be.[2]

Without the driving force of Ballou and his reform-minded colleagues, the MAUR ceased to be a viable organization. The 1840 annual meeting turned out to be the last ever held.

Ballou and his associates founded a newspaper, the *Practical Christian*, to promote their ideas about social reform. In September 1840 he wrote an editorial urging the formation of a community dedicated to Practical Christian ideals. By January 1841 he had drafted a constitution and recruited about thirty members for "Fraternal Community No. 1." That summer he purchased for the organization a 250-acre farm in Milford, Massachusetts, which he christened "Hopedale."

In March 1842, Ballou resigned his pastorate and moved, with his wife, two children, and twenty-four other men, women, and children, into the old farmhouse. "We boarded at common tables and lodged in small but distinct apartments, too small and cluttered for comfort, yet passably endurable," he recalled. "Our faith, hope, and zeal enabled us to bear many privations, inconveniences, trials, vexations, disgusts, with reasonable patience and composure."[3] They began farming the first summer, but found almost immediately that a mechanics' shop, utilizing the water power of the Mill River which ran through the property, was a more important source of sustenance. Unlike the Transcendentalist communitarians at Brook Farm and Fruitlands, the Practical Christians entertained no back-to-the-land romanticism, but participated enthusiastically in the industrial economy from the start.

The community struggled in its first years. There was too little money, too small and cramped a dwelling place, too large an influx of indigent members. As Ballou later admitted, "My hope was too large and my economic judgment too small." The people attracted to the Standard of Practical Christianity tended to be of a stubborn and self-righteous bent, and the community's leaders had a hard time of it, adjudicating disputes arising from "some peculiarity of judgment, idiosyncratic opinion, or question of expediency exalted into the place of a supposed ethical principle."[4]

A persistent source of tension was the balance between communal ownership and private property. The community was organized as a joint-stock company, in which members, and some non-members, owned varying numbers of shares. Some years the enterprise prospered; other years it operated at a loss, which had to be made up by loans and donations from the wealthier members. Although in theory large and small shareholders participated equally in community decision-making, some of the poorer members felt that the inequality in the ownership fostered an "aristocratic spirit." Those who contributed most, whether of capital, labor, care, or responsibility, resented members who did less, yet shared equally in community property. A complicated system of record-keeping, "wheels succeeding wheels and wheels within wheels" designed to ensure that every member was doing a fair amount of work, only increased resentment and distrust.[5]

Five years after its founding, its funds at low ebb and its members demoralized, the community was on the brink of dissolution. It emerged from the crisis with a new, simplified constitution and a complete reorganization of the economy along more individualistic lines. The printing press, shoemaking shop, stables, medical practice, and several other small businesses were sold back to the members who had brought them into the community. The machine shop, sawmill, and mechanic shop were leased to groups of residents. On the whole the community found that the benefits of rewarding the most hard-working and productive members outweighed the risks of inequality. The system which evolved came to be more like social democracy than like communism: private ownership was allowed and individual initiative was rewarded, but a basic minimum standard of living was guaranteed for all. The community owned all of the land and public buildings; operated the farm and store; provided employment for all who were able to work, and care for those who could not; and served the members as a savings bank and a fire and casualty insurance company. In return all able-bodied men, women, and children served in the "Industrial Army" (the name was later changed to the less bellicose "Industrial Union") whose duties included caring for the sick, maintaining roads and sidewalks, and landscaping public spaces.

Out of the crisis and the arduous process of reaching consensus came a more realistic appreciation of the difficulty of creating a truly just society, even on a small scale. Setting aside the "over-confident comprehensiveness" that had led them to call their venture "Fraternal Community No. 1," the members agreed that "it were the part of wisdom to be more modest in our pretensions and claims ... and with our none too large equipment of moral and spiritual ammunition, to confine our ambition and our efforts for the present to our own single experiment."[6] Accordingly they rebaptized themselves with a new, more homely name, "The Hopedale Community."

The community continued to tinker with its economic arrangements, "steering the vessel of our social system," as Ballou put it, "between the Scylla of organic arrangements and the Charybdis of individual license."[7] With practice the members also learned to disagree without endangering the cohesiveness of the community. The daughter of a Hopedale family recalled that the fads and foibles of the grown-up people made Community meetings "a 'continuous performance' of vast entertainment." In endless discussion of the pros and cons of smoking, shaving, vegetarianism, and spiritualism, "neither party convinced the other, but the war of words afforded a certain relief to strenuous natures who, as good non-resistants could indulge in no other form of warfare."[8] The experiment proved more successful as time went on. Experience had tempered the extravagant expectations of the early days, but left the vision largely intact.

In their concern with perfecting their social system, the members of the community did not forget their commitment to moral reform in the world outside Hopedale. They were particularly active in the antislavery cause. The annual "Anti-Slavery Picnic" drew hundreds to hear such prominent speakers as William Lloyd Garrison, Frederick Douglass, and Sojourner Truth. The community sheltered escaping slaves, sometimes for a day or two, sometimes for months. Women's rights activists Lucy Stone and Abby Kelley Foster spoke at Hopedale, and on one occasion "twenty-five women, all clad in bloomers, went in a barge to Worcester to attend a Women's Rights Convention."[9] Abby Hills Price, Hopedale's resident poet and most outspoken women's rights advocate, spoke at the convention. Public meetings on reform topics were held weekly, as were Lyceum lectures and classes in such subjects as chemistry, botany, and philosophy. Both black and white children, including children of abolitionists William Lloyd Garrison and Samuel J. May, attended the Hopedale Home School. The Home School, like the public library and the Lyceum, survived the breakup of the community proper.

By 1852 Hopedale had been so successful in overcoming its early challenges that Ballou felt able to step down as president, "trusting that all would go well with another at the helm to direct our richly-freighted bark." He was succeeded as president by Ebenezer D. Draper, the community's treasurer and largest shareholder, a charter member and Ballou's long-time trusted friend. Ballou turned his attention from the day-to-day management of community affairs to the task of extending "our excellent social system … to the ends of the earth" by speaking, writing and publishing, expanding and improving the Hopedale schools, and eventually, he hoped, by initiating new communities.[10]

Practical Christian Socialism was written as part of this effort to spread the gospel of Practical Christianity. At the time of its composition, in early 1854, the community was in what Ballou called "the palmiest period of its history." President Draper reported at the 1854 annual meeting, "We do not think that the Community for a long time has exhibited … so much unity, kindliness and good feeling."[11] Ballou's son-in-law, William Heywood, reported in the *Practical Christian* that there had been no recent withdrawals, and a good number of prospective members. The community was building new streets and houses, a large barn, an addition to the school. A new chapel, "more commodious and imposing" than the old, was planned. The Agricultural Branch, consisting of a nursery, orchard, and vegetable gardens, was in "a remarkably prosperous and hopeful state." The Machine Branch, which made tools and machine parts, had more orders than it could fill. And if the market for boots and shoes was "dull," it was made up for by the brisk demand for Hopedale soap.[12] People in Pennsylvania, Wisconsin, and Ohio expressed interest in forming communities similar to Hopedale. This gave Ballou the impetus to develop a plan for a "Practical Christian Republic," or union of communities, which he set forth in *Practical Christian Socialism*. Unlike the naïve overconfidence of Fraternal Community No. 1, the Practical Christian Republic was based on a solid foundation of twelve years' experience of communal living. Under the circumstances, Ballou can perhaps be pardoned for the smug tone that occasionally crept into his writing:

> All classes of readers are respectfully entreated to examine the Work patiently, carefully and thoroughly, before passing judgment for or against it. Many of its doctrines, ideas and views will at first seem strange to the majority of minds … Yet, if they will candidly peruse the whole volume, and take ample time for reflection, they will probably be convinced that nearly all the author's positions are impregnable … Its leading conceptions and ideas are large, generous, sublime and magnificent, without being fanciful, romantic, extravagant, unreal and impracticable. (pp. 2-3)

The Hopedale experiment came to an end, quite suddenly, in the spring of 1856. The key actor in the drama was Ebenezer Draper. As one of the community's wealthiest and most generous members, Draper had repeatedly been called upon to lend the community money, or to make up a deficit by buying additional shares in the joint stock company. By this means he had, almost by accident, acquired a controlling interest in the community's assets.

The source of the Draper family's wealth was the patent on the self-acting temple, a device invented by Ebenezer Draper's father to regulate the extension of cloth on a power loom, allowing for more efficient weaving. In 1853, Ebenezer entered into a partnership with his brother George to manufacture the temple at Hopedale. Though he had "only dubious faith in Community life," George joined the community and quickly became one of its major shareholders.[13] In 1855 he brought into the business (and into the community) Warren Dutcher of Vermont, who held the patent on an improved version of the loom temple. With Dutcher as a partner instead of a rival, the Drapers' business was in a position to become much more profitable. This could not happen, however, within the confines of the community, with its restricted, carefully screened work force, its standard rate of pay for all hands, and its limitation of profit to four percent.

The Drapers made their move at the annual meeting in February 1856, by calling attention to the fact that the community had never taken into account depreciation when determining the value of its assets. "A shrewd business man or an expert on finance," Adin Ballou wrote, "could easily see by looking over the situation, that the Community liabilities actually exceeded its assets by several thousand dollars." There is little doubt as to the identity of the shrewd businessman who brought to light this defect in Hopedale's accounting system. "Bro. George Draper," it seemed, "was becoming weary of Community financiering, especially when his capital was involved and when it blocked the way of his money-making ambition."[14] Ebenezer, whatever his feelings about Community financiering, was not in a position to save the situation. His money was tied up in the loom temple business; he was dependent upon his brother, just as Hopedale was dependent upon him.

With good will all around, the community could have survived the crisis, as they had survived economic setbacks before. But if there had been good will all around, the crisis would never have arisen. The community's leaders, never very sophisticated financially, reacted with bewilderment – had they done something improper or, worse, dishonest? Unable to determine precisely where the fault lay, the leaders wrangled amongst themselves and finally allowed themselves to be convinced that the entire economic system was fatally flawed and unworkable. When Ebenezer Draper joined his brother in withdrawing his capital from the common treasury, the community's doom was sealed. "My distress and mortification at this issue of our Community enterprise – at this overthrow of my most cherished hopes and plans for the regeneration and progress of individual and social humanity, were inexpressible – almost unendurable." Ballou wrote. "I felt like one prematurely consigned to a tomb."[15]

The great experiment in Practical Christianity was over. Under the benevolent dictatorship of the Drapers, Hopedale became a different kind of Utopia, a model industrial town.[16] Adin Ballou received a pension from the Draper brothers, and served as pastor of the Hopedale church (affiliated with the American Unitarian Association and renamed Hopedale Unitarian Parish) until his retirement in 1880. He remained active in reform causes, especially in the peace movement. In later years he found comfort in the belief that Hopedale failed because the world was not yet ready for it.

> In the wisdom of God all is for the best, and nothing true and good is forever lost. The final verdict is not rendered yet, and my case and cause are adjourned to a more auspicious future. Times and generations are coming that will justly estimate me and my work, and assign both to their proper place in the providential plan for the progress and redemption of humanity. For them, as it has proved, have I lived and labored, rather than for my contemporaries.[17]

ABIGAIL ALCOTT, searching for a community to join after the failure of the Alcotts' communal experiment at Fruitlands, recorded in her journal, "At Hopedale I could find nothing higher than living quiet inoffensive lives and aiding all the moral reforms by going into the world and lecturing."[18] These accomplishments are not to be despised. Of the forty utopian communities founded between 1841 and 1845, only four – Hopedale among them – survived for more than eight years. Seventeen failed within the first two years. Most of them collapsed due to some combination of dissension, bankruptcy, and inability to supply their members' basic needs for food and shelter. A previous spate of new communities, inspired by the ideas of Robert Owen in the 1820s, had fared even worse: none of them, including Owen's own New Harmony, lasted more than three years.[19] The dismal record of most "utopian" communities highlights the achievement of the Hopedale community in remaining united for a period of fourteen years. It is particularly impressive that it was able to do this without relying on authoritarian rule by a charismatic leader. The only comparable success was North American Phalanx in Monmouth County, New Jersey, the longest-lived of the Fourierist communities.

At the root of the Hopedale system lay an inherent contradiction: the desire to remain uncontaminated by the evils of the outside world while actively participating in it as buyer and seller, teacher, evangelist and moral exemplar. The Standard of Practical Christianity proclaimed "All that we are and have, with all that God shall ever bestow upon us, we unreservedly dedicate to the cause of universal righteousness," while at the same time "expecting for ourselves in the order of divine providence ... a comfortable subsistence until death." The Standard did not admit that these two goals could be in conflict, or specify which would take precedence if they were. The same criticism has been made of Ballou's pacifism: in arguing for the tactical superiority of non-resistance as opposed to violence, he failed to face squarely the fact that principled refusal to use force sometimes demands self-sacrifice.[20] Protected, in spite of themselves, by the laws of the United States and the Commonwealth of Massachusetts, contained within the orderly and law-abiding town of Milford, the people of Hopedale were never threatened with anything worse than an attempted burglary and the theft of a few chickens. They did not have to confront the full implications of their non-resistant stand, or develop workable alternatives to the "sword-sustained" governments they rejected.

Like their businesses, the domestic arrangements of the people of Hopedale became less communal as time went on. In the earliest days of the Hopedale community, the members "were all domiciled under one roof, lived as one family, stocked a common larder, spread and sat at a common table, ... [and] placed our children under common regulations and restraints." Lucy Ballou was elected "Director of Housekeeping," while Adin became "the governing father of the younger members of the household."[21] After eight months of this life, the community adopted a new constitution which allowed members to build, own, and occupy private family dwellings.

In theory, Hopedale stood for complete equality between men and women. Within the community, women could vote and hold office. (Hopedale's non-resistant principles barred both sexes from political participation outside the community.) Ballou's writings on marriage are completely egalitarian. In *Practical Christian Socialism* he wrote, "I mean by companionship in marriage a mutually respectful, cordial, confidential, coequal intimacy – the relationship of real companions, as distinguished from that of master and slave, ruler and subject, numeral and cipher, proprietor and property, superior and inferior" (pp. 212-213). But the move from the unitary household to individual family dwellings was a move in the direction of a conventional gender-based division of labor. In a series of articles in the *Practical Christian* in 1852 and 1853, Abby Hills Price asked the community to reconsider the rejection of the communal household. "Without some practical reformation in housekeeping," she wrote, "woman's elevation must advance but slowly. Indeed, can it advance at all with such a load of care for petty detail resting upon her?"[22] But the hoped-for reformation never came, and Hopedale's commitment to gender equality remained more theoretical than actual.

Hopedale was never a paradise, nor was it the embodiment of an abstract social theory. It was a fluid, contingent, improvisational communal creation, always on the brink of triumph or disaster. It outlasted almost all other contemporary experiments because it was flexible rather than doctrinaire, democratic rather than authoritarian, accepting of compromise and imperfection – in a word, *practical*. It did not succeed in re-making society, but did succeed in giving its members both a reasonable standard of living and a meaningful life, while doing some good in the surrounding world.

One woman who lived in Hopedale as a child, recalling the fugitive slaves the community had helped and sheltered, wrote, "There can be no doubt that the early inhabitants of Hopedale were earnest and conscientious in their devotion to convictions of duty, whatever its cost and penalties." Another wrote that at Hopedale "what may seem plain and prosaic village life [was] beautiful in its round and noble in its outlook."[23] Most of us would be happy to be able to say as much of the communities we live in. Hopedale continues to capture the imagination because, more than most of its rivals, it holds up before us a goal lofty enough to be inspiring, and modest enough to be achievable.

Notes

[1] Adin Ballou, *Autobiography of Adin Ballou* (Lowell, MA, 1896), 291-293.

[2] Ballou, *Autobiography*, 331-332.

[3] Ballou, *Autobiography*, 331.

[4] Ballou, *Autobiography*, 342, 344-345.

[5] Adin Ballou, *History of the Hopedale Community* (Lowell, MA, 1897), 155.

[6] Ballou, *History of Hopedale*, 170-171.

[7] Ballou, *Autobiography*, 358.

[8] Sarah E. Bradbury, "Community Life as Seen by One of the 'Young People,'" in *Hopedale Reminiscences* (Hopedale, 1910), 12-13.

[9] Ida D. Smith, "Recollections of Hopedale" in *Hopedale Reminiscences*, 29.

[10] Ballou, *History of Hopedale*, 224, 228.

[11] Ballou, *History of Hopedale*, 253, 251.

[12] Ballou, *History of Hopedale*, 254-256.

[13] Ballou, *Autobiography*, 401-402.

[14] Ballou, *History of Hopedale*, 287.

[15] Ballou, *Autobiography*, 403.

[16] See John S. Garner, *The Model Company Town* (Amherst: University of Massachusetts Press, 1984).

[17] Ballou, *Autobiography*, vii.

[18] *The Journals of Bronson Alcott* (Boston: Little. Brown and Co., 1938), 17.

[19] Foster Stockwell, *Encyclopedia of American Communes, 1663-1963* (Jefferson, NC: McFarland & Company, Inc., 1998).

[20] Peter Brock, "The Pacifism of Adin Ballou" in *Freedom From War: Nonsectarian Pacifism 1814-1914* (Toronto: University of Toronto Press, 1991), 91-99.

[21] Ballou, *History of Hopedale*, 72.

[22] Abby H. Price, "Combined Household," *Practical Christian*, 20 Nov. 1852.

[23] Anna Thwing Field, "Anti-Slavery and Other Visitors to the Community," in *Hopedale Reminiscences*, 25; Ellen Patrick, "Our Community School and its Teacher," in *Hopedale Reminiscences*, 39.

Practical Christianity and Practical Christian Socialism

PRACTICAL CHRISTIANITY is an edited and arranged version of Adin Ballou's *Practical Christian Socialism*, first published in 1854. It is intended as an accessible introduction to Ballou's theological and social thought. My aim has been to make the work shorter and more accessible without compromising the integrity of Ballou's ideas or style of expression.

Practical Christian Socialism consists of three parts. In Part I, "Fundamental Principles," Ballou laid the groundwork for his Christian socialism by setting forth his understanding of the Christian religion. This is the clearest and most complete statement Ballou ever made of his personal theology. Part II, "Constitutional Polity," presents and discusses the proposed constitution of the Practical Christian Republic. In Part III, "Superiority to Other Systems," Ballou compared Practical Christian Socialism to competing varieties of utopian socialism, including those of Charles Fourier, Robert Owen, the Oneida Community, and the Shakers.

Practical Christianity also consists of three parts, but not exactly the same three. This edition does not include Ballou's Part III, which is part of an argument that has long since run its course. Whereas in 1854 Ballou could elucidate his program by comparing it with what were then popular movements, today's readers cannot be expected to bring this background with them. Fortunately, the most dated part of the book is also the least essential. Omitting it allows the focus to remain on the power of Ballou's ideas and their continuing relevance to the state of American society in the twenty-first century. The subject of how to live a life of "holiness and happiness" in an unregenerate world is as timely now as it was in 1854.

I have divided Ballou's Part II into two sections. "The Practical Christian Republic" contains Ballou's reflections on the experience of twelve years of large and small adjustments to the constitution of the Hopedale community, and looks forward to a time when Hopedale would be just one of many similar communities. This section deals with such matters as the objects and principles of a Practical Christian community, terms of membership, ownership of property, and methods of discipline and decision-making. The final section, which I have called "Education for Practical Christianity," is ostensibly a commentary on the articles of the constitution dealing with education and marriage. In fact, it is something quite different: a comprehensive vision of the well-lived life. The intimate topics it addresses – marriage, sexuality, child-rearing, mental and physical health – do not depend on the existence of Practical Christian communities, or any other specific social and political institutions.

For this reason I have dropped the word "socialism" from the title of this book. In our time, the term inevitably conjures up images of a very specific set of social and political structures, remote from any that Ballou would have had in mind. The events of the past 150 years have made it all but impossible to recover the comprehensive sense in which Ballou understood the word:

> Individuals can realize their highest good only when rightly associated. In true association all the essential interests of individuals and families will be harmonized. Such a harmonic order of Society is possible here on earth, and ought to be instituted. This is Socialism. It is a Theory of Society. All who embrace this Social Theory are Socialists. (p. 9)

Even in Ballou's sense, the term "socialism" hardly does justice to a book which ranges from the loftiest abstractions of theology and political theory to detailed instructions concerning dress, diet, work, and recreation. The only comparable work I can think of, in its combination of visionary social theory with minute particulars of daily life, is Rousseau's *Emile, ou l'Education.* "Practical Christianity" is an accurate title for a book which explores what would happen if the "essential divine principles" of the Christian religion, introduced in Part I, were "heartily embraced, and reduced to practice" (p.14).

BALLOU IS often considered, and tended to consider himself, an idealist, and it is true that he looked forward to a day when human nature and society would be perfect. Yet he was also a realist, with a shrewd appreciation of the pitfalls on the road to perfection. To the Charitive Circle – his term for those community members specially devoted to "the reformation, elevation, improvement and welfare of the world's suffering classes" – he offered this hard-headed advice:

Expend most of your energies on those whom you can induce to *help themselves*. It is of little use to feed idleness and vice ... Actual distress ought to be relieved, at least in its crises; but I have seen so much of that sort of charity which pumps itself out of breath to keep filthy ships from sinking, all their leaks still left unstopped, that I sincerely hope the Charitive Circle will not exhaust its energies in such fruitless labors. (pp. 133-134)

Some of his observations are startling in their modernity: "The almost universal watchword in the market place is, Look out for number one" (p. 75). Or consider this analysis of the working of "sword-sustained" governments:

They take everything up by pieces, and look at it in the light of expediency. And their expediency is like the child's world, bounded by the sensible horizon, which terminates in all directions where the sky seems to shut down upon the earth. It is a very short-sighted expediency. But they are none the less confident it comprehends all things. Such is their mole-eyed wisdom. (p. 110)

Ballou's frankness on sexual matters retains the ability to surprise, even to shock. I was struck by both the bluntness and the prescience of his picture of the plight of women in a state of "free love" (pp. 208-211). Even those ideas that seem dated, such as the strictures against "self-pollution" (pp. 200-201), turn out to be worth a closer look. In this case, Ballou's point is that sexual overstimulation leads to restlessness and discontent – a fact well known to the modern advertising industry.

Ballou's idealism was tempered by experience, common sense, even a vein of earthy humor. His idealism, in turn, relieved the bitterness of his many disappointments. Contemplating the vastness of God's Infinitarium – his word for "the *absolute infinity* of things and beings which God governs" – he came to understand that it was unreasonable to expect God's plan for creation to be scaled to the measure of a human lifetime. He did not expect to witness *much* progress. All he wished to do, all he wished to inspire others to do, was to make "a fair beginning" (p. 96). Believing that God created the world imperfect so that his creatures might have the pleasure of improving it, he took a generous view of human frailty. He looked on the world around him with compassion, sometimes with indulgence, sometimes with indignation, but always without illusions, and without despair. Even the failure of the Hopedale experiment did not embitter him. It merely persuaded him that he wrote and wrought not for his own time, but for generations yet unborn – for us and our own posterity.

The program outlined in *Practical Christianity* incorporates, alongside the lofty vision of the goal, a realistic estimate of the starting point. The Hopedale

Home School, for example, had extremely ambitious aims for the mental, physical, and moral education of its students: it was "designed that in connection with scholastic training the pupil should be taught the laws of health, in order that a symmetrical development of the body be secured; also the conditions and laws of moral and spiritual life, so that the roots of selfishness and sin should be eliminated from the nature of the child."[1] At the same time, however, the community tolerated a surprising amount of misbehavior on the part of its young members. In the early days of the community, Ballou recalled, the children were "rude and uncouth in their manners, and unused to self-discipline and self-regulation." In 1847 there were "frequent complaints of lawless ways and growing disrespect of proper authority" among the older boys. A statute of 1849 required parents to ensure that their children "refrain from all profanity, from all vulgarities in word or action, and from all obscene utterances or writings; that in their recreations they indulge in no habits of injuring, annoying or vexing their playmates."[2] Ballou reported all of this without surprise or dismay. He accepted that it was the nature of young people, especially young men, to be rebellious. It had no bearing on their ability to grow into highly responsible adults. Hence, he always treated young people with respect and unfailingly high expectations; and in the end they did not disappoint him. The Hopedale educational system – with its physical, emotional, and moral components, its emphasis on ascertaining "what department of useful industry the young are predisposed to prefer," its incorporation of meaningful work experience, and its frequent "amusements" to vary the routine of work and study – is in many ways similar to the philosophy of the "alternative" high school that my daughter attended in the first years of the twenty-first century.

PRACTICAL CHRISTIAN SOCIALISM is written as a dialogue between the "Inquirer," who asks questions about Practical Christian Socialism, and the "Expositor," who answers them. Ballou explained that he chose the conversational form to relieve the "formidable solidity" of the work. His use of the dialogue form was inspired by such classics as Plato's *Republic*, the dialogues between Christ and the Disciple in *The Imitation of Christ*, and, especially, Elhanan Winchester's *The Universal Restoration: Exhibited in Four Dialogues between a Minister and his Friend*, the book which Ballou credited with converting him to Universalism.

The dialogue form introduces a good deal of redundancy into the text. Typically, the Inquirer asks the Expositor to speak on a certain topic; the

Expositor does so; the Inquirer repeats the Expositor's answer to make sure he has understood it correctly; the Expositor may then repeat or paraphrase it by way of commending the Inquirer's grasp of the subject.

As literary characters, the Expositor and the Inquirer leave much to be desired. The Expositor is, of course, a transparent mask for Ballou himself. The Inquirer's contributions are generally restricted to questions that serve as subheadings for sections of the text ("I would inquire what your views are concerning the Atonement"); exclamations of amazement at the novelty of the Expositor's ideas ("It is all so new, amazing and overwhelming to my mind"); and fulsome expressions of admiration and agreement ("I feel myself enlightened and spiritually elevated by your answers to my inquiries"). This has the unfortunate effect of emphasizing what is probably the least attractive feature of Ballou's writing: his confident, not to say smug, belief in the soundness and originality of his own ideas. I happen to believe that many of them *are* sound and original, but I think most readers would prefer to make this judgment for themselves. It seemed more straightforward to me, therefore, to omit the device of the Inquirer, and allow Adin Ballou to make his case directly and succinctly to the reader.

I have used chapter titles and subheadings to take the place of the Inquirer's questions which introduced new topics. In cases where the Inquirer's part contains more substance, I have incorporated material from both the Inquirer's and the Expositor's lines into the integrated text. For example, the discussion of Christian Non-Resistance (pp. 72-75) begins with a long statement by the Expositor, preserved unchanged in this edition. This is followed by a number of Biblical quotations in support of the Expositor's position. The passage in the original work then continues:

Ex. Are these samples sufficient?

Inq. They are. I have no doubt that Jesus Christ and his apostles taught your seventh principle of Social Order – The non-resistance of evil-doers with evil. But how such a principle can be carried out into practice, in the present state of this selfish, and often outrageously wicked world, is more than I can know. I greatly doubt whether the thing is practicable. *That* would be my chief difficulty in joining one of your Practical Christian Communities. I should acknowledge the principle to be Christian and most excellent, and should fear nothing but the trial of it under evil circumstances.

Ex. If you had a firm faith in two truths respecting this principle, you would give yourself no further anxiety about its practicability.

Inq. What are those?

Ex. 1. That this principle will cost vastly less of human suffering in practice than its opposite does. 2. That it will certainly make this wicked world better, and ultimately do away with all evil aggression.

In this edition, this conversation is rendered as:

> How can such a principle be carried out into practice, in the present state of this selfish, and often outrageously wicked world? We may acknowledge the principle to be Christian and most excellent, yet fear the trial of it under evil circumstances. Yet if we had a firm faith in two truths respecting this principle, we would have no further anxiety about its practicability. These are, that this principle will cost vastly less of human suffering in practice than its opposite does; and that it will certainly make this wicked world better, and ultimately do away with all evil aggression.

In a few cases, where I felt that the Inquirer's part could not be merged into the text without loss of meaning, I give it in a footnote. For example, in the discussion of "the Infinitarium of universes, earths, heavens, things and beings," I have preserved the Inquirer's interjection, "I must crave some explanation of such terms and expressions as these. How many earths and heavens would you intimate there are? I have not been accustomed to think of more than *one Earth, one Heaven*, and *one Universe*," and the Expositor's reply, "Then your mind needs to be expanded" (p. 20).

Especially in Part I, the Expositor's speeches, and some of the Inquirer's, are filled with collections of proof texts from the Old and New Testaments; indeed, requesting such texts is one of the Inquirer's principal functions. Since this style of discourse is less common now than it was a century and a half ago, the inclusion of these quotations may make it harder, not easier, to follow the thread of the argument. I have retained a few of these passages, where they seemed an integral part of the argument, but I have replaced the majority of the quotations with notes giving chapter and verse. I have also used notes to identify quotations, from the Bible and elsewhere, that Ballou used without attribution (or, in a few cases, with incorrect attribution). I have not, however, annotated every instance of Ballou's favorite quotations, such as "that God may be all in all" or "by their fruits you shall know them," which occur many times throughout the book.

In eliminating the dialogue, I have restructured the book into chapters instead of "conversations." I have also rearranged some material in order to present the topics in a more logical sequence. Ballou himself was aware that organization was not his strongest point; he would often make wry reference to his habit of digressing. For example, in the discussion of the principle of "reverence for the Divine and spiritual," the Expositor – led astray, perhaps, by the Inquirer's questions – makes a long excursion through his ideas on the varieties of matter and spirit, the nature of space and time, reincarnation, and the afterlife. "And this brings me back to my first grand principle of Personal Righteousness," he says, before proceeding to the stated topic. I have moved this material from chapter 3, "Principles of Personal Righteousness," to a more congenial location in chapter 2, "Principles of Theological Truth." For those interested in comparing this work with Ballou's original, the correspondence between the chapters of *Practical Christianity* and the conversations in *Practical Christian Socialism* is given in a table at the end of the book.

I have to the best of my ability preserved Ballou's authentic voice, in all of its poetry and also its occasional awkwardness. He adopted many terms from phrenology, such as "amativeness," which now sound strange in our ears. He did not hesitate to coin words when he could not find one to suit his purpose. Some of his coinages are graceless; one feels that with a little more thought he could have come up with alternatives to "amusemental," "interiorating," "charitive," and "humanital." But I for one feel my mind expanded by "God's Infinitarium," just as Ballou intended.

Ballou's style is for the most part simple and straightforward, valuing force and clarity over elegance. The magisterial confidence with which he pronounces his opinions – as if the Inquirer were more a disciple than a critic – is lightened by occasional flashes of wry humor; as when, in his rules for health, he says the head needs little clothing except "the hair, while that lasts." Occasionally he rises to heights of eloquence. Among the most striking is the passage on selfishness in the advice to practical Christians that concludes the book (pp. 233-234). "Too many communists," he wrote, "think that if individual property can be abolished, all goods held in common, and trade superseded, selfishness will have been annihilated, and a paradise established at once. But they greatly mistake ... Selfishness manifests itself through many lusts." There follows a remarkable 171-word sentence detailing the many varieties of human selfishness, from "the lust of power, authority, leadership, management, dictation, usurpation, tyranny" to "the lust of secretiveness, slyness, cunning, craftiness, guile, deceit, under-working and over-reaching."

It is my hope that this book will make Adin Ballou's thought more widely available to readers in this twenty-first century, who still hunger and thirst for a time which shall see *the people all righteous, the nations learn war no more, knowledge cover the earth, poverty cease, human misery finally become extinct, and "God be all in all."* Written at a high point in his life and that of the community he loved, this work reflects all that was most characteristic in Ballou's personality: his frank, unembarrassed gaze, his shrewd observations, his dreams and visions, his earnestness, his stern morality and his tolerant good sense. I hope that in its new guise, *Practical Christianity* will retain its capacity to surprise and delight as well as to instruct.

MY APPRECIATION of *Practical Christian Socialism*, and my sense of how it could be made more approachable, developed in the course of reading and discussing portions of it at meetings of Friends of Adin Ballou, a study group which since 1999 has met quarterly, in Hopedale, to explore Ballou's life and thought and to seek ways to keep his legacy alive in the modern world.

In discussing Ballou's theology at Friends of Adin Ballou meetings, we found it convenient to use a non-dialogue form of Part I of *Practical Christian Socialism* which I had prepared some years before, in the course of my research for a still-to-be-written biography of Ballou. I was encouraged to complete and publish it by the response of the group, who found my version easier to use – shorter, more direct, less distracting – than the original. Determined to give the dialogue a chance, we devoted a meeting to reading one of the conversations aloud, with people taking the roles of the Expositor and the Inquirer. Despite the efforts of some enthusiastic performers, we came away from the meeting convinced that the dialogue really was irredeemable.

Several members of Friends of Adin Ballou read and commented on various sections of the manuscript. In particular I thank Jeanne Kinney for her thoughtful comments and unfailing enthusiasm. The staff of the Bancroft Memorial Library in Hopedale encouraged this and my other Ballou-related projects, and kept the library open for me past closing time. I am grateful to my fellow pacifists, present-day successors of Adin Ballou, for reassuring me that this work is valuable and for keeping me, most of the time, from giving way to fear or hopelessness. In the words of peace activist Michael True, "Adin Ballou lives! And oh, how we need him *right now!*"

Lynn Gordon Hughes
October 2002

Notes

[1] Adin Ballou, *History of the Hopedale Community* (Lowell, MA, 1897), 268.

[2] Ballou, *History of Hopedale*, 72, 174, 192.

Preface

The author desires that this book should be read and thoroughly studied by all who are capable of appreciating it. It was not written to amuse the votaries of light literature, but to instruct susceptible and ingenuous minds. It is commended to honest, earnest, patient, discriminating, comprehensive thinkers, who are endeavoring to be judicious, uncompromising, indomitable workers for humanity. It is the fruit of patient reflection and ripe experience. It is not perfect, and will hereafter be improved; but it is worthy of all the consideration solicited in its behalf. It claims to be an EXPOSITION OF THE TRUE SYSTEM OF HUMAN SOCIETY; and such it is. It presents, theoretically, a complete Social Superstructure, from foundation to pinnacle. Let friend and foe inspect every part of it critically.

Every important idea involved in the vast subject of *Practical Christian Socialism* has received more or less attention in some part of the Work. And the author has faithfully declared his highest convictions of Truth and Right on every point discussed, without mystification of language, compromise, or the fear of man. He has studiously endeavored to make himself understood on all topics, even the most delicate, regardless of fashionable fastidiousness. Some may deem his plainness of speech too great on sexual matters, and his severity against certain alleged errors extreme. But he has no pardons to ask, nor apologies to offer, with reference to these demonstrations. He has written in love of the truth, and without ill will to any human being. He has sought the glory of God in the highest good of all mankind; and, having done his duty, he has no distrust of consequences. Nevertheless, if convinced of error, injustice, wrong, or even impropriety, he holds himself bound to make the best correction in his power. He has done as he would be done unto.

1

Particular portions of the Work will probably be read with different degrees of interest by different persons. Some will be interested most in its theology, some in its personal righteousness, some in its principles of social order, some in its Constitutions and practical details, some in its educational elucidations, some in its discussion of marriage and divorce, and some in its controversial criticisms. Let each follow his or her own preference. And yet the author hopes that no one who may become deeply interested in what is said on a favorite topic will long neglect to read the book *as a whole.* There are several classes of persons to whom this Work will be eminently useful.

1. To those who are already Practical Christian Socialists, or strongly inclined to become such. Here they will find a Treatise which states, illustrates and defends their peculiar doctrines in the most systematic, thorough and conclusive manner. They can study it every day with profit. They can confidently place it in the hands of all who inquire into the nature of their Socialistic Movement. They can draw from it inexhaustible munitions of mental and moral strength wherewith to contend successfully against opposers. And they can safely challenge their adversaries to examine and refute it at their leisure.

2. To writers, preachers and lecturers engaged in promulgating Practical Christian Socialism. These will have a complete system of objects, principles, polity and institutional arrangements always before them. Such a multitude of themes, propositions, texts, suggestions and hints, admitting of endless amplifications, will enable them to serve the cause effectually on all occasions; leaving them, at the same time, full scope for originality of thought, peculiarity of illustration and excellence of expression.

3. To parents, educators and all who are devoted to mental improvement. Such will find in the educational sections a fund of information, direction and suggestion which must afford them invaluable aid. Those also who are seeking light on the subject of marriage and the questions therewith connected will find, under that head, much profitable instruction.

All classes of readers are respectfully entreated to examine the Work patiently, carefully and thoroughly, before passing judgment for or against it. Many of its doctrines, ideas and views will at first seem strange to the majority of minds. They will find it difficult to adjust their old habits of thinking and educational prejudices to such singular inculcations. Yet, if they will candidly peruse the whole volume, and take ample time for reflection, they will probably be convinced that nearly all the author's positions are impregnable. Let them give due consideration to the following characteristics of the Treatise:

1. It comprehends a vast field of primary, secondary, collateral and incidental subjects. Theology, Christology, Pneumatology, Ethics, Anthropology, Natural and Moral Philosophy, Social Polity, Political Economy, Education, Amusements, Marriage, etc., are all more or less expounded and discussed.

2. It is discriminating, definite and specific with reference to all these themes and their subordinate topics. It does not confound natural distinctions. Things, names, terms and ideas are carefully defined. The reader can clearly see just what is stated, asserted, denied, accepted, rejected, conceded, condemned or recommended.

3. It is methodical, systematic and orderly. It begins at the natural beginning of its subjects, follows them through their natural development, and ends them at their natural acme. Common sense will find the links of each elaborated chain very nearly in their proper consecutive order.

4. Its leading conceptions and ideas are large, generous, sublime and magnificent, without being fanciful, romantic, extravagant, unreal and impracticable.

5. It is self-consistent and unitary. Fundamental objects are kept in view from beginning to end. Its fundamental principles are constantly held sacred, and their just application is made universal. Its fundamental social polity runs in straight lines from center to circumference. The just critic will find no contradiction or incongruity of essential ideas. He may scrutinize its theology, piety, morality, philanthropy, and social order as closely as he pleases; he will find everywhere an invulnerable consistency.

The author does not expect that this Work will receive much attention from the general public at present. It is not of a nature to excite, dazzle, amuse or please the popular masses, nor their leaders. It is above their standard of motive and action. The devotees of mammon will stick to their idol, the lovers of self and pleasure to theirs, the politicians to theirs, the worshipers of Mars to theirs, the popular sectarians to theirs, the philosophers to theirs, the light literati to theirs, the ignorami to theirs, the petrified conservatives to theirs, the high flying radicals to theirs, the fashionables to theirs, and the nothingarians to theirs. It is a pity; but so must it be for a long time to come. Yet there is progress. A noble few scattered here and there, through all these bustling, jostling masses, are aspiring after truth and goodness, after light and love, after a purer and higher order of society, after individual and social regeneration, after universal righteousness, harmony and happiness. These will gradually come to the knowledge of this Work, and will read it with delight. They will espouse the cause it advocates, and will noiselessly flow together into Practical Christian Communities. It is to such minds, regardless of their present associations, positions and denominations, that this book makes its special appeal. Such will welcome, rejoice in, and profit by it. The author would be happy to believe that such minds were *numerous;* but he knows that they are *not,* and has no disposition to flatter himself with false anticipations. He therefore commences with an edition of only one thousand copies, and expects to be a considerable time in disposing of these.

While the author firmly believes that in process of time the purest, most disinterested and most enlightened minds will embrace the system of religion, moral order and social polity expounded in this Work, with perhaps minor modifications and improvements, he expects that many Socialists of the present day will deem it objectionable. With some it will be too religious and illiberal; with others the reverse. Some will deem its theology too orthodox; others too heterodox. Some will object to its creed-like Declarations; others to its want of external ordinances, ceremonies and forms. Some will revolt at its asceticism; others at its too great conformity to the world. Some will dislike its uncompromising Non-Resistance and non-participation in sword-sustained governments; others its spiritual and moral intolerance – its discipline and disfellowship of evildoers. Some will think it too Individualistic; others too Communistic. Be it so. Let each class of dissenters stand aloof from our Republic and experiment to their heart's content on their own wiser systems. It is desirable that they should do so, in order that it may be demonstrated as soon as possible which the true social system is. When the radically defective have failed, there will be a harmonious concentration of all the true and good around the Practical Christian Standard. Meantime the author confides this Cause calmly to the guidance, guardianship and benediction of God, even that heavenly Father who once manifested his divine excellency in Jesus Christ, and whoever manifests himself through the Christ-Spirit to all upright souls. He sincerely believes the movement to have been originated and thus far supervised by that Holy Spirit. He is confident that well appointed ministering angels have watched over it, and will never cease to do so. This strong confidence has sustained him from the beginning, under all temporary discouragements, and now animates him with unwavering hopes for the future.

The Hopedale Community, the first constituent body of the new social order, commenced the settlement of its Domain, in the Spring of 1842, very small in numbers and pecuniary resources. Its disadvantages were so multiform and obvious, that most Associationists of that period regarded it as little better than a desperate undertaking – alike contracted in its social platform, its funds, and other fundamental requisites of success. Yet it has lived and flourished, while its supposed superiors have nearly all perished. Such was the will of God; such his promise to its founders; such their trust in him; such the realization of their hopes; and such the recompense of their persevering toils. And such is the benignant Providence which will bear the Practical Christian Republic onward through all its struggles to the actualization of its sublime destiny.

To all who are willing to read this Volume with candor and care, the author respectfully commends it. He long contemplated its execution, and has been enabled at length to complete it. He has done so with a good degree of self-satisfaction, with devout gratitude to God for his assistance, with the pleasant consciousness of having discharged faithfully a great duty, and with the cheering assurance that it will exert a regenerating influence on mankind.

Go then, faithful Volume, to thy task. Thou art sent forth on an arduous and responsible mission; but thou goest not forth unprepared. Thy loins are girded about with truth. The breast-plate of righteousness covers thy bosom. Thy feet are shod with the good will and peace of the gospel. Thy helmet is the hope of a world's salvation. Faith is thy shield. Let thy voice be heard in the wilderness, saying, "Prepare ye the way of the Lord, make his paths straight."[1] Proclaim the Jubilee of humanity on earth. Be thou a tireless herald of that long-predicted Republic, whose "officers shall be peace and its exactors righteousness"[2];wherein the Sovereignty of Divine Principles shall be supreme, the people all righteous, the nations learn war no more, knowledge cover the earth, poverty cease, human misery finally become extinct, and "God be all in all."[3]

ADIN BALLOU
Hopedale, Dec. 1, 1854

PART I

Fundamental Principles

Introduction

Mankind are by nature social beings. No individual alone possesses all the capabilities of human nature for happiness. One individual supplies the deficiency of another. Individuals can realize their highest good only when rightly associated. In true association all the essential interests of individuals and families will be harmonized. Such a harmonic order of Society is possible here on earth, and ought to be instituted. This is Socialism. It is a Theory of Society.

All who embrace this Social Theory are Socialists; and all opposed to it are Anti-Socialists. But you will not thence conclude, that all Socialists agree in other particulars. They differ as widely as do the Anti-Socialists in respect to principles, opinions, plans of arrangement, morals, forms, methods, ways and means.

One often hears Socialists spoken of and denounced as one homogeneous class of visionaries, fanatics, disorganizers, levelers and destructives, against whom the friends of religion, the family, the state and the present order of society, ought to be on their guard. This error is a very common one. Anti-Socialists, like all other anti-progressives, are sometimes very ignorant, prejudiced and undiscriminating. Whatever evil such may know, suspect, or imagine of the most exceptionable Socialists in any part of the world, they ascribe to Socialism *per se*, and so denounce all Socialists together as infamous. We might with equal justice treat all Anti-Socialists in the same manner. The most notorious murderers, pirates, robbers, oppressors, extortioners, etc., have been found among Anti-Socialists, from Cain to our modern kidnappers. What then if we should represent all who are opposed to Socialism as one common gang of murderers, pirates and robbers! Would it be truthful and just? No. But it would be quite as truthful and just, as the indiscriminate denunciations thundered from many pulpits and presses against Socialism and Socialists.

Chapter 1

Christianity and Socialism

Socialists and Socialisms

In ancient times there were the Pythagoreans, the Platonists, the Essenes, the primitive Christians, the Egyptian Canobites, etc. In modern times there are the Moravians, the Shakers, the Rappites, the Zoarites, the Owenites, the St. Simonians, the Fourierists or Phalansterians, the Icarians, the French and German Communists, the Church of England Villagers calling themselves Christian Socialists, the Noyesite Perfectionists, and, besides several others, our *Practical Christian Socialists*. All these agree substantially in the great doctrine of Socialism; but in almost everything else they differ as widely from each other, as do the different sects of professed Christians, or as do Pagans, Jews, Christians, Mahometans, and Mormons. All these believe in the social harmony of heaven in the next world. In this they are agreed, but in very little else. We Socialists all believe in the social harmony of a rudimental heaven to be established on earth. In this we are all agreed, but in very little else.

The terms Socialism, Socialist, etc. are odious to many people, chiefly on account of principles, practices and peculiarities prominent in certain classes of Socialists, with whom we have little or no fellowship. Why then do we use these terms, which must confound us with them in popular opinion? Would it not be good policy to drop these terms, and to substitute others less obnoxious to popular prejudice?

Nothing would be finally gained by such a policy. "Speak the truth and shame the Devil" is a good maxim. The truth is, we really are Socialists; we believe in Socialism; Socialism must ultimately be accepted by mankind; its day is coming; and it is not a doctrine for honest, noble souls to be ashamed of. As to justice from the opposition, no great Reformer ever received it; and Reformers only betray their cause, when they resort to a timid, evasive, and time-serving policy.

I am certain that Anti-Progressives hate the vital principles and require-ments of true Socialism more than they hate what is really abominable in its wrongheaded and vicious professors. Therefore they would hate the same thing no less under another name. I am certain that I can make the world understand the merits of *Practical Christian Socialism*, in contradistinction to all other kinds, as well without substituting new terms, as I could by means of them.

The word *Christian* denotes that our kind of Socialism is based on the essential Principles of the Christian Religion. The word *Practical* denotes that the essential principles of the Christian Religion, as held by our kind of Socialists, are *interior* to all external ceremonies, formalities, ecclesiasticisms, scholasticisms, sectarianisms, localisms, temporisms and mere incidentals; are of universal application to human relations and conduct; are such as imperatively require of all individuals, and all societies, divine love in their affections, divine purity in their motives, divine wisdom in their understand-ings, divine rectitude in their conduct, and divine order in their relations. Practical Christian Socialism proposes to harmonize all the important interests of individuals and families in a *true social state* on this basis, by the moral force of these principles rightly expounded, organized and applied. And it affirms that such a result can never be effected in any other way.

The Christian Religion

Now there seem to be a great many Christian Religions. We have a multi-tude of sects, all professing and extolling the Christian Religion, and yet all giving it an aspect to suit themselves; so that virtually there are many Christian Religions. Practical Christian Socialists do undoubtedly regard the Christian Religion in a very different light from that in which it is viewed and represented by the great mass of nominal Christians comprising what is called Christendom.

In the first place, the term *Religion* should be understood. This term is said to be derived from the Latin verb *religio*, to tie hard, to bind, to make fast – to impose solemn obligation. Religion consists of *truths* to be *believed* and *duties* to be *performed*, or at least what are *assumed* to be such. Truths and duties thus prescribed are collectively termed Religion, because they impose the highest obligations of faith and conscience on the human soul. Every Religion claims that mankind are under the highest and most solemn obligation to venerate its declared truths, and practice its prescribed require-ments. This is true of what is called Natural Religion, of Pagan Religions, of the Jewish Religion, of the Mahometan Religion, and of the Christian Religion. They all assume that unless mankind believe certain declared truths, and obey certain precepts of duty, they cannot escape indescribable privations and woes, cannot be acceptable to God, cannot be happy, either in this life or in that which is to come. All Religions recognize a God, or a plurality of gods, as their central and supreme Authority, to whom everything stands in a subjective relation. Hence all the Worships, and Priesthoods, and External-isms of the various religions that have prevailed in our world.

To ascertain what the Christian Religion really is, I depend entirely on the Scriptures of the New Testament, together with their necessary refer-ences in the more ancient Scriptures, and in Nature. I pay no deference to the dogmas, opinions, expositions and representations of the Christian Religion, as now held by the *nominal Church* of the various denomina-tions; nor to the decisions of Councils; nor to Ecclesiastical traditions, commentaries, glosses, catechisms, systems of scholastic divinity, or creeds; nor to any Writings subsequent to those of the Evangelists and Apostles. I go directly to the Bible, especially to the Scriptures of the New Testament, and *most confidently* to the *four Gospels.*

I learn from the closing paragraph of St. John's Gospel, that if all the things said and done by Jesus Christ had been written, "even the world itself could not contain the books."[1] I infer from this that the New Testament Scriptures do not record a hundredth part of Christ's words and works. But we ought not to infer that anything *absolutely essential* was left out of these records; nor that professed Christians of later generations have reliably sup-plied any important deficiencies. We must depend on the primitive histories and expositions alone. What cannot be learned from them must remain unknown. We cannot depend on the mere opinions and judgments of men who had no higher sources of information than are accessible to ourselves.

Jesus Christ did not leave writings under his own hand, containing a com-plete statement of the doctrines and duties of his religion. We are left without one word purporting to have been penned by him; and with nothing from his disciples but synoptical reports of his teachings and life – very brief sketches of the more important particulars of what he said, did, and experienced. I regard this not as a defect, but as a capital excellence. To systematize, expound in detail, and amplify the applications of Religion, is a work which can be done by sub-ordinate teachers. But to be the oracular Medium of essential divine principles – eternal, fundamental, universal principles – required a mind at the very head of the human race, a representative of the highest spiritual capabilities, one through whom the Divine Love and Wisdom might flow forth to all ages in incorruptible purity. Such a One was the man Christ Jesus. His Religion is one of essential divine principles. It is therefore a universal Religion, proper for all men, and all spiritual intelligences, in all progressive states of existence. It does not consist of mere words. It was never designed to wear the livery of any one particular nation, or age. It cannot be petrified into external forms, nor crystallized into mere human language. Therefore its Mediator did not write it out in systematic detail, nor provide for its being so written out. He knew that the language in which he must express his Religion, and the external forms which it must then take on, would become obsolete to after generations. He knew that change is inevitable in all mere human externals – and that there must be ceaseless *progress*, as well as *change*. He knew that the same Spirit of Truth which had spoken through his visible humanity, would flow into the minds of men in all coming time, and would magnify the same divine principles, in ever-living applications to the wants of each succeeding age. Hence those memorable words:

> I have many things to say unto you, but ye cannot bear them now. Howbeit, when he, the Spirit of Truth, is come, he will guide you into all truth; for he shall not speak of himself; but whatsoever he shall hear, that shall he speak: and he will show you things to come. He shall glorify me; for he shall receive of mine, and shall show it unto you. All things that the Father hath are mine; therefore said I, That he shall take of mine and shew unto you. [2]

It was far wiser for Jesus to have taught and exemplified his Religion in its essential principles, as he did, leaving just such synoptical, artless sketches of it as have come down to after times, than to have given it an artificial, systematic elaboration in writing.

It is declaratively a Religion, "not of the *letter*, but of the *spirit*," not in mere "*word*, but in *power*."[3] Therefore, if we have only enough of letter and word to signify plainly what its principles are, we need no more. Indeed, more would embarrass, rather than facilitate, the progress of such a Religion. Even as it is, nine-tenths of nominal Christians pay nearly all their reverence to the "letter" which has reached them; very little to the essential divine principles and "spirit."

I do not affirm that none of these principles was ever revealed or taught except through Jesus Christ. They have been partially and imperfectly taught in all Religions, and in all spiritual Philosophies. What is called the light of

Nature reveals some of them. Divine inspiration, wherever it has acted strongly on human minds, has revealed them to a greater or less extent. The Seers, Prophets and Sages of all ages and countries have discovered and inculcated these principles with more or less distinctness. The Hebrew religion, as set forth in the Old Testament Scriptures, contained many of these principles. But Jesus Christ taught and exemplified them all in their purity, in one complete embodiment. He focalized all the scattered, fragmentary and obscure illuminations of the Past into one resplendent Sun of truth and righteousness; and this Sun will radiate the ever-waxing luminosity through all the Progressive Future.

Such is the Christian religion. It transcends all other Religions, because it contains the essential truth and good of them all, without their errors and evils; because it contains higher unfoldings of divine principles than any or all of them together; and because, in its cardinal principles, it is a universal, perfect, and immortal Religion. If those principles were heartily embraced, and reduced to practice, by individual and social man, the Earth would be an Eden, swarming with the holy and happy millions of a redeemed race.

Practical Christianity

Practical Christianity is altogether a different thing from *nominal* Christianity; but I will show you that it is the Christianity of Jesus Christ. I will now proceed to demonstrate that these are the cardinal principles of the Christian Religion, and, in so doing, illustrate their nature and scope.

Then you will begin to see that Practical Christianity has a broad and solid religious basis; that there is nothing narrow and superficial about it; that it is not a petty, arbitrary, purblind sectarianism; but an infinitarian harmonialism, recognizing the Deific Interior Spirit of innumerable earths and heavens, with his various manifestations, as affecting the progress and happiness of all spiritual intelligences.

You will henceforth understand why Practical Christian Socialists, unlike some other Socialists, cannot ignore Christ, nor contemn his authority, nor hold his Religion in light esteem; but feel impelled to reverence him as the exteriorization, the Apparition, "the Image of the invisible God," and to exalt his name "above every name." For to them Christ is not only a beautiful and perfect man, one "altogether lovely" in the highest attributes of humanity; but a heavenly and divine Spirit.[4] He is the outer and perceptible essence of the one

Deific Nature that inherently and most interiorly vitalizes the whole Infinitarium of worlds and beings – the manifested Father – the communicable Life, Love and Wisdom of God to all moral and spiritual beings. All they expect to know of THE ABSOLUTE God, even in the highest heavens, they expect to know in his Christ-form of Deific Personalization, by the Christ-Spirit of Love and Wisdom illuminating their own spiritual interiors. All they have yet known of the true God, they have learned in these ways. They see all truth by the Christ-Light. They feel all absolute Good by the Christ-Heat. Therefore it does not stumble them to read the uncompromising testimonies of Jesus Christ, that men must believe in him, or abide in spiritual darkness and condemnation; for they see that this is the simple truth, necessitated by the moral and spiritual constitution of human nature. He says, "I am the Way, the Truth and the Life; no man cometh unto the Father but by me," and truly this is so. He says, "God so loved the world that he gave his only begotten Son, that whosoever believeth in him should not perish, but have everlasting life," and it is even so. He says, "He that believeth on the Son hath everlasting life: and he that believeth not the Son shall not see life: but the wrath of God abideth on him" (i.e. he necessarily remaineth in spiritual darkness and moral death); and surely this is so. He says, "He that hateth me, hateth my Father also," and elsewhere, "all they that hate me love death."[5]

Practical Christian Socialists see that all this is truth. They see that when any individual soul is brought right, the Christ-Spirit must have done it, and that this Spirit must have taken up his abode within such a soul; even as it is written: "If a man love me, he will keep my words; and my Father will love him, and we will come unto him, and make our abode with him."[6] They see that when Society is brought right the Christ-Spirit will have done it, and must take up its abode in the constitutions, laws and organic administration of such Society; because Society is a man, a complex man, a Social man. Therefore, they have no more hope of regenerating Society without faith in Christ, without reconstructing it on Christ-Principles, and breathing into its organism the Christ-Spirit, the true breath of divine Life, than they have of regenerating individual sinners without the Faith, Hope and Charity of the same eternal Christ-Spirit; or than they have of saving a wicked man in his sins. This is their grand reason for making the interior, essential principles of the Christian Religion the basis of their Social Superstructure.

The Essential Divine Principles of the Christian Religion

Here are twenty-four cardinal principles: eight of Theological Truth, to be embraced by faith; eight of Personal Righteousness, to be illustrated in practice; and eight of Social Order, to be acknowledged and acted upon in the constitution, organization and establishment of a true harmonic Society.

Before I proceed, I wish to critically define what I mean by the term *principle*. I mean by the word principle, *chief root of originating life*. When I speak of the essential divine principles, or fundamental principles, or cardinal principles of the Christian Religion, I mean those chief roots of Truth, Duty and Order, in which inhere the vitality of the Christian Religion. When I speak of principles of Theological Truth, I mean those great truths, respecting God and spiritual natures, which must be acknowledged and acted upon, in order to the true spiritual life and happiness of all moral intelligences. When I speak of principles of Personal Righteousness, I mean those great Duties of affection, intention and action which all moral intelligences must illustrate, or be personally more or less sinful and miserable. When I speak of principles of Social Order, I mean those great truths of relation, condition, affection and action between moral intelligences, which they must sacredly respect, or be socially discordant, disorderly and miserable.

Now a chief root implies outgrowing branches. So a principle always implies branches dependent on it as its natural outgrowth. What I call an essential principle always has several sub-principles, minor principles or branch principles, from each of which grow minuter branches, twigs, stems, leaves, fruits, as from a tree or vine. What is it that immediately produces and sustains the fruit? We see the stem growing out of the twig, the twig out of the small branch or limb, the limb out of the large branch, this out of the main trunk, and this last, with a few great roots, we find established in the ground. The whole life-power of the tree inheres in its main root or roots; and without these the trunk, large branches, limbs, twigs, stems, leaves, blossoms, fruits, could not have been produced. Just so in religion and morals. Just so with my system of Practical Christian Socialism. It must have its life-originating roots, alias essential principles.

These are the essential divine principles of the Christian Religion. With their sub-principles and indispensable cognates, they include all that is vital in that Religion. Taken together, they constitute its soul, its spirit.

The Essential Divine Principles
of the Christian Religion

I. Principles of Theological Truth

1. The existence of one All-Perfect Infinite God.
2. The mediatorial manifestation of God through Christ.
3. Divine revelations and inspirations given to men.
4. The immortal existence of human and angelic spirits.
5. The moral agency and religious obligation of mankind.
6. The certainty of a perfect divine retribution.
7. The necessity of man's spiritual regeneration.
8. The final universal triumph of good over evil.

II. Principles of Personal Righteousness

1. Reverence for the Divine and spiritual.
2. Self-denial for righteousness' sake.
3. Justice to all beings.
4. Truth in all manifestations of mind.
5. Love in all spiritual relations.
6. Purity in all things.
7. Patience in all right aims and pursuits.
8. Unceasing progress towards perfection.

III. Principles of Social Order

1. The supreme Fatherhood of God.
2. The universal Brotherhood of Man.
3. The declared perfect love of God to Man.
4. The required perfect love of Man to God.
5. The required perfect love of Man to Man.
6. The required just reproof and disfellowship of evildoers.
7. The required non-resistance of evildoers with evil.
8. The designed unity of the righteous.

Practical Christian Socialists hold these to be essential, eternal, universal, divine principles; positively practical in their natural tendency, and interior to all external ceremonies, formalities, scholasticisms, ecclesiasticisms, sectarianisms, localisms, temporisms and mere incidentalisms.

By *external ceremonies* I mean what are commonly called the public ordinances of religion, such as water baptism, the Lord's supper, the several sacraments, etc. By *formalities* I mean all stated forms and observances as to days, times and seasons, places, postures and modes of address, in the worship of God, in fasting, prayer, thanksgiving, praise, etc. By *scholasticisms* I mean studied propositions in which metaphysical doctrinaries of different ages, either individually or in conclave, have stated the articles of their faith, such as the Trinity, Transubstantiation, Election and Reprobation, Foreordination, Total Depravity, Vicarious Atonement, etc.; which may have more or less of truth as their original basis, but are not warranted by the simplicity of Scripture, or its plain testimony as a *whole*. By *ecclesiasticisms* I mean Church Constitutions, Confessions, Covenants, Clerical Orders, and all kinds of Ecclesiastical Polity, Rules, Regulations and usages; which may be good, bad, or indifferent, according to their nature, use, and circumstances. By *sectarianisms* I mean all peculiarities of faith or practice which appertain to a particular sect as *such*, and which merely distinguish it from other sects, but are not essential, universal principles of truth and righteousness. By *localisms* and *temporisms* I mean those peculiarities of religious action or manner, observance or form, which become customary in a particular locality or age, which may be proper, or even indispensable *there* and *then*, but which are neither necessary, nor useful, when circumstances have greatly changed. By *incidentalisms* I mean all little peculiarities of fashion, custom, habit, or eccentricity, into which religious leaders sometimes fall, without intending to make them any way essential, or expecting them to be insisted on by their followers; but which, nevertheless, through human weakness, become sanctified, and magnified into great importance.

Now when I assert that the essential divine principles of the Christian Religion, stated in my Table, are INTERIOR to all external ceremonies, formalities, scholasticisms, ecclesiasticisms, sectarianisms, localisms, temporisms and mere incidentalisms, I do not mean to condemn and discard all these as necessarily evil, or useless, nor to raise a quarrel against them, but to affirm that the PRINCIPLES are absolutely essential to the Christian religion, as its vital, unchangeable *interiors*; whilst all these are, at best, non-essentials – mere *changeable exteriors* of the Religion, every one of which may pass away, or be modified, without impairing its inherent life.

Chapter 2

Principles of Theological Truth

The All-Perfect Infinite God

I commence with my first stated principle of Theological Truth: *the existence of one All-Perfect, Infinite God.* That the Christian Religion distinctly reaffirms the existence of one, and but one, self-existent God – an All-Perfect, Infinite Spirit – the Source, Sustainer and Controller of Universal Nature, will not be questioned. He "is the blessed and only Potentate, the King of Kings, and Lord of Lords; who only hath immortality, dwelling in the light which no man can approach unto, whom no man hath seen, nor can see; to whom be honor and power everlasting."[1] Such is the manner in which our first fundamental principle is declared in the Scriptures of the New Testament. To deny the existence of one All-Perfect, Infinite God, or to hold that there is more than one such God, or to make God imperfect and finite in any of his attributes, is to discard the Christian Religion.

This principle is a *practical*, as well as a theoretical one. I am confident that Atheism, Polytheism, Pantheism, etc., are incompatible with the living of a true *individual*, or a true *social* life. Human nature needs to recognize, confide in and worship *one All-Perfect, Infinite God.* The individual needs this, the family needs it, the community needs it, the nation needs it, the race needs it. Without this, solid virtue, order, and happiness are impossible to mankind. Practical Christian Socialists expect to accomplish nothing towards the establishment of their grand superstructure without this first essential divine principle of the Christian Religion.

God's Infinitarium

By God's Infinitarium I mean the *absolute infinity* of things and beings which God governs. Space is without any common center, or circumference. It has innumerable grand centers. It is infinite. Duration had no beginning,

19

and can have no end. It is infinite. There are things and beings everywhere throughout all Space. Their number must be infinite. There have been things and beings in all Space, throughout all past Duration, and will be through all coming Duration. Therefore I speak of all these together as God's Infinitarium.

There never was a time of NOTHING; never a time when God did not exist; never a time when he existed in solitude; and never a time when he had not this Infinitarium of universes, earths, heavens, things and beings to govern.* It follows that God cannot be limited, either in Space or Duration. He must be as old and endless as Infinite Duration, and as diffusive and omnipresent as Infinite Space. Else there would be supposable periods of Duration in which God was not; and there would be regions of Space in whose earths and heavens God *is* not. But this cannot be.

God is a Spirit. He fills immensity. He is the most interior, vitalizing Essence of the Infinitarium. God cannot be limited, either in Space or Duration. All motion, formation, organization, sensation, affection, sentiment, reason, happiness – all power, love and wisdom, in all universes, earths and heavens, must originate in him as the Infinite Father-Spirit. There is no one grand center of the Infinitarium, in which he has all exclusive personal presence. He must be essentially an omnipresent Spirit. Hence the Israelites were strictly forbidden to make any visible image, likeness or similitude of God. Hence David truly apostrophized God, when he said: "Whither shall I go from thy spirit? or whither shall I flee from thy presence? If I ascend up into heaven, thou art there: if I make my bed in hell, behold, thou art there. If I take the wings of the morning, and dwell in the uttermost parts of the sea, even there shall thy hand lead me, and thy right hand shall hold me."[2]

I have been led to contemplate the Infinitarium of existence as exhibiting six different, yet harmonious infinities: the Deific Spirit, Soul-Spirit, Matter, Space, Duration and Diversity. The Deific Spirit comprehends all that belongs to the Divine Nature, whether spoken of as God the Father, Christ the Son, the Holy Ghost, the Christ-Spirit, or absolute Divine Principles. Soul-Spirit comprehends all angels, spirits, humans, and all the lower grades of spirit that give motion and life to Matter.

---

* Inquirer: "I must crave some explanation of such terms and expressions as these. How many earths and heavens would you intimate there are? I have not been accustomed to think of more than *one Earth*, *one Heaven*, and *one Universe*."
Expositor: "Then your mind needs to be expanded."

Matter comprehends all gradations and varieties of inert, passive substance. These three, Deific Spirit, Soul-Spirit, and Matter, are substantial Infinities; they consist of real substance, or essence. Matter is the most exterior of these. Soul-Spirit interiorates, pervades and controls Matter. And the Deific Spirit interiorates, pervades and controls Soul-Spirit, thus through that controlling all Matter. So the Deific Spirit, God, is the inmost, and the Supreme Controlling Nature of the Infinitarium.

The other three Infinities are unsubstantial: Space, which has no common center, no circumference and no limits; Duration, which had no beginning and will have no end, comprehending all ages and eternities; and Diversity, which is the unlikeness of all individualizations, whether of Soul-Spirit or Matter, to each other, giving an Infinity of distinction and variety. Thus the three *substantial* Infinities exist in Infinite Space, in all eternity of Duration, and with such differences and peculiarities as exhibit an Infinite Diversity – an infinite divisibility and variety in general unity. Space gives room, Duration gives time, and Diversity gives variety to all things. Such are the infinities of the Infinitarium.

I hold that there never was a time when God existed alone, or when he was not exercising control over innumerable worlds, with their multitudinous populations. Many earths and universes, with their appropriate inhabitants, are ever in a state or formation, progression and perfection; while others are decaying, and vanishing away so that at no period in all the possible eternities of infinite duration, past, present or future, is there any absolute increase, or decrease, of spirit, matter, beings, worlds or universes; but only change and revolution, according to their nature and appropriate cycles. From this I infer the co-eternity of Spirit and Matter; and that the aggregate substance of neither can be increased by creation, or diminished by annihilation; also, that as many individuations of Spirit and Matter, on the great average of the Infinitarium, are always being dissolved as are being generated.

Matter and Spirit

I hold that Matter exists in seven states or grades: *mineral, vegetable, animal, aqueous, aerial, igneous* and *ethereal*, culminating in the most subtle electrical, magnetic and aromal imponderables. Each of these seven grades of matter would seem to be more refined than the other. But Spirit in its lowest state or grade is more subtle than the most refined Matter, and can interiorate it so as to impart to it motion and life.

I rank Spirit also into seven states or grades, exclusive of the Infinite Deific Spirit: motific, formatic, organic, sensific, intellectic, rationic, and moralic. (I coin some of these words, for want of any already coined that answer my purpose.) By *motific* spirit I mean that grade of Spirit which merely gives motion, attractive or projective, vibratory, circular or vertical, to Matter. By *formatic* spirit I would designate the next higher grade, which is induced by chemical attractions and repulsions, causing naturally the formation of crystalline bodies, and all material bodies that exhibit small complexity of structure. By *organic* spirit I would denote the next higher grade, which operates in all vegetable and animal organizations. Next comes the *sensific*, which gives sensation – beginning with the highest vegetable, and rising through the animal kingdom to man. Out of sensation spring the instinctive propensities and affections of animal nature. Next comes the *intellectic*, which gives distinct individual consciousness, perception of related individualities, and all the knowing faculties. Then follows the *rationic*, which develops reason with all its powers. And last comes the *moralic*, which renders man a moral agent, a religious being, and a temple for the divine spirit to dwell in.

But the Deific Spirit is higher and more interior still. He is All-Perfect and Infinite. He interiorates, pervades and comprehends the Infinitarium of Spiritual and Material Nature. I cannot define Him, except in those manifestations, attributes and qualities of nature which he has reduced to finite comprehension. He is "Light ineffable,"[3] "without variableness, or shadow of turning."[4] But all Spirit below him, and all Matter, is subject to mutations and variations innumerable, from and to all eternity.

Reflect and be devout! Matter is everywhere, always was and always will be, in infinite variety. Soul-Spirit is everywhere, always was and always will be, in infinite variety – interiorating, pervading, actuating, animating and controlling all Matter. God, the Deific Spirit, is everywhere, always was and always will be; interiorating, pervading, inspiring and controlling all Soul-Spirit, and through that all Matter; rolling on all universes and worlds through their incalculable cycles of generation, progression, perfection, and dissolution; doing all this in infinite Love, with infinite Wisdom, and by infinite Power; adapting his divine essence to all diversities and varieties of changing being; Himself unchanged, unwearied, and undisturbed, from everlasting to everlasting, through interminable Duration! In the thought of all this, what is man that he should magnify himself! or the son of man that his soul should be lifted up with pride![5]

The Christ-Spirit and the Man Jesus

My second stated principle of Theological Truth is *the mediatorial manifestation of God through Christ.* My views are these: God is an All-Perfect, Infinite Spirit. Men, angels, and all created spirits are finite. It is certain that no one finite mind, no one society, no one earth, no one heaven, no one universe of minds, can see God as a WHOLE, or conceive of him in his absolute Infinity. His WHOLE cannot be contained within the prescribed bounds of Space. To be seen and known, even *finitely*, he must manifest himself in some manner conceivable and comprehensible by finite spiritual intelligences. He must adapt himself to their limited capacities. This is a necessity of the case.

The human form, being the highest and most perfect known to man, must have been assumed by the Deific Spirit as the suitable one in which to manifest himself to men, and in this form he must needs illustrate superhuman excellences; otherwise we would not have recognized any divine manifestation. Human beings innately desire, and absolutely need, personal manifestations of the Divine Nature, in order to their progress and happiness. God actually makes such manifestations of himself to his finite children whenever proper. This is done by a certain capability of his divine nature, exercised at will, which concentrates any requisite measure of his omnipresent Spirit, personalizes it with a chosen exterior form, and inspires that form in the degree necessary to make any manifestation he pleases. The form so chosen is the exterior Christ. The concentrated personalization of the Divine essence within that form is the interior Christ. The omnipresent Spirit or essence, thus concentrated and personalized at will, is the Eternal Christ-Spirit, concerning which John says, "In the beginning was the Word, and the Word was with God, and the Word was God."[6]

It is indispensable to the progress and happiness of all moral intelligences that God should make all such adaptable manifestations to them of his divine nature, attributes, and will. Accordingly, we find that he does so by what I have termed his Christhood. By means of this he is able, at will, to appear to his creatures as a Deific Person; adapting his divine personality to the necessities of the case in whatever manifestation he may make in any particular earth, or heaven. Thus he may manifest his perfections, with very different yet equally suitable degrees of excellence, in each earth, and each heaven. He can do this at different times, or, if he please, in numberless earths, heavens and universes, at the same time; all his personal manifestations being only various and multiform demonstrations of one Infinite Spirit, perfect in Love, Wisdom and Power. In every such adaptable manifestation, the Apparition or Image, of the otherwise invisible God, is called Christ, or the Son of God; and it represents God to finite minds in the most perfect personality which for the time being they are capable of conceiving.

Christ is not the Infinite God. Christ is only a comprehensible Apparition, Image, or Personalized Manifestation of the invisible God, made in condescension to the necessities of finite minds. Doubtless there are innumerable Personalized Manifestations of God, considering the countless universes which exist; and in this sense innumerable Christs; but the Divine Apparitions or Images are all of one essence. There is but one Holy Christ Spirit, and one Christhood whereby God manifests himself. And all this without the least real division, or confusion, of his own absolute Unity.

Minor and less personal manifestations of God are also made in every part of the Infinitarium, to individuals, and circles of minds, as occasion requires. Hence come extraordinary divine revelations, inspirations, visions, impressions, gifts and excellences. These minor manifestations are spoken of in Scripture as immediately wrought by the Holy Ghost; which, in fact, is only a certain concentration of the universal Christ-Spirit, whereby God acts communicably within and upon his creatures. Hence God, contemplated in his wholeness, is called the FATHER. When contemplated through his manifest Christhood, as a comprehensible Deific Personality, his Apparition or image is called the Christ, or Son of God. When his Spiritic Essence gives forth its less personal manifestations, it is called the Holy Ghost or the Holy Spirit. So there is really one and but one God – one omnipresent, all-interiorating, all-vitalizing, Infinite Parental Spirit, however manifested. There is no difference in essence between the Infinite Father-Spirit, the Christ-Spirit, and the Holy Spirit, but there are differences of degree and function.[7] Such, I think, are the true distinctions to be made between the Father, Son and Holy Ghost of the Christian Scriptures. I am not a Trinitarian, nor a Unitarian. I am a Practical Christian.

The word *Christ* is of Greek origin, and signifies literally *The Anointed*. The Hebrew word *Messiah* has precisely the same signification. Prophets, Priests and Kings were anointed in ancient times with holy oil. Thus consecrated, they were considered God's representatives before the people. Their persons were held sacred, and their authority divine. To treat them with contempt was to insult, and rebel against, God himself. They were regarded as divinely commissioned, divinely consecrated, and divinely protected. They acted declaratively in the name, and by the authority of God. Through them God spoke and acted. They stood forth as God's visible representatives. They were his Messiahs or Christs – his ANOINTED ONES.

But all the Hebrew Prophets appear to have been inspired with the prophetic conception of a coming Christ, incomparably more exalted than any of these. He was to combine in himself all the dignified functions of Prophet, Priest and King. He was to be transcendently and emphatically, THE ANOINTED of God – his most illustrious representative to mankind.[8] It is plain enough that Jesus claimed to be the predicted Messiah, and unqualifiedly applied various prophetic Scriptures of the Old Testament concerning Christ to himself.[9]

What was he in his nature? Was he *divine*, or was he *human*? Both the divine and human natures were manifested in him. And being so constituted, he was truly the Son of man and the Son of God. He was truly and properly a man – a model man – the best possible specimen of a rightly generated, rightly organized, rightly balanced, rightly developed man. Hence he was appropriately and most significantly called "the Son of man." This pure and true man was the exterior Christ. But the Spirit of the Infinite Father flowed into him, pervaded him, anointed him, spoke through him, and wrought wonders by him. God effected all this by what I have called his Christhood. This interior Christ dwelt within, spoke, and wrought at pleasure, through the exterior Christ. The exterior and interior Christs were exactly adapted to each other. Both the *Man* and the *Spirit* could speak and act freely, either separately or jointly, without discord. The properly *human*, and the properly *divine* natures, acted in complete unison, the interior Christ within the exterior Christ. And because of the interior Christ, the person, Jesus Christ, was appropriately and most significantly called "the Son of God."

Thus constituted, he takes the pre-eminence in our earth and heaven, as it is written: "The Word was made flesh, and dwelt among us, and we beheld his glory, the glory as of the only begotten of the Father, full of grace and truth."[10] Such is the mediatorial manifestation of God through Christ. Embracing this great theological truth as an essential divine principle of the Christian Religion, we look up to Jesus Christ as the Head of the true Church; the Lord, Judge, and Savior of the world; the Mediator between God and men; the Way, the Truth, and the Life; by whom alone we can truly know the Father; whose principles and spirit must govern us in all things; and without whom we can do nothing for ourselves or the world, *as it ought to be done.*

Scripture speaks of the Christ-Spirit as existing prior to, and distinct from, the man Christ Jesus. "In the beginning was the Word," (*Logos*, the God-manifesting Spirit, the Christ-Spirit) "and the Word was with God, and the Word was God" (was God's communicable, self-expressing, exteriorizing essence). "The same was in the beginning with God. All things were made" (mediately) "by him; and without him was not anything made that was made. In him was life; and the life was the light of men ... This was the true Light which lighteth every man that cometh into the world. He was in the world, and the world was made by" (by means of or through) "him ... And the Word was made flesh" (tabernacled in the man Jesus of Nazareth) "and dwelt among us."[11] This same word is spoken of in the eighth chapter of Proverbs, as the eternal Wisdom of God:

> The Lord possessed me in the beginning of his way, before his works of old. I was set up from everlasting, from the beginning, or ever the earth was. When there were no depths I was brought forth; when there were no fountains abounding with water. Before the mountains were settled, before the hills I was brought forth... When he prepared the heavens, I was there ... When he appointed the foundations of the earth: then I was by him, as one brought up with him; and I was daily his delight, rejoicing always before him ... Whoso findeth me findeth life, and shall obtain favor of the Lord. But he that sinneth against me wrongeth his own soul: all they that hate me love death.[12]

This was no other than the Christ-Spirit – the light which lighteth every man that cometh into the world.

All men, in all ages and countries of the world, who have formed any just conceptions of the Deity, of man's spiritual nature, relations and obligations – who have unfolded any great truths of Wisdom, or practically illustrated any heavenly virtues, have done so under the inspirations of the eternal Christ-Spirit, the Wisdom element, which is the true Light that lighteth every man in all earths, and in all heavens.

Some of this light shone through Moses, some through Pythagoras, some through Confucius, some through Zoroaster, some through Plato, Socrates, etc. I determine what is Christlike in all these manifold illuminees by reducing everything to fundamental principles, and comparing them with the essentials clearly illustrated by the teachings, life and death of our great Prince Messiah, the man Christ Jesus. The manifestation of God through him is the highest ever made to man. God gave him the Christ-Spirit "without measure."[13] The interior Christ spake the truths of God through him without obstruction, and with absolute personal authority.

The Christ-Spirit in Jesus sometimes exercised Deific Personality, and spoke as one superior to the Christ-*man*. "I am the bread of life." "I came down from heaven, not to do mine own will, but the will of him that sent me." "I am the light of the world." "Before Abraham was, I am."[14] In other passages, the exterior Christ, the *man*, as distinguishable from the interior Christ, spoke: "Why callest thou me *good*? there is none good but one, that is God." "My soul is exceedingly sorrowful even unto death." "My God, my God, why hast thou forsaken me?"[15] In these instances the exterior Christ, the simple Christ-man, spoke.

Atonement and Reconciliation

The popular doctrine of Atonement, if I understand it, affirms that the death of Jesus Christ on the cross was of the nature of a punishment suffered in the place of guilty man; whereby divine justice was satisfied, the divine wrath appeased, and divine forgiveness purchased for all the penitent. I do not believe in any such atonement. This doctrine is what I call a *scholasticism*, invented by the metaphysical Doctors of the Church. The word atonement occurs but once in the Christian Scriptures: "We also joy in God, through our Lord Jesus Christ, by whom we have now received the atonement."[16] The original word, here rendered atonement, is elsewhere rendered, more properly, *reconciliation*.

The entire manifestation of God through Jesus Christ in the flesh constitutes the true Christian atonement. It was a complex demonstration of truth declared, righteousness exemplified, and self-sacrifice suffered, for the reconciliation of mankind to God. It was necessary to that end; not as a vicarious punishment to appease divine justice; but as an efficacious illustration of divine Truth and Love, appealing to the deepest spiritual and moral sensibilities of human nature. Nothing less than such a demonstration could make man feel how low, sinful and lost he was; how much God loved and desired to save him; and how holy salvation would render him, by making him Christlike.

The work of atonement culminated in the death of Jesus on the cross; and therefore the sufferings and bloodshed of that great event have often been made to stand for the entire process. But it was not literally the whole; it was rather the finale and consummation of the work. We must never separate the self-sacrifice of the cross from the chain of its inductives, nor the efficacy of literal blood, shed for the remission of sins, from that spiritual life of which it was only the external representative. All that Jesus Christ said, did and suffered as the Medium of Divine Manifestation, through his entire life in the flesh, is comprehended in and constitutes the atonement. The atonement was as necessary, and is as important to man's salvation, as it has been represented to be in the popular Church; but is of a very different nature, and was necessary for very different reasons. It is an inseparable accompaniment of the mediatorial manifestation of God to mankind through Jesus Christ.

Revelation and Inspiration

The next principle is my third: *divine revelations and inspirations given to men*. That this is an essential of the Christian Religion is very obvious. It is either affirmed or taken for granted, all the way through the Scriptures, both of the Old and New Testaments, that God gave supernatural revelations or his existence, attributes, will, law and purposes to particular persons, and special inspirations to enlighten and guide their thought, speech, writing and action. Here it is written: "God, who at sundry times and in divers manners spake in times past unto the fathers by the prophets, hath in these last days spoken unto us by his Son, whom he hath appointed heir of all things, by whom also he made the worlds."[17] The entire Bible is characterized be records of divine revelations and inspirations to patriarchs, prophets, apostles, etc. To deny that God has ever revealed, or does ever reveal himself to man, except through the ordinary activities of the mind, is to discard the Christian Religion.

These divine revelations and inspirations have been given to man in various ways. That all-pervading, omnipresent divine essence, which I have called the Christ-Spirit, and which in Scripture is called the Holy Ghost, the Holy Spirit, the Spirit of God, etc., I have described as concentratable and personalizable in any degree, at any point, or within any susceptible created mind. I have said that God can do this, at will, whenever and wherever necessary to the good of his finite children. It is by means of this concentrating and personalizing capability that all special divine revelations and inspirations are given. Sometimes they are given through angels and departed spirits, who render themselves visible and audible, or manifest themselves in a striking manner to the senses of the recipient. Sometimes through extraordinary visions, trances, and dreams. Sometimes by powerful impressions and presentiments of a purely mental and spiritual nature. And sometimes by deep, distinct and irresistible suggestions to the inmost soul. Underlying all these there is a *general*, perhaps I may say *universal*, divine inspiration acting with greater or less effect on human nature.

When I speak of supernatural and special divine revelations, I mean not *contra*-natural, but *higher*-natural. It is as natural for the Divine Nature to act in its own way, as for any subordinate nature to act in *its* own way. The activities and manifestations of a higher nature are *super*natural to every lower nature. Mineral natures have their modes of action under given conditions, vegetable natures theirs, animal natures theirs, rational natures theirs, angelic natures theirs, and the Divine nature its own. The higher is always capable of transcending, modifying and even suspending the modes of action peculiar to a lower nature. And yet superior natures act as naturally in their sphere as inferior ones do in theirs. The higher are supernatural to the lower, and are miraculous to them, only because above their plane of natural action.

I do not believe that Divine revelations and inspirations have ceased, or ever will cease, till God shall be all in all. What I have denominated *general* inspiration certainly has not ceased, and never can. Nor do I see why special revelations and inspirations should cease. The ancient revelations and inspirations intimate no long cessation of their like, but plainly point forward to fresh and even more glorious ones to be enjoyed by mankind.

I do not regard Divine inspiration as *perfect* or *plenary*, so as to preclude all possibility of human error on the part of the inspired person. Jesus Christ alone claimed such perfection for himself, and stands honored by prophets and apostles, as the only one plenarily inspired, or perfectly God-possessed. All the Bible inspirees are declared to have received the Divine Spirit "by measure," but *he* without measure. All the prophets and apostles of both Testaments, confess the limitation of their inspiration, and that they were more or less erring and frail. But they all make *him* perfect in the Divine Spirit, Wisdom, and Love – and sinless. And, without the least seeming vanity or boasting, he represents himself as dwelling perpetually in God, and having the Father within him; as speaking the words, doing the works, and cherishing the Spirit of the Highest; as always pleasing Him. He alone, then, stands forth the living illustration of a *perfect, plenary, infallible* inspiration. All others, ancient and modern, however gloriously and reliably inspired at times, have been, are and must be, liable to error in a greater or less degree.

Immortal Spirits and the Resurrection of the Dead

I will now consider the fourth of my principles of Theological Truth: *the immortal existence of human and angelic spirits.* That there is a world of spiritual and immortal existence, into which all mankind pass at or soon after the death of the body – a world wherein are innumerable angels and spirits of various grades – is certainly a cardinal principle of the Christian Religion. The world to come, the resurrection of the dead, and the existence of angels and spirits, are prominently spoken of throughout I the Christian Scriptures, as realities of the sublimest importance.

> The children of this world marry, and are given in marriage; but they who shall be accounted worthy to obtain that world, and the resurrection of the dead, neither marry nor are given in marriage; neither can they die any more; for they are equal unto the angels; and are the children of God, being the children of the resurrection. Now that the dead are raised, even Moses showed at the bush, when called the Lord the God of Abraham, and the God of Isaac, and the God of Jacob. For he is not a God of the dead, but of the living; for all live unto him.[18]

I think both Scripture and reason lead us to the conclusion, that there are *evil* angels and spirits, as well as good ones. Many passages either declare, or plainly imply it, all the way through the New Testament; and reason cannot show us how the millions of men who leave this world in wickedness should suddenly and radically change at the instant of death. My belief is, that there are many grades of angels and spirits in the other world, including every conceivable variety of intellectual and moral character. I do not, however, believe that any are *totally* and *absolutely* evil there; nor that any are so low as to be incurable, or incapable of final progress to a higher grade. I see no reason why the beings of that world should not be good and evil *comparatively*, as men are here; though the scale of gradation, variety and comparison is probably greater there than in this mortal state; since if none are lower than our lowest, innumerable millions must be higher than our highest.

I believe that man has a body in the resurrectional or immortal state, as truly as in this life, and that it corresponds to the mortal body in every respect necessary to personal identity. But I do not believe that the gross substance of bones, flesh and blood, constituting the mortal body, ever goes into the immortal state. So far as the popular scholastic Theology teaches this, I reject it.

I think the Christian Scriptures do affirm the literal resurrection of Christ's body, but not as finally immortal; rather, as an absolute and unmistakable demonstration to his doubting disciples, that he had risen to the immortal existence. They needed such a demonstration to bring their faith to a sufficient intensity for the work before them. They needed to see, feel and know that he whom, in black despair, they had seen crucified, was alive again. It was granted them, and the end was answered. But being answered, it is altogether probable to my mind, that Jesus laid aside his flesh and bones to mingle with their kindred dust. His appearance, sometimes in a manner to vanish out of sight, and sometimes with a tangible body that could be felt and handled, indicates to me that he sometimes used his mortal body, and sometimes manifested himself to the spiritual senses of his disciples in his immortal body alone. When he said, "A spirit hath not flesh and bones as ye see me have," and when he said to Thomas, "Reach hither thy finger, and behold my hands; and reach hither thy hand and thrust it into my side," I think he must have had his body of flesh and bones with him.[19] But when he vanished out of sight on breaking bread with the disciples at Emmaus, when he suddenly stood in the midst of the disciples sitting with the closed doors, and when he ascended into a cloud out of their sight, when Saul heard his voice on the road to Damascus, and also when he was seen of more than five hundred brethren at once, I think he appeared in his proper resurrectional, spiritual, immortal body.

It is plainly declared by the apostle Paul, that "flesh and blood cannot inherit the kingdom of God"; that the body sown is not the body that shall be raised; that there is a natural body and a spiritual body; that the resurrection body is the spiritual one; that this earthly body is dissolved before we are clothed upon with our incorruptible one; and that then we are absent from our fleshly body, being present with the Lord.[20] It is contrary to the order of ascending nature, that Christ's earthly body, or any of our earthly bodies, should go into the immortal state. The common doctrine of the Church is, that the soul leaves the body at death, and exists in some intermediate state of being until a certain appointed time, when there is to be a general resurrection of men's bodies, and the soul and body are to be reunited forever. My view is that all mankind enter the immortal or resurrection state, at or soon after the death of the body.

Certain passages of New Testament Scripture speak of a general resurrection at a particular period. I understand such passages to speak, not of the *universal absolute* resurrection of man into the immortal state, which takes place at or soon after physical death, but rather of a *manifestive* or *demonstrative* resurrection; whereby the moral character or the personal condition of the immortals should be manifested in a conspicuous manner to others. It must be remembered that the word resurrection is used in Scripture with somewhat different significations. It does not always signify the renewal of man's conscious existence. Its radical generic meaning is *a raising up* of something which is in a fallen, or low, or unobservable condition. Hence that is properly called a resurrection which raises up persons or things so as to render them conspicuous, eminent or publicly observable. "The hour is coming in the which all that are in the graves shall hear his voice, and shall come forth; they that have done good to the resurrection of life; and they that have done evil to the resurrection of damnation."[21]

Now this passage describes a judicial resurrection of the departed dead, i.e. of departed spirits. It asserts that they should be so raised up, and rendered publicly observable, as that their true moral character, whether good or bad, should be unequivocally known. They that had done good were to come forth to life, i.e. to divine approval and universal honor; and they that had done evil to condemnation and rebuke. All this would be perfectly proper, as a judicial process executed in the immortal state. Its design must be to remove all obscurity from the moral character of the departed, and to reveal all conspicuously to themselves and each other in a true light. That such judicial processes are executed in the world of spirits, I have no reason to doubt. If so, they are *manifestive* resurrections of the departed to each other and to the public of that world, for some necessary, wise, an beneficent purpose.

> Behold, I show you a mystery; We shall not all sleep, but we shall all be changed, in a moment, in the twinkling of any eye, at the last trump; for the trumpet shall sound, and the dead shall be raised incorruptible; and we shall be changed.[22]

> For the Lord himself shall descend from heaven with a shout, with the voice of an archangel, and with the trump of God; and the dead in Christ shall rise first. Then we who are alive and remain shall be caught up together with them in the clouds to meet the Lord in the air; and so shall we ever be with the Lord.[23]

These passages also relate to a *manifestive* resurrection; but to one of a different character. In both these passages Paul points forward to a grand consummation of the immortalizing process, when Jesus Christ shall manifest himself on earth in his perfect glory, together with the departed saints in their immortal forms, and when the living saints shall be instantly changed, without passing through death, into immortals. These, and several other passages, appear to me to declare that such a consummation will be realized; and I can see nothing in the idea contrary to reason. I am therefore strongly inclined to believe it will ultimately take place. Indeed, the idea is to me delightful and sublime, as well as Scriptural and reasonable.

In this understanding, these passages present no incompatibility with those which teach the universal and absolute resurrectional immortality of mankind at or soon after physical death. Because the immortalization of all may very fitly and gloriously culminate in just such a manifestive resurrection. Probably all the earths of all the solar systems in the Infinitarium have their grand cycles and epochs of change through which their respective races of human inhabitants pass onward and upward to perfection. Our earth is not likely to be an exception. If so, the period will come when "mortality shall be swallowed up of life;" when "there shall be no more death;" when all things shall have been made new; when the tabernacle of God shall be made with men, when our glorious Lord Jesus Christ, with innumerable angels and saints, shall freely manifest themselves to the dwellers on earth; and when the communion of all shall have been rendered complete by the immortalization of all.[24] This perfectly accords with the holy prophecies and prayers of all ages, and with the ineffable design of the mediatorial manifestation of God through Christ; who must reign till he hath put all enemies, even death, the last enemy, under his feet. "And when all things shall be subdued unto him, then shall the Son also be subject unto him that put all things under him, that God may be all in all."[25]

Unity with God

Soul-Spirit, through all its individuations, from those nearest the animal to those nearest God, has probably a close connection with some kind of material body, grosser or more refined. Man has a gross body here in this mortal state. He will have a far more refined one after death. As he rises in excellence, he will be clothed with finer and finer forms, till the cycle of his eternity be completed, and his identity becomes constituted at last purely of the Divine essence. Then will his unity with God become absolutely perfect. And then what will follow? Just what God is doing with his own Essence throughout the Infinitarium, from and to all eternity of eternities: the perpetual interiorating, blessing and gradually perfecting of new souls innumerable. God's happiness consists in such activities as these; and good angels and good men, the nearer they shall be developed into the divine likeness, must find a similar happiness. Our identity will arrive at such an ultimate perfection as to unite our consciousness, and our very being, with God's.* At the completion of our individualship, the eternity of our selfhood, we come to be constituted purely of the divine essence. And so, instead of

---

* Inquirer: "What will be become of me then? I shall be annihilated! I shall be nothing! That will be dreadful!"

Expositor: "Are you afraid of becoming *too* perfect, and *too* happy? Are you afraid of becoming so near like God, in affection, will and action, that you cannot distinguish your selfhood from his?"

Inquirer: "Not exactly that; but I am afraid of losing my separate conscious identity."

losing our consciousness, we find it expand indefinitely into the omnipresent consciousness of God, and our happiness into the all-perfect bliss of God. Would that be a loss of either consciousness or happiness? Would it not be the consummation of all that the divinitized soul craves? O glorious thought! "Of him, and through him, and *to* him are all things."[26]

These thoughts – I can hardly call them my own thoughts – have come to me within a few years, in my meditative hours, unbidden, new and striking, by suggestion and impression from some higher sphere of intelligence. Afterwards I revolved and re-revolved, and considered their reasonableness, till they have become riveted in my convictions as sublime and heavenly truths.

Moral Nature and Responsibility

My fifth principle is: *the moral agency and religious obligation of mankind*. The whole Christian Religion assumes as self-evident, that man is by nature a moral agent and a religious being; that is, that he is capable of distinguishing between right and wrong, and that he is conscious of a religious obligation to choose the right, and to eschew the wrong. All its addresses and appeals to mankind presuppose this. It instructs, commands, warns, encourages, admonishes, exhorts and comforts man, as such a being. To deny the moral agency and religious obligation of mankind; to say that man is incapable of distinguishing right from wrong; that he has no sense of religious obligation; that he is not at all accountable to God for what he *does* or *is*; that he is a mere automaton of fate, or of necessity, or of circumstances; and that he is in no degree deserving of approbation or condemnation for his conduct; is to trample the Christian Religion under foot.

I do not mean to say that all human beings are *equally* and *unqualifiedly* moral agents. I speak of man generically, and of human nature in general. I speak of the proper normal, moral and religious capabilities of mankind, at the proper age of understanding, when of ordinary mental development and sanity. The infantile, idiotic, *non compos*, insane and abnormally eccentric, are to receive proper consideration, as undeveloped or diseased humans. Christianity shows them proper consideration, and treats them both justly and kindly. It also recognizes all the inequalities and conditional differences of those who are proper moral agents – their constitutional peculiarities, education, ignorance, knowledge, natural talent and powers of mind, circumstances and whatever increases or diminishes their moral responsibility. Where much is given much is required; where little, less in due proportion; and where nothing, of course, nothing. He who has one talent is required to improve and account for it; he who has two to improve and account for two; and he who has five to improve and account for five.[27] It is required of a man according to what he hath, not what he hath not. The Christian Religion assumes the moral agency and religious obligation of mankind to be just what it is, and represents the Divine Father as treating all accordingly, with due reasonableness, equity and merciful consideration of circumstances.

Circumstances direct all more or less; some extremely; others partially; but none, who are moral agents at all, so as wholly to do away their responsibility. Some are eminently capable of creating and controlling circumstances; others less capable; others very incapable. Moral responsibilities are proportionate. But the doctrine that man is a mere creature of circumstances, of blind fate or of irresistible necessity – that he is no moral agent by nature – is as repugnant to Christianity as it is to common consciousness, reason and moral order. Practical Christian Socialism can have nothing to do with such a pernicious negation of essential divine principles.

Some very well-meaning and benevolent persons of my acquaintance, have philosophized themselves into the theory that mankind are in no degree moral agents; but are the mere creatures of circumstances, totally unsuitable subjects of command, prohibition, reward, punishment, praise or blame. I should as soon think of commencing a house at the ridge of the roof, or of building a granite tower on quicksand, as of establishing a permanent Community with minds cherishing such irresponsible and impractical notions. Man must be taken for what he really is in natural capabilities and normal development, and *as such* made the most of. While nothing is unjustly required of him, or laid upon him, he must be made to feel the full responsibility of his proper moral agency and religious obligation. Without this he remains at best only a good-natured animal, and is always in danger of becoming a very troublesome one to his fellows. But bring him up to his capabilities, quicken his conscience, enlighten his understanding, inspire him with high aims and hopes, subject him to patient discipline under the yoke of acknowledged duty, attach him to Jesus Christ, enlist him fully in the great work of human progress, and make him feel all his responsibility to God, man and himself, and he becomes a noble being, a true child of the Highest, an angel of light and love, a happy realizer of his heavenly destiny.

Divine Retribution and Judgment

I now proceed to the consideration of my sixth principle of Theological Truth: *the certainty of perfect divine retribution.* That God causes all mankind to experience, at one time or another, in one way or another, a perfect retribution, is clearly a fundamental principle of the Christian Religion. This appears from many passages in the Christian Scriptures, as "He shall reward every man according to his works" and "We must all appear before the judgment seat of Christ; that every one may receive the things done in his body, according to that he hath done, whether it be good or bad."[28]

By divine retribution, I mean that causation by God of all enjoyment and all suffering in mankind, whereby the right and the wrong of their conduct is perfectly attested, as approved or condemned. The nature and qualities of a tree are perfectly known by their fruits.[29] The essential right or wrong of motives, feelings, words and actions is fully attested by their good or evil effects; i.e. by the good which God causes to be enjoyed, or the evil which he causes to be suffered, on account of them. This enjoyment and this suffering are experienced primarily and chiefly by the right and wrong doers, but secondarily, in some degree, by all connected with the prime actors. This enjoyment of good and suffering of evil, on account of the conduct of moral agents, I call divine retribution.

I make no radical distinction between natural consequences and special judgments. All divine retributions are natural consequences in their way and place; and all natural consequences are special judgments, so far as regards the ever-present, living, causing agency of God.

The common notion of natural laws is a fallacy. They are presumed to constitute a code of rules, which, having been established a great while ago by the Deity, have ever since executed themselves with perfect precision, without any accompanying and positive exercise of his will. That this is a fallacy may be seen at once, by just reflecting and questioning thus: Was there ever a time when these natural laws did not exist and operate? If so, did God before that time do everything by a positive exercise of his omnipresent will? If so, have natural laws been any improvement on the ancient specialty plan? If so, is not God imperfect, and gradually making progress? And if so, may not natural laws themselves be abolished sometime in favor of "a more excellent way"?[30] But if God from unbegun eternity operated *perfectly* until a certain time, *without* this self-executing Code of natural laws, what need was there of establishing any such Code? Or again, if there never was a time when these natural laws did not exist, then are they not as *old* as God, and as *unmade* as God? And if as old and as self-existent as God, are they in any way separable from God? If separable from God, and self-executing, what need is there of a God? Is not this Code of natural laws a competent and all-sufficient God? Why then have *two* Gods, to cause results which one might accomplish *alone*? But if these natural laws are inseparable from God, then they are nothing but *modes* of his causation and operation. And if so, God is everywhere present and acting, with a positive will and judgment, just as much and just as truly, as if there were no natural laws; which is undoubtedly the fact. Therefore the notion of a sometime-established code of self-executing natural laws, which take care of Nature, is a fallacy. The one All-Perfect, Infinite God is omnipresent, and by a positive unwearied exercise of his own proper power, will and judgment, carries on all the processes of causation throughout the Infinitarium. And thus, from moment to moment, he causes *that* to take place which is best, all things considered; regard being had to the grade of nature, the circumstances of the case, and all proper resulting effects. Hence I make no radical distinction between natural consequences and special judgments. All the difference to be made between them is, that ordinary effects or consequences, which to human apprehension seem to be regular and uniform, are called *natural*; whilst those which seem very peculiar and extraordinary are called *special*. In truth they are all *natural* and all *special*. Finite creatures make the distinctions, according to their imperfect apprehensions of cause and effect.

A perfect divine retribution must be a *just* retribution; a *benevolent* retribution; and a *salutary* retribution. A *just* retribution must be one which is universal, impartial and equitable. It must take effect on all the proper subjects of retribution. It must be without respect of persons. It must be according to the exact deserts of all, with such adaptations, discriminations and modifications as strict equity demands. It must truly express and demonstrate the divine approbation or disapprobation of the conduct to which it relates. Such would be a just retribution. To suppose a retribution which was not executed on moral agents impartially, equitably and fitly, would be to suppose an *unjust* retribution. But the divine retribution is perfectly just.

It is also *benevolent*. God can do nothing that is not benevolent. "God is love."[31] A benevolent retribution must be one which aims at the highest good of all the parties concerned. God himself is a party concerned. Each individual rewarded or punished is a party concerned. All the individuals connected with the retributed one, or cognizant of the case, are parties concerned. The general public are parties concerned. The whole race, yes, the whole universe are parties concerned. The father, the child, and the whole family are concerned. The highest good of each and all these parties must be desired and aimed at in a benevolent retribution. To imagine any act of divine retribution which disregards God's highest good as the Supreme Father, or the highest good of any connected relative, or witness, or the highest good of the whole, is to imagine an *un*-benevolent retribution. But the divine retribution is a perfectly benevolent one.

It is also *salutary*. A salutary retribution is one which has the effect, on the whole, to make *right* understood and received, wrong understood and detested, duty loved and delighted in; it must be an exemplary and corrective retribution. To suppose a divine retribution which makes any of its recipients or beholders, worse in moral character, or no better, is to suppose an *un*-salutary one – a useless, or worse than useless retribution. But the divine retribution is a perfectly salutary one. And so it is written: "We have had fathers of our flesh which corrected us, and we gave them reverence; shall we not much rather be in subjection to the Father of spirits, and live? For they verily for a few days chastened us after their pleasure; but he for our profit, that we might be partakers of his holiness."[32]

I am very sure that the abominable doctrine that God will punish the wicked after death to all eternity without any regard to their good, is not warranted by a fair construction of the Christian scriptures. By a fair construction, I mean a construction which always respects clearly declared fundamental principles, and makes due allowance for the mere sound of figurative and intensive language. Now I contend that the clearly declared fundamental principles of the New Testament, those which set forth the moral attributes, perfections, will, character, purposes and government of God, make it an utter impossibility that he should punish the wicked to all eternity without any regard to their good. If there are any passages of Scripture the words or phrases of which seem to teach any such doctrine, their *literal* import is contrary to clearly declared fundamental principles, and probably contrary to their true internal import. And whoever makes the *literal* import of such passages override fundamental principles, and withal their own true *internal* import, gives them a grossly unfair construction.

Such a text as, "These shall go away into everlasting punishment; but the righteous into life eternal"[33] would perplex me, if I did not know that such terms and phrases are often used in an accommodated sense throughout the

Scriptures, not in a strict, literal and philosophical sense; and if I did not also know that the clearly declared fundamental principles of the Christian Religion preclude the possibility of Christ's having intended to teach that God's retributions will ever be repugnant to justice, love and wisdom. It is absolutely impossible that the same Teacher, who enjoins us to love and do good to our enemies that we may be like God, should have intended to teach us that the same God will consign his enemies to a *hopeless, endless punishment*. It is much easier for me to presume that his language, in such passages, requires an accommodated construction. Therefore I give it such a construction; nor do I find the least difficulty in so doing.

Here Jesus puts the punishment of the wicked in exact contrast with the happiness of the righteous; both are to be everlasting. Why should he have done so, if the one is to end and the other not?

The original terms rendered *eternal, everlasting, forever* and *forever and ever*, have not a strict and literal meaning, nor a uniformly precise meaning, either in the Old or New Testaments. But they are used with a wide latitude and variety of meaning. Every person decently informed on the subject knows this. The everlasting covenant of circumcision, everlasting priesthood of Aaron, everlasting possession of the land of Canaan, eternal God, everlasting hills, everlasting reproach of the Jews in the Babylonian captivity terminating in seventy years, eternal damnation of wicked men, everlasting life of the righteous, eternal judgment, everlasting gospel, etc., are all spoken of in these terms, with a various, general, but accommodated meaning, which may be easily enough understood by minds that have a proper veneration for fundamental principles, are not pre-committed to make out a case, and are not idolaters of the *mere letter* of Scripture. Such truthful and enlightened minds know very well that though the covenant of circumcision, priesthood of Aaron, possession of Canaan and reproach of the Babylonian captives, were not literally and philosophically *endless*, there was no impropriety in their being called *everlasting*. They see that though God and the hills are both called eternal or everlasting, yet that the hills are not as everlasting as God is. They see that though the gospel is called everlasting, it is not necessarily to be preached to all eternity. They see that eternal life has nothing in the mere adjective to guarantee its endlessness, and that the naked word *life* in many passages just as certainly means unlimited happiness, as does the phrase *everlasting life*; because in the nature of the case there is nothing to limit its duration. They see that "eternal damnation" and "everlasting punishment" must have a limitation somewhere; because neither the plainly declared justice of God, benevolence of God, wisdom of God, nor promises of God, admit the idea of a literally endless punishment. At the same time, they see that there was no falsehood nor impropriety in Christ's denominating the *damnation* of the willfully wicked *eternal*, or their punishment *everlasting*; because that damnation and punishment will be of long continuance, will extend into the future world, will be administered in accordance with immutable divine principles, and will be everlastingly effectual and salutary on its subjects. Therefore, rooted and grounded in fundamental principles, enlightened as to the usage and meaning of Scripture terms, and full of confidence both in the justice and love of God, such texts no longer give them the least perplexity or uneasiness.

The popular doctrine of the nominal Church is, that the life of man in this world is his only absolute probation for all eternity beyond, and that at death his case is sealed up till the final *judgment day*. That the life of man on earth is more or less probationary for the next life in the immortal state is very natural, reasonable and probable. But that this earthly life is man's *only* and *absolute* probation, for all the eternity or eternities to come is unnatural, unreasonable, improbable, and without one particle of warrant from Scripture, either in the letter or spirit. I know what I say and whereof I affirm, in respect tot his point, and consent to be held responsible for my assertion.

As to the day of judgment, it is a Scripture term, but has been greatly misconstrued, misapplied and overstrained. That God has appointed a particular day of judgment, at which all mankind are to be assembled, tried and finally sentenced to heaven or hell, is a fiction, founded partly on a falsely literal construction of a few parabolic and highly figurative passages of Scripture, but chiefly on the speculations of imaginative and scholastic theologians. It is indefensible by either Scripture or reason. But it has this underlying truth beneath it, that there are periods of judgment, harvest periods, for nations, cities, families and individuals; some in this life and others in the immortal state. These are judgment days to their respective subjects. They are periods of judicial visitation, marked and distinguished by strong demonstrations. Nations, states, cities, communities, families and individuals, all have their seed time and harvest, their probationary and retributionary periods in orderly succession. This is true to some extent on earth, and is probably more completely illustrated in the world to come, at least with respect to individuals and the race at large. So all mankind *have* had, *are* having, or *will* hereafter have, their respective day or days of judgment, in the true and proper meaning of that Scripture term. But there is no reason for believing in *one*, exclusive, universal, final DAY OF JUDGMENT for the entire human race. It is a mere scholasticism.

Spiritual Regeneration and the New Birth

My seventh principle is: *the necessity of man's spiritual regeneration.* What do I mean by spiritual regeneration? What is *generation*? It is that process of nature whereby human beings are developed into sentient and mental life, so as to be conscious of natural existence, and to exercise its appropriate loves. What then is *re*-generation? It is that process whereby human beings are developed into spiritual, moral and eternal life, so as to be conscious of their true spiritual existence, and to exercise its appropriate loves.

The appropriate loves of man's first or mere natural existence are essentially selfish. He loves himself supremely, and all others only as subordinate to the presumed good of self. This is the condition of all merely generate; i.e. *un*-regenerate human beings. The appropriate loves of the true spiritual existence are unselfish; love to the great Parent Spirit with all the heart; love to the neighbor as one's self; love of all goodness; and love of the universal highest good. This is the condition, and these are the predominant loves of all truly regenerate human beings.

The unregenerate man is governed by essentially carnal, animal, selfish loves; and his intellectual faculties are chiefly exercised in searching out and employing the means of self-gratification. The germ of spiritual life is within him, but is undeveloped. He has no distinct consciousness of being an immortal spirit, or of his proper relations to God or to fellow man. He is not inherently and necessarily evil in his nature. But he is yet chiefly an intellectual animal. He therefore acts out the intellectual animal. And if the great spiritual law of truth and love presses upon him, the resists it as a cross upon his loves. How *could* it be otherwise? The ovum of his spiritual nature is latent within him, but it must be impregnated by the Divine Spirit, and caused to germinate. He must be begotten and born again – born from above – spiritually regenerated – born of God. All must be. This is an indispensable process in the grand order of human progress. Without it man cannot see the kingdom of God, and enter into the joy of its pure filial and fraternal loves. There is nothing *contra*-natural, nothing unreasonable, in the doctrine of regeneration. It is a fundamental principle of the Christian Religion.

This accounts for the universal sinfulness of mankind in their natural development, before spiritual regeneration. It could not be otherwise with human nature, in its first plane of development. Hence the entire Christian Religion justly assumes that all mankind need to be regenerated – that they must be enlightened, quickened, called to the exercise of faith and repentance, placed under the wholesome discipline of the cross, and sanctified by the all-cleansing influence of the Holy Spirit. Just assume that mankind in their primary development are truly spiritual, governed by heavenly and unselfish loves, naturally addicted to spiritual truth and good, and what then? If this were true, you would have naturally a sinless, holy, happy world of human beings, already unfolded for the kingdom of God – blooming and fragrant trees of the divine paradise. *Then*, what need of a gospel, a Savior, a universal regeneration? None at all.

But it *was* not so, *is* not so. It is quite the reverse. Eschewing the scholastic device of absolute and total depravity, with all its overstrained accompaniments; and also eschewing the equally scholastic device of man's absolute native purity and heavenly-mindedness; let us take the facts as they are: that universal human nature is generated and developed *first* on the low plane of animal intellectuality, innocent indeed at birth, but naturally selfish, and therefore universally manifesting various degrees of folly and sin; that in the order of progress the spiritual man is developed *after* the animal man; that the process of this second development is spiritual regeneration; and that this spiritual regeneration is *necessary* for mankind. "Verily, verily I say unto thee, except a man be born again, he cannot see the kingdom of God ... That which is born of the flesh is flesh, and that which is born of the Spirit is spirit."[34]

I reject the doctrine of absolute total depravity; and also the opposite doctrine of absolute native purity and holiness. I regard both these doctrines as mere scholasticisms and untrue in their extreme assumed facts. I regard the popular doctrine of the Fall of human nature in Adam as another theological scholasticism. I have no objection to the idea of Adam's fall from original simplicity and innocence into transgression, physical perversion and moral perversion. Nor have I any objection to the idea that mental and moral qualities are hereditarily transmissible from generation to generation, in a greater or less degree. All this seems natural and reasonable. But I do object to the notion that our first parents fell from a state of pure holiness and moral perfection into a state of total depravity, and thereby involved universal human nature in such depravity. I see nothing in Scripture, nature, or reason, to warrant such a sweeping and extravagant doctrine.

Man is born unspiritual, carnal. He is selfish, frail and prone to sin, as naturally developed on the primary plane of his being. But his selfishness, frailty, sinfulness is of all grades, shades and modifications, from very low and hateful, to very tolerable and amiable. The differences and varieties of manifestation in individuals of the race have this wide range. The suscepti-bility of and the undeveloped germ of spirituality are latent in all; and so all are capable of spiritual regeneration under the proper excitabilities and conditions.

The grand agent in producing spiritual regeneration is the holy Spirit of God – the Christ Spirit, as I have called it – the Divine Spirit of Truth, Wisdom and Love. But man is always and necessarily active and cooperative in regeneration. He exercises faith in the divine and spiritual, and in the possi-bilities of his higher development. He prays, seeks, knocks, strives. He repents, denies himself for righteousness' sake, and struggles after reformation.

Spiritual regeneration is necessarily gradual; but of variously gradual degrees in different individuals. It may commence very suddenly and strik-ingly, or very insensibly and noiselessly. So it may progress, and develop the spiritual nature, rapidly or slowly. First there is the seed, then the germ, then the blade, and then in due time the full corn in the ear.[35]

The infallible evidence of spiritual regeneration is a developed con-sciousness of spiritual, moral and eternal life in the soul; selfishness morti-fied willingly by the cross of self-denial; true love of God, of brother man, of divine principles, and of the universal good. These are the appropriate fruits of regeneration. There is no other sufficient evidence that any human being has experienced spiritual regeneration. I think you must see that *the necessity of spiritual regeneration* is a cardinal principle of the Christian Religion; and that without this grand essential we cannot expect ever to build up true Practical Christian Communities, much less hope for the regeneration of universal humanity.

The Triumph of Good over Evil

The eighth and last principle of Theological Truth to be considered is *the final universal triumph of good over evil*. The Christian Religion contem-plates human nature as struggling through a long and severe conflict for deliverance from its frailty, error, sin and misery. This is a struggle of the spiritual mind with the carnal mind. It is a conflict of truth with error, light with darkness, love with selfishness, right with wrong, good with evil. Once commenced, it constantly goes on in each individual until truth and love, right and good, gain the victory. Likewise between higher and lower souls, the more carnal and the more spiritual. Likewise between the carnal and the carnal, the selfish and the selfish, the revengeful and the revengeful. Likewise between classes, parties, sects and nations – the wicked against the wicked, the wicked against the righteous, the less righteous against the more righteous, and the less progressive against the more progressive. Hence Jesus declared that he came not to bring peace, but a sword of division among mankind; well knowing that so long as the world was low, dark, corrupt and unwilling to reform, opposition, hatred and persecution would certainly be drawn forth against those who should embrace truth and righteousness. He also knew that the animal man would war with the spiritual man, so soon as the latter should be born in every individual; and that the cross must be taken up daily, in order to the triumph of the spiritual mind over the carnal. Hence Paul wrote:

> For we know that the law is spiritual; but I am carnal, sold under sin ... For I know that in me (that is in my flesh) dwelleth no good thing; for to will is present with me, but how to perform that which is good I find not ... I delight in the law of God after the inward man: But I see another law in my members, warring against the law of my mind, and bringing me into captivity to the law of sin which is in my members. O wretched man that I am! who shall deliver me from the body of this death?[36]

This individual, social, universal conflict or warfare is going on and will go on in the soul between the carnal and spiritual minds, between souls variously more or less carnal or spiritual, between societies variously carnal or spiritual, in fine, between all the powers of Light and Darkness manifestable in human nature, till at last Truth and Righteousness shall triumph over their opposites.

> Then shall be brought to pass the saying that is written, Death is swallowed up in victory. O death, where is thy sting? O grave, where is thy victory? The sting of death is sin; and the strength of sin is the law. But thanks be to God, who giveth us the victory through our Lord Jesus Christ. Therefore, my beloved brethren, be ye steadfast, unmovable, always abounding in the work of the Lord, forasmuch as ye know that your labor is not in vain in the Lord.[37]

By such testimonies we perceive what the will, aim, purpose of God is; what he manifested himself through Jesus Christ to accomplish; what the reign of Christ is designed to effect; what all the holy prophets have predicted as the grand consummation; and what all true saints are taught to pray for in faith, and labor for in patient hope. Is it any thing less than *the final universal triumph of Good over Evil – the triumph of truth and righteousness*, holiness and happiness?

Why should an All-Perfect, Infinite God should create universes that require such a severe and protracted struggle to reach a state of perfection? The triumph of truth and righteousness, holiness and happiness is unspeakably sublime and glorious; but would it not have been better to have constituted all things perfect at once, without any struggle at all?

I do not believe it would have been better for any universe of rational and moral intelligences. I believe that God has done wisely in constituting his universes with all the imperfection, variety, contrast and other requisites to the long struggling progress I have been contemplating; and that the final triumph of truth and righteousness, order, harmony and bliss, is more glorious with, than it could have been without such a struggle. I say this for three general reasons. Perfect beings could not be happy without imperfect beings to love, bless and elevate. Imperfect beings could not be happy without progress from a lower to a higher condition. Neither perfect nor imperfect beings could be happy without multiform variety, contrast and change in the scale of being, in the condition of things, and in the course of events. Let us test these three reasons.

We say God is an All-Perfect Being. If so he must be capable of all-perfect happiness. In what then must that happiness consist? It cannot consist in any thing given to him from without himself as a supply for his needs; since an All-Perfect Being has no needs that can be thus supplied. It cannot consist in the gratification of self-esteem, self-will, self-aggrandizement or any other selfish attribute; since an all-Perfect Being is infinitely above all pride and selfishness. It must consist in creating, disciplining, providing for, and blessing beings that are finite and imperfect. What would Love be without beings on whom to bestow it? What would Wisdom be without beings to discipline, to guide, to inspire and elevate? What would Power be that was never exercised? The happiness of all beings consists in the proper exercise of their normal affection, intelligence and ability. This must be as true of God as of all other beings. Therefore, in order to the highest happiness of his divine nature, God must be in the legitimate exercise of all his attributes. And in order to this, he must be a Creator, Governor and Benefactor of numberless creatures.

But this could not be without imperfection in those creatures of numberless degrees and variety. If they were perfect, they would be his own equals – mere repetitions of himself, or at least existing on the exact plane of his own nature. And in that case, neither he nor they could be happy without inferiors – needy and dependent children toward whom to exercise all-perfect Love, Wisdom and Power. Besides, the creation of one All-Perfect, Infinite Being by another is a self-evident absurdity. But even were this possible, divine happiness would still be impossible, for want of dependent beings to bless. The divine nature, being perfect in itself and without the least selfishness, must find all its own blessedness in blessing others – in *giving*, not in *receiving*.

Why might not God have created beings so nearly perfect, that they should commence existence as good as the angels, or at least as good as the very best of human beings in this world? Then an inconceivable amount of error, folly, sin and suffering would have been prevented, which now exist. But perhaps a still greater amount of wisdom, righteousness and happiness would have been prevented. For, how are *comparatively good* angels and men are to find happiness? In loving, worshipping and progressing towards their All-Perfect Father; and, of course, in loving each other. But the nearer they become like God, the more necessarily will their happiness consist in imparting good to inferiors. And in the same ratio of progress will they cease to need each other's aid and sympathy. Now how are they to be rendered happy, without adjoining to them several descending grades of beings more imperfect than themselves? We are not quite sure that there is a grade so low as to take no interest in a still lower, till at least we get below the humans. But if there were such a grade, it might be one capable of progress; and that progress might require for its stimulus the variety and contrast of beings, things and conditions beneath itself; so that nothing, on the whole, is absolutely unwise in the grand system of things.

Does this mean that there is neither error, folly, sin, nor wrong in our universe, nor in any other universe of the whole Infinitarium? Not exactly. I only make out that on God's part there was none; and that in his infinite Wisdom and Goodness he so governs the grand system of his operations as to render even the error, follies, sins and wrongs, exhibited by his imperfect creatures in the lower stages of their progress, conducive to the highest good of all; so that, in HIS designs and overrulings, all things considered, "whatsoever is, is right" – is BEST.

Can no man then be blamed, condemned or chastised for sin? I answer this question with another: are we obliged to impeach the Wisdom and Goodness of God, in order to find just causes for the condemnation and correction of sinful creatures? Every being is morally responsible for his conduct according to the degree of his light and ability, and according to the motive from which he acts. Each has a standard of right, higher or lower. Each is conscious of a certain ability to do right or wrong. And each knows within himself whether his leading motive in any case was to do right or not. Therefore it is just that each sinner should be condemned and corrected by his own standard, and in strict accordance with his infidelity to that standard. This is for the highest good of all beings. It is therefore an integral part of the divine system of government.

Now suppose further that God also takes care that all partial evil shall be made to work out universal good; that all the errors, follies, sins and punishments of his imperfect creatures shall be rendered harmless, and even beneficent, *on the whole*. Suppose this, I say; and what then? Does it exculpate the real guilt of his creatures? By no means. They meant what they did unto evil; but he overrules it unto good, no thanks to them. "Let God be true, and every man a liar." Let man stand for what he is, and God be glorified for what he has done and is doing in his own infinite perfection; "of whom, through whom, and to whom, are all things."[38]

I close with the following pertinent quotations from two eminent poets:

> Of systems possible, if 'tis confest
> That wisdom infinite must form the best,
> Where all must full or not coherent be,
> And all that rises, rise in due degree;
> Then in the scale of reasoning life 'tis plain
> There must be, somewhere, such a rank as man;
> And all the question (wrangle e'er so long)
> Is only this, – If God has placed him wrong?
> Respecting man, whatever wrong we call,
> May, – must be right as relative to all.
> . . . .
>
> Then say not man's imperfect, Heaven in fault;
> Say rather, man's as perfect as he ought;
> His knowledge measured to his state and place,
> His time a moment, and a point his space.
> If to be perfect in a certain sphere,
> What matter soon or late, or here, or there?
> The blessed to-day is as completely so
> As who began a thousand years ago.
> . . . .
>
> Cease then, nor Order imperfection name;
> Our proper bliss depends on what we blame.
> Know thy own point; this kind, this due degree
> Of blindness, weakness, Heaven bestows on thee.
> Submit – in this or any other sphere,
> Secure to be as blest as thou canst bear;

Safe in the hand of one disposing Power,
Or in the natal, or the mortal hour.
All nature is but art unknown to thee;
All chance, direction which thou canst not see;
All discord, harmony not understood;
All partial evil, universal good;
And spite of pride, in erring reason's spite,
One truth is clear, *Whatever is, is right.* [39]

I cannot go
Where *Universal Love* not smiles around,
Sustaining all yon orbs, and all their suns;
From seeming evil still educing good,
And better thence again, and better still
In infinite progression. – But I lose
Myself in Him, in *Light ineffable*;
Come then, expressive Silence, muse His praise. [40]

Chapter 3

Principles of Personal Righteousness

The Nature of Personal Righteousness

I am now to treat of the principles of Personal Righteousness. By Personal Righteousness I mean all that is necessary to render an individual human being, or moral agent of any class, truly righteous. Personal Righteousness consists in right action or conduct, right intention, aim, or will, and right affection, spirit or temper. If the external action or conduct be right, the main intention, aim or will be right, and the ruling affection, spirit or temper be right, there is a true personal righteousness. And if these three requisites were all perfectly right, there would be a *perfect* personal righteousness. If either be imperfect in any individual, the resultant righteousness must be correspondingly imperfect.

Thus a man's external action or conduct may be right, or chiefly right, but his intention, aim or will may be wrong; his governing motive may be low, or unworthy. Such a one is not truly a righteous person. Another may be nearly right in his external conduct, and also in his predominant intention, but nevertheless be in such an unholy affection, spirit or temper as quite to neutralize his good conduct, and good general intention. Such a man is not truly righteous. He may be much less unrighteous than others, but he is deficient in a right spirit. Another may have a right spirit or temper of mind, and a right general affection, yet really lack a clear, well-settled right intention or aim. He will therefore be a good-natured, kind feeling, pleasant man, who means well so far as he knows; but his righteousness will be a haphazard, inconsistent and often self-destroying one – in many cases giving the strongest undesigned aid and countenance to real wickedness. And yet again, a man may be righteous in his grand intention, aim or will, but so wrong both in his spirit and external conduct as to neutralize nearly all the good influence of his right aim. Hence a true personal righteousness must be one growing out of and sustained by essential divine principles.

Reverence for the Divine

I will commence with the principle of *reverence for the Divine and spiritual.* Truly, "the fear of the Lord [reverence for the Divine] is the beginning of wisdom."[1] Without something of this, man is but an intellectual beast. It is the first and indispensable step in personal righteousness.

I have defined reverence for the Divine and spiritual to be a just and sacred respect for God, all manifestations of God, all divine moral attributes, principles and qualities, and all spiritual realities, as distinguished from external, material, sensuously known Nature. This reverence I call a *principle* of personal righteousness; by which I mean that it is a cardinal duty to be acknowledged and fulfilled by all moral agents.

Phrenologists say that Reverence or Veneration is a natural organ of the religious sentiment, which gives the *feeling* or *desire* to worship God, pray, be submissive, humble etc. If one has this organ large and strong, he will have full flow of reverential feeling. If small and weak, he will have little or none of this feeling. Is not reverence for the Divine and spiritual, then, a spontaneous *feeling* where it exists at all, and not a *duty* which men must acknowledge and act to from *principle*?

Human nature has in its very constitution all the susceptibilities and rudimental capabilities of doing and becoming just what it ought, in order to happiness in all its relations. Or to speak Phrenologically, it has all the organs necessary to this result, if properly excited, conditioned and disciplined. But this IF must not be disregarded. Physiologists have demonstrated that all the mental and moral, as well as physical constitutionalities and marked peculiarities are transmissible from parents to their children; and that remarkable accidents and strongly impressive circumstances, occurring about the time of gestation, or during gestation, often greatly affect the predispositions of the offspring. Hence many are born with ill-balanced brains, or what are called *badly organized heads.* Then, it is to be remembered that *education* works mighty effects all the way up from infancy to maturity. I include in education every description of direct or indirect influence by which the habits and character of the young are formed. We cannot unmake badly organized heads already in existence; but, doing the best we can by and for them, we must guard against evil in the future generation, gestation and education of children.

Here, then, is this organ of Veneration. If large and strong, very well; it may require comparatively little pains to excite, condition and discipline it properly. Neglected, mis-influenced, or poorly trained, it will not fulfill its promise. The Christian Religion is replete with ministries for its proper development. Its exercise under these various stimuli is therefore made a cardinal duty – an essential principle of personal righteousness. All who have the organ large enough to feel the appeal which the Christian Religion makes to it, will embrace this principle with a profound conviction of its fundamental importance, and will set about making others respect it.

As I have already said, right affection, intention and action *together* constitute personal righteousness. This is as true of reverencing the Divine and spiritual as of any other duty. Reverence must not be a blind spontaneous sentimentality. It must be an *enlightened, well-considered, well-disciplined* reverence. It must be right in external action, right in intention and right in spirit. Such is reverence for the Divine, regarded as a fundamental principle of duty.

True Reverence for the Divine and spiritual is the root or radical principle out of which grow humility, submission, contrition, prayer, gratitude, adoration and all holy worship. It also inspires proper deference for all divine attributes, principles and qualities, in whomsoever manifested or wheresoever existent; and predisposes the soul to appreciate the inherent and high superiority of spiritual beings, things, and interests, over those of a mere material and sensuous nature. When a human being begins to be spiritually developed, he recognizes himself as a rational and moral spirit destined to an immortal existence. He perceives that the same is true of all of the Adamic race. He looks upward and thinks of the great world of angels and spiritual intelligences. He contemplates the All-Perfect and Infinite God. He studies his divine manifestations. He inquires into his laws, into his attributes, into his moral qualities and perfections. He turns back and sees himself; how ignorant, weak, erring, sinful, dependent, necessitous he is. He bows himself in the dust before the Highest. He submits himself to the majesty of the Almighty. He melts into penitence and contrition. He becomes as a little child. He prays; he confesses his unworthiness; he implores divine mercy; he feels all the excellence and goodness of God; he gives thanks; he worships the Infinite Father in spirit and in truth; he devotes himself to His service; and conscientiously inquires day by day what is his duty – what is *right*.

In closing on this point, permit me to notice its *practical* bearings. Contemplate the individual who is a stranger to this first grand principle of personal righteousness; who is so undeveloped in spirit that he scarcely recognizes himself as anything more than an intellectual animal. To him, who is God or Christ, that he should reverence them? Who and what and where are angels and immortal spirits, that he should concern himself about them? What is duty, what is righteousness, that he should trouble himself anything further about them than to keep out of the way of human penalties and public disgrace? Behold his self-conceit and pride! Behold his sensualism, his sordidness, his coarse brutality or refined selfishness! Behold how little he cares for the enlightenment, elevation and moral progress of his fellow creatures! Behold his ambition, his tastes, his pursuits, the ignoble ends for which he lives! Behold his prayerlessness, his impenitence, his contempt of all true worship, all true devotion to principle! Whether learned or unlearned, in high life or low life, behold this carnal, animal man, unborn of God, rushing irreverently onward like the horse into the battle, without any just appreciation of God, of himself, of mankind, of this life or the next; without true righteousness, without real happiness, like the troubled sea when agitated by a storm, casting up mire and dirt; discordant in himself, in his family, in his neighborhood, and really at war with God and man. And behold, at length, he passeth away into the lower spheres of the next life, there to experience a protracted discipline before he can fairly begin to reverence the divine and spiritual!

Shall I ask if any man or woman, greatly lacking in Reverence for the Divine and spiritual, is a fit candidate for membership in a Practical Christian Community? What could be done with such an unhewn stone in the edifice of a new social state? Self-conceited and self-willed, revolting at the most wholesome restraint, and incapable of government of divine principles, he or she would never rest till self-precipitated into the uproar and violence of antagonistic, man-governed society. Such souls must be born again, in order either to individual or social happiness. Without a tolerable degree of reverence for the Divine and spiritual, and without the humility, submission, contrition, prayerfulness, gratitude, worshipfulness and devotion to divine principles, men and women could not harmoniously cooperate in building up a new social order. They would be too proud, selfish, turbulent and contentious.

Self-Denial

The principle of *self-denial for righteousness' sake* follows naturally after reverence for the Divine. The Divine and spiritual once fairly seen and truly reverenced, a standard of righteousness immediately unfurls itself to the mind. But it is one thing to behold, acknowledge and reverence the standard of righteousness, and another thing to follow it faithfully.

The animal man revolts against the spiritual man. The carnal mind delights not in the obedience of the spiritual. There is a warfare to be accomplished. There is a cross to be taken up and borne daily, for a long time, before the crown of life and glory can be put on. There is no escape from this conflict, from this crucifixion of the old man. Christ and Belial cannot both be followed. God and Mammon cannot both be served. The carnal mind and the spiritual mind cannot both bear rule. The will of the flesh and the will of God cannot both be done. So the cross of self-sacrifice and self-denial for righteousness' sake must be borne till the new man, created in righteousness and true holiness, has gained a complete ascendancy. Then the narrow way, that was entered through the strait gate, will be a way of pleasantness and a path of peace, shining more and more unto the perfect day.[2]

The cross is the grand distinctive emblem of the Christian Religion, to indicate the way of human salvation, and the indispensable process of its accomplishment. Jesus Christ took it up, bore it through life, endured its aggravated sufferings in death, and was exalted from it to the throne of mediatorial glory. He consecrated it to the sacrifice of himself for the redemption and reconciliation of the world. He knew that he must lead human nature over it into the glorious liberty of the sons of God. He knew that it must be taken up and borne by every regenerate soul. Hence he said, "If any man will come after me, let him deny himself, and take up his cross daily, and follow me."[3]

This then is a fundamental principle of personal righteousness: the cross of self-sacrifice and self-denial for righteousness' sake. Without this neither individuals, nor society, nor the race, can be saved from sin, folly and evil – can be reformed, purified, elevated, regenerated and perfected. It must be taken up and victoriously borne forward over the vanquished hosts of darkness.

There is a great mystery in the cross, and yet, when viewed as a *principle*, no mystery at all. Who does not see that righteousness must be put first and foremost in the veneration and devotion of every soul, in order to deliverance from all sin and evil? If any human being love sin and evil, or love the wrong which inevitably drags evil in its train, there is no power in earth or heaven that can save him from the consequences. *Right, duty* must be held supreme. Whatever love, or will, or interest, or convenience comes in competition with these must be promptly and unreservedly sacrificed. There must be no compromise of absolute divine principle. This is the indispensable condition of human salvation and progress. And who would soften this condition? It could only be done to the ruin of our highest hopes, and to the loss of our highest ultimate good. Divine and glorious principle! Nothing truly great and good ever was or ever can be accomplished for mankind without it. We must have it in the individual, in the family, in the community, in the nation, and throughout the race, or perish in our carnal lusts, evil ambition and selfish expediency. You can imagine how unfit a man must be to work out the happiness of himself, or family, or community, who has not a tolerable devotion to this all-redeeming principle. He would halt, and turn aside at every temptation or trial. His law would be appetite, passion, ease, convenience, expediency, selfishness, mere human enactments, customs, fashions and public opinion, however low; and his career would end in perdition.

Justice

The principle of *justice to all beings* includes justice to God, to angels and spirits, to friends, to strangers, to enemies, to all mankind, to one's self, to the very animals and to all sensitive creatures. And what is justice? It is that divine principle which constantly prompts us to respect the rights of all beings, to render to them all that they may rightfully demand of us, or what is fit and right under the well-considered circumstances of the case, and to exact nothing of any being which we have not a good right, and a good reason to claim. To be scrupulously just to all beings, in all our dealings, all our expectations, all our words and all our feelings, would be a most exalted illustration of personal righteousness. That this is a cardinal principle of the Christian Religion, no one needs an array of texts to prove.

Alas, how deficient are mankind in Justice! Behold how little of it toward God, toward fellow man, toward inferiors, toward the animals and toward their own immortal spirits! See their irreverence, ingratitude, impiety, rebellion and murmurings against the Father of all! See the tyranny, oppression, outrage, covetousness, iniquity and violence, which man experiences from man in all ranks of society! See the inferior creatures of the earth wronged without reason or stint! Finally, see man cripple himself, dwarf himself, poison himself, torment and degrade himself, commit perpetual suicide against his better nature, and, without seeming to know it, inflict on himself all the evil blows he inflicts on others! For no man can wrong another without doing himself an ultimately greater wrong. Man cannot become elevated, and truly happy, without bowing implicitly and reverently to the dictates of Justice – the divine principle of Justice to all beings.

Truth

Sincerity, candor, honesty, veracity and fidelity are various manifestations of the principle of Truth in all manifestations of mind. This principle inspires truthfulness in feeling, intention, action, speech and every other manifestation of mind, whether toward God or man, friend or foe. It fills the soul with a profound love of truth for its own sake, whatever it be, wherever found, or however regarded by others. It is utterly opposed to hypocrisy, duplicity, dissimulation, deceit, falsehood, dishonesty, treachery and perfidy. It makes no compromise with known error and wrong, however popular or carnally advantageous.

It would be superfluous to quote even a sample of the numerous texts which inculcate and enforce this divine principle. Its importance to human regeneration, progress and happiness, is great beyond demonstration, whether considered with reference to the individual, or to society. How lovely is the soul that exemplifies preeminent truthfulness! Frank, candid, sincere, honest, veracious and faithful in all things, everywhere, toward God and fellow creatures, toward friend and foe, that soul is the delight of God, angels and good men. How noble, how reliable, how trustworthy, how happy, how instrumental of good to humankind! Contrast with such a one the cunning, guileful, hypocritical, knavish, lying, treacherous, perfidious soul! Such souls have falsehood within, and falsehood without. Their words lie; their countenances, tones and gestures lie; their whole appearance lies; their most solemn prayers, professions, promises, and even oaths, are lies. There is no dependence, trust, reliability. What a spectacle to God, angels and upright men!

I have many times been ready to say with one of old, "All men are liars."[4] It is painful to reflect how little of genuine truthfulness there is in our world; and at the same time how much mischief and misery mankind suffer from its opposite. If the generality of what are called moral people could fairly see the amount of insincerity, uncandor, dishonesty, deception and falsehood which even they practice in various ways, they would be overwhelmed with condemnation and shame. And then again, how deficient most of us are in love for the truth! If any truth be unpopular, or inconvenient, or likely to procure us any temporal loss, or be mortifying to our pride, or unpleasant to our self-complacency, or require any considerable pains to obtain it, how very ready we are to ignore it, contemn it, avoid it, run away from it or excuse ourselves for neglecting the pursuit of it! And yet I know that our real interest and highest good must be connected with Truth. Practical Christian Socialism would erect its proposed new social state on a sandy foundation, without Truth for one of its principal stones.

Love

I will pass on to my fifth grand principle of Personal Righteousness, *Love in all spiritual relations.* Man's spiritual relations are those which he sustains to God, Christ, divine principles, angels and his fellow humans; i.e. the relations which exist between himself and all other spiritual beings. I have already made a distinction between Material and Spiritual natures, and also between the Divine-Spiritual and Soul-Spiritual natures. Man belongs to the Soul-Spiritual nature. His spiritual relations are to the Divine- and Soul-Spiritual. These he is to love. And what is love? It is that divine principle which prompts one moral being to desire, seek and delight in the highest good of all other moral beings. Benevolence, kindness, mercy, compassion, forgiveness, etc. all flow out of love. This is the only love of which I can speak in this connection. There are many lower loves; but this is the one meant in my Table.

This love regards all that is truly divine as inseparable from the highest good of moral beings. Therefore it is a love for God, for all that is right and good, and for the highest welfare of all moral beings. And being such a love, it worketh no ill to any Divine thing or moral being; neither to God, nor to his righteousness, nor to a fellow spirit; neither to friends nor to foes, to the righteous nor to the wicked. It blesses, and curses not. It moves its possessor to desire nothing, aim at nothing, do nothing, but what it deems conducive to the highest good of all moral beings. This is love – the Divine principle of love. It is the highest and purest of all the loves which moral beings can exercise. It is this love which man is commanded to exercise toward God with all his heart, toward his neighbor as himself, toward his offenders and enemies, and toward the most unthankful and evil of his fellow moral beings. This is the love that God exercises toward all moral beings, that he manifested in Christ, that he breathes into men by the Holy Christ Spirit, and that constitutes the essence of his very nature. Hence it is declared that "God is love, and he that loveth is born of God."[5]

How radical and comprehensive is this Love Principle! It strikes deep damnation into all selfishness, revenge, wrath, war, violence, hatred, envy and injury; as well as into all impiety, irreligion and ungodliness. Nothing must be desired, intended, said or done, that is against God, against any divine principle, or against the highest goal of any moral being in existence, not even though he be the bitterest of enemies and the vilest of criminals! What would become of all our military and death-inflicting social institutions, if men generally bowed themselves to such a principle? They would wax old, vanish away, and be superseded by benevolent, peace-promoting, life-preserving, bliss-ensuring institutions. And the whole vast undercurrent of personal selfishness, oppression, insult, resentment, retaliation, revenge, hatred, violence and injury, which now renders most men Ishmaelites to their fellows, and of which existing institutions are the legitimate outgrowth, would give place to peace on earth and good will among men. The kingdom of God would then have come, and his will would be done on earth as in heaven. All things would indeed have become new, and tears be wiped from off all faces.[6] Love would do all this, if well enthroned in human souls and human institutions.

The popular Christian Religion of the Sects makes the principle of love perfectly compatible with the infliction of the greatest injuries on offenders and enemies, and with a total disregard of their good; I speak of offenders and enemies who carry their offenses and enmity beyond certain sufferable bounds. God, we are taught, consigns his offenders and enemies to an endless hell, where they must sin on, and suffer unutterable miseries to all eternity. And Christians may kill their intolerable offenders outright, in personal self-defense, in justifiable war, or on the gibbet, or by some other penal process: and they may inflict a great variety of cruel and injurious punishments, short of death, on their criminal fellow creatures, having little or no regard to their good, but only to the supposed public good. Indeed, the popular doctrine is, that when offenders and enemies pass a certain point of forbearance, they forfeit all right to have their good regarded, and it would be a wrong to the rest of mankind to regard the good of such wicked beings. All this the popular expounders of Christianity, as well as Jews, Mahometans, Pagans and infidels affirm. My interpretation of the Love Principle transcends all this. But it does not transcend the Christianity of Jesus in the Sermon on the Mount, and throughout the New Testament.

> Ye have heard that it hath been said, Thou shalt love thy neighbor, and hate thine enemy. But I say unto you, Love your enemies, bless them that curse you, do good to them that hate you, and pray for them who despitefully use you and persecute you; that ye may be the children of your Father which is in heaven. For he maketh his sun to rise on the evil and on the good, and sendeth rain on the just and on the unjust. For if ye love them which love you, what reward have ye? Do not even the publicans the same? And if ye salute your brethren only, what do ye more than others? Do not even the publicans so? Be ye therefore perfect, even as your Father which is in heaven is perfect.[7]

Does it transcend this? Let popular Christendom be ashamed of its infidelity to this divine primitive Christianity of the Son of God. I mean to do what little I can to make it ashamed of such infidelity, and to bring it to repentance.

And now what need I add? You feel and see that *Love in all spiritual relations* is a grand fundamental principle of the Christian Religion. And though we have given our views a wide social range, this love is a principle indispensable to personal righteousness. What would God be without it? What would Christ be without it? What would any angel, spirit or man be without it? Nothing. It is that *charity* without which Paul said, "I am nothing."[8] As to personal righteousness and happiness, no moral intelligence is any thing, without this LOVE.

> Did sweeter sounds adorn my flowing tongue
> Than ever man pronounced, or angel sung;
> Had I all knowledge, human and divine,
> That thought can reach, or science can define
> And had I power to give that knowledge birth
> In all the speeches of the babbling earth;
> Did Shadrach's zeal my glowing breast inspire
> To weary tortures, and rejoice in fire;
> Or had I faith like that which Israel saw,
> When Moses gave them miracles and law;
> Yet gracious Charity, indulgent guest,
> Were not thy power exerted in my breast,
> Those speeches would send up unheeded prayer;
> That scorn of life would be but wild despair;
> A cymbal's sound were better than my voice,
> My faith were form, my eloquence were noise.[9]

Purity

The next principle of Personal Righteousness is the sixth: *Purity in all things*. By purity is meant freedom from defiling or polluting admixtures. That which exists in its own proper simplicity, unmixed with and undefiled by any thing repugnant to its own nature, order or right condition, is said to be *pure*. The principle of purity has numerous applications, relations and branches: hence we speak of purity of heart, purity of mind, purity of faith, purity of conversation, purity of life, purity of principle, etc. Also, purity in our relation to God, purity in our sexual relations, purity in our various social relations, and purity in our own persons. Holiness is spiritual and moral purity. Chastity is sexual purity. Temperance is purity in the indulgence of the appetites, etc.

Impurity is the opposite of these, in whatever application, relation or branch existing. Then we may be impure in our hearts, impure in our minds, impure in our consciences, impure in our faith, impure in our conversation, impure in our life, impure in our principles. We are impure in our relation to God, if we are insincere, hypocritical, ungrateful, rebellious or impious in any degree. We are impure in our sexual relations, if we commit adultery, fornication, lasciviousness, lewdness, self-pollution, or allow ourselves to cherish the desire to commit such acts, i.e. to lust after impure sexual indulgence. We are impure if we are unjust, untruthful, malicious, revengeful, envious, or in any way injurious to our fellow moral agents. We are impure, if we are abusing ourselves by any habitual perversion of our bodies or our minds. We are impure, if we are unholy in *any* respect; if we knowingly violate any law of our being. Impiety, selfishness, injustice, falsehood, hatred, cruelty, drunkenness, gluttony, debauchery, sexual pollution, idleness and all the vices of the carnal mind, are manifestations of impurity; and, I may add, all physical personal filthiness, voluntarily and habitually indulged.

I make a clean sweep, from center to circumference – from the inmost affection to the most exterior act and habit – even to personal physical cleanliness. The principle of Purity in all things – mental, moral physical – internal and external – God-ward and man-ward; in feeling, purpose, thought, word, deed; in the exercise of every propensity, appetite, passion, sentiment, and faculty; in the use of all that is within our reach; in eating, drinking, sleeping, dressing, recreating; in our stomachs, our mouths, our skins, our clothes, our habitations, our door yards, our gardens, our fields and our streets; in ALL THINGS. Filthiness, uncleanness, disorder, impurity, are to be eschewed everywhere, at all times, in all things; that our whole body, spirit, soul and condition may be more and more sanctified; till "HOLINESS UNTO THE LORD" be inscribed on our entire being and all its accessories. "All filthiness of the flesh and spirit" is to be put away; that true holiness may be perfected.[10]

Patience

I will pass to the seventh principle in this division of my Table: Patience in all right aims and pursuits. Webster gives a very good definition of patience:

> 1. The suffering of afflictions, pain, toil, calamity, provocation or other evil, with a calm, unruffled temper. 2. A calm temper, which bears evils without murmuring or discontent. 3. The act or quality of waiting long for justice or expected good, without discontent. 4. Perseverance; constancy in labor or exertion. 5. The quality of bearing offenses and injuries without anger or revenge.

Thus Patience includes calmness, firmness, constancy, endurance, perseverance, meekness, forbearance, gentleness, long-suffering, etc. And it stands opposed to restlessness, fickle-mindedness, instability, despondency, fretfulness, resentfulness, rashness, vindictiveness and all manner of violence.

Now we are to cherish and cultivate *Patience in all right aims and pursuits*, as a cardinal principle of personal righteousness. Being sure that our aims and efforts are right, that they are in accordance with essential divine principles, that they look to the highest good of all moral beings, we are to confide ourselves to God without distrust of consequences; we are to be calm, firm, steadfast and persevering; we are to hope on and ever, to toil on and ever, to suffer whatever calamities may overtake us with unmurmuring composure; we are to face all opposition, meet all contradictions, endure all persecutions, bear all provocations and suffer all evils, resolutely, meekly, gently, forgivingly, heroically; without fretfulness, without resentment, without returning evil for evil, and without seriously doubting that the right, the good and the true will finally triumph.

The severe and protracted struggle through which human nature passes in its progress, from its rudimental to its celestial and divine development, has already been considered. This struggle involves innumerable incidental trials which cannot be endured and overcome without Patience. No one can read the New Testament, or call to remembrance its teachings, with the least doubt that Patience is an essential of the personal righteousness inculcated by Jesus Christ and his apostles.

Progress towards Perfection

My eighth principle of Personal Righteousness is *unceasing progress toward perfection*. I have declared my belief to be that each universe of worlds in the Infinitarium is composed of Soul-Spirit and Matter, interiorated by the Deific Spirit, and has its seasons of generation, progress, perfection and dissolution. The same I hold to be true of all the individuals and associations, which make up the Diversity of each universe. Each grand cycle of a universe may be called its eternity, as including all the ages of Duration from its generation to its dissolution. Then commences another generation of individuations in that universe, another grand Cycle, another of the eternities through which the aggregate of its Soul-Spirit and Matter exists, perpetually changing, but, in its elements and aggregate, neither increased nor diminished. So each earth has its birth, growth, perfection and dissolution. So each race of animated beings. So each race of moral beings; and therefore man. So each man in particular. So the body of man in each sphere of his progressive existence. When a man arrives at his absolute perfection, his essence will no longer consist of Soul-Spirit and Matter conjoined, but of Deific Spirit alone; and then the affection, will, action and bliss of each man will be strictly DIVINE, so that his very consciousness will be one with God's.

How can it be, that a man's very consciousness can be one with God's? I will further explain. I have said that the Deific Spirit interiorates all Soul-Spirit, and thus all matter; so that from the moment a man's soul is conscious of moral development, there must be in his inmost an ever-present portion of the Deific Spirit. That same portion of the Deity has divine consciousness, affection, will, intelligence and power; in me, in you, in all moral beings. And these portions of divine love and divine wisdom in us all have a common consciousness, a common affection, a common will, a common intelligence, and a common good. The least conceivable portion of the Deific Spirit must have the attributes of the Divine Nature, whether in my spiritual inmost, or yours, or another man's, or an angel's, or an archangel's. And yet the consciousness of divine personal identity must be one, however existing in all individuations; because Deific Spirit has everywhere precisely the same perfect love, wisdom, will and good. You may see, then, that the more room God occupies in a man, the larger his inmost must be; and consequently that the more he is conscious of being actuated by God's Love, God's Wisdom and God's Will, the less he is conscious of distinguishing his own original selfhood. Thus as he consists more and more of the Divine Nature, he will consist less and less of Soul-Spirit and Matter; or, in other words, as God expands within him, his external selfhood diminishes and vanishes away. But that which vanishes away is not annihilated, any more than the Matter of our bodies is, when superseded by fresh supplies received within. It goes to its own place to be used over again. So with the Matter in all our personal individualities. But not so with Deific Spirit, which by degrees comes to constitute our most interior identities. That has an essential, unchanging perfection of its own. When, therefore, after the process of incomputable ages of progress towards perfection, we finally reach it, the last particle of our selfhood will have passed away, and our consciousness of existence, love, wisdom, will and bliss, will be indistinguishable from God's, – not lost, but perfected in his own divine unity. Hence the sublime expression, "God all in all." Accordingly we find that the highest and purest of human beings on earth, as they approximate God, long to be one with him. It is their meat and drink to do his will; their very life to feel, think, speak and act only as moved by him. Hear how the good Kempis expressed himself:

> Thou, O Lord God! art above all, in all perfection! Thou art most high, most powerful, most sufficient, and most full! Thou art most sweet, and most abundantly comforting! Thou art most lovely, and most loving; most noble and most glorious! In thee all good centers, from eternity to eternity! Therefore, whatever thou bestowest upon me, that is not thyself; whatsoever thou revealest or promisest, while I am not permitted truly to behold and enjoy thee; is insufficient to fill the boundless desires of my soul, which, stretching beyond all creatures, and even beyond all thy gifts, can only be satisfied in union with thy all-perfect Spirit ... When will it be granted me, in silent and peaceful abstraction from all created being, to taste and see how good thou art, O Lord, my God! When shall I be wholly absorbed in thy fullness! When shall I lose, in the love of thee, all perception of myself; and have no sense of any being but thine![11]

The principle before us impels the man who embraces it to make all the progress he can towards this perfection; and by every means in his power to promote the progress of the whole human race toward their destined perfection. In himself he unceasingly aspires after and presses towards perfection; perfection of Reverence for the divine and spiritual; perfection of Self-denial for righteousness' sake; perfection of Justice to all beings; perfection of Truth in all manifestations of mind; perfection of Love in all spiritual relations; perfection of Purity in all things; perfection of Patience in all right aims and pursuits; absolute divine perfection. "And this also we wish, even your perfection." "Be ye perfect, even as your Father which is in heaven is perfect."[12]

Chapter 4

Principles of Social Order

By Social Order I mean the true harmonic conditions, relations and operations of Society – in the family, in the neighborhood community, in the municipality, in the state, in the nation, in the human race, in the universe of spiritual races. The least form of Society is the family; the greatest form on earth is a fraternity of nations. When we extend our thoughts to other earths, suns, systems and universes, we only follow Social Order into its more and more comprehensive combinations. But I need not contemplate Society, for the purposes of this exposition, beyond the limits of our own earth.

I believe that human Society *may* be happy. But to be happy, it must be harmonic; and to be harmonic, its conditions, relations and operations must be in true order. There is, I am confident, a true and right Social Order somewhere among the possibilities and destinies of human nature. That right Social Order must have its fundamental principles. And as man must have a very responsible part to act in the establishment of true Social Order, it is obvious that he should understand, embrace and practically carry out these principles.

The Fatherhood of God and the Brotherhood of Man

The first Principle of Social Order is *the supreme Fatherhood of God*. Does the Christian Religion declare that God is the supreme common Father of the human race? Or does it leave use to presume that some of the human race are the offspring of one Father, and some of another?

> Jesus said unto them, If God were your father, ye would love me; for I proceeded forth and came from God ... Ye are of your father the devil, and the lusts of your father ye will do: he was a murderer from the beginning, and abode not in the truth, because there is no truth in him. When he speaketh a lie, he speaketh of his own; for he is a liar and the father of it.[1]

Is not this text against our principle of the supreme Fatherhood of God? Does it not involve the existence of two hostile Fathers of mankind – God, the Father of the righteous; and Satan, the father of the wicked?*

I learn from the context that the Jews were justifying their hatred and persecution of Jesus, by the plea that they had Abraham for their honored ancestor, and acknowledged one God as their Father. But Jesus charged them with being actuated by a spirit the reverse of Abraham's, and doing works morally unlike his. The fatherhood of the devil is one which relates, not to the proper *being* of men, but to their affections, temper, intentions, will, conduct and moral character. It is utterly absurd, as well as impious, to conclude that wicked men were created by a great infernal Spirit, called the devil; or that there is a single human being not created and paternally treated by the one All-Perfect, Infinite God; or that the devil is any man's *father*, save only in a figurative and moral sense. For then the devil would be made the rival of God, and would have as good a right to demand the worship, love and service of *his* children, as God those of *his*. Also, if all are sinners before becoming saints, and God has nothing but sinners out of whom to make saints, then it would follow that the devil created all mankind, and God only converts a part of them into his children.

FATHER is the profoundly significant and adorable appellation by which Jesus almost uniformly designated God. The four Gospels are every where adorned with this name, "*My* Father," "*your* Father," "*the* Father," "heavenly Father," "Father which is in heaven," etc. are phrases which everywhere glisten like precious stones sprinkled with a liberal hand over that hallowed ground. We are enjoined to believe in God, to pray to him, confide in him, obey him, imitate him, worship him, as our *Father*; who is more ready to give good things to them that ask him than earthly parents are to their children; who is "kind to the unthankful and evil;" and who meeteth his penitent prodigals on their return to his house with compassion and holy rejoicings. He even says in one instance, "Call no man your Father upon the earth; for ONE is your FATHER, which is in heaven." The apostles appear to have become thoroughly imbued with the principle of the supreme Fatherhood of God: "There is one God and Father of

---

* At this point the Inquirer and the Expositor exchange roles, as the Expositor asks the Inquirer to "try your skill a little" with an explanation of this passage. The next paragraph is the Inquirer's response.

all, who is above all, and through all, and in you all."[2] Now then let us see what is implied in the supreme Fatherhood of God: A Father's love for all mankind; a Father's care and providence toward them all; a Father's authority, government and discipline over them all; and a Father's right to be loved, trusted, honored and obeyed by them all.

This brings out my second Principle of Social Order: The universal Brotherhood of Man. It is necessarily involved in, and evolved from the Supreme Fatherhood of God. So if we have established the first of these principles, we have as certainly established the second. So we may pass on to inquire what is implied in the Universal Brotherhood of Man. It is clearly implied that all men have a common Father; that they owe him a common love, worship, confidence and obedience; that they have a common nature, as to wants, capabilities, rights and responsibilities; that they are equals in their essential rights; that they have a common good, which involves the obligation of each and all to seek it; that they have a common final destiny; and that they ought to love each his neighbor as himself.

The Great Principles of Love

And where are we now? We are already acknowledging by anticipation the third, fourth and fifth principles of Social Order: *the declared perfect love of God to Man, the required perfect love of Man to God*, and *the required perfect love of Man to Man*. How naturally, consistently and beautifully do these principles grow out of their divine root!

The declared perfect love of God to man appears in such passages as:

He that loveth not knoweth not God; for God is love. In this was manifested the love of God toward us, because that God sent his only begotten Son into the world, that we might live through him. Herein is love, not that we loved God, but that he loved us, and sent his Son to be the propitiation for our sins ... And we have known and believed the love that God hath to us. God is love; and he that dwelleth in love dwelleth in God, and God in him ... We love him because he first loved us.[3]

The sum of all such testimonies is condensed into those three words above quoted, "GOD IS LOVE."

The required perfect love of Man to God is comprehended in the first great commandment, "Thou shalt love the Lord thy God with all thy heart, and with all thy soul, and with all thy mind, and with all thy strength."[4] The required perfect love of Man to Man is set forth in the second great command-ment, "Thou shalt love they neighbor as thyself." It is urged and enforced in such passages as, "All things whatsoever ye would that men should do to you, do ye even so to them" and "If any man say, I love God, and hateth his brother, he is a liar; for he that loveth not his brother whom he hath seen, how can he love God whom he hath not seen?"[5]

And lest men should plead that they are not required to love their enemies, but their friends only, Jesus was explicit and special, in his injunc-tions, to include all enemies and offenders in the obligation of the second great commandment.

> Ye have heard that it hath been said, Thou shalt love thy neighbor, and hate thine
> enemy; but I say unto you, Love your enemies, bless them that curse you, do good
> to them that hate you, and pray for them which despitefully use you and persecute
> you; that ye may be the children of your Father which is in heaven; for he maketh
> his sun to rise on the evil and on the good, and sendeth his rain on the just and
> on the unjust. For if ye love them which love you, what reward have you? Do not
> even the publicans do the same?[6]

Treatment of Evildoers

Our first five principles of Social Order are certainly fundamentals of the Christian Religion. And now we may proceed to the sixth: *the required just reproof and disfellowship of evildoers*. This is a principle not inferior in impor-tance to the others. We must give it a serious and critical consideration. It is a great stumbling stone to many. One class of minds stumble over it into vindictiveness, violence and cruelty; another class stumble at it as irreconcil-able with the great Love-Principle, which ever seeks the good of evildoers. The first class *persecute* evildoers; the second class *indulge* them to their own hurt, as well as to the corruption and damage of others.

Evildoers are those who violate the principles of Personal Righteousness and Social Order, and especially those who knowingly and persistently violate these principles. Every violation of these principles is a sin against one's own soul, against mankind, and against the Supreme Father. Its legitimate and inevitable effect is, disturbance and pain in the moral and social sphere. It is therefore an imperative dictate, both of charity and justice, that evil-doing should be justly reproved and disfellowshipped by all who acknowledge themselves under the government of divine principles. And this can be done only by making evildoers understand and feel, that their conduct is regarded as evil, and will neither be sanctioned nor morally tolerated. Therefore the Christian Religion requires us to be true to divine principles and to human welfare, by always opposing sin. We must never approve, fellowship, countenance or connive at evil-doing, though it be in our most intimate, beloved and honored friends.

> If thy brother shall trespass against thee, go and tell him his fault between thee and him alone. If he shall hear thee, thou hast gained thy brother. But if he will not hear thee, then take with thee one or two more, that in the mouth of two or three witnesses every word may be established. And if he shall neglect to hear them, tell it unto the church; but if he neglect to hear the church, let him be unto thee as a heathen man and a publican. [7]

If an evildoer acknowledge no fraternity with us, and work his iniquity boldly, or hypocritically, or self-righteously, or presumptuously, he must be rebuked and even denounced sharply in the sphere of his evil-doing, whether it be private or public. The true and faithful adherent of divine principles must place himself in unmistakable, uncompromising protest against all persistent evil-doing. But he must never reprove, rebuke and disfellowship evildoers with hatred, vindictiveness, cruelty or any kind of injury to their bodies or their souls. If he does, he becomes an evildoer himself and deserves to be reproved, rebuked and corrected, or disfellowshipped. He must abide in the spirit of God, whose rebukes, disfellowships and chastisements all flow out from love, and are directed in wisdom to the highest good of those who experience them. "Have no fellowship with the unfruitful works of darkness, but rather reprove them."[8] Thus the Christian Religion prohibits with equal explicitness all approval and fellowship of evildoers on the one hand, and all hatred and injury to them on the other.

Treatment of Unbelievers

Both precept and example in Jesus and his apostles demonstrate the great fact, that there are essentials of faith and practice which the Christian Religion insists on as indispensable to human salvation, progress and happiness. And it requires its disciples to reprove and disfellowship as evildoers all who set at naught these essentials. Indeed the Christian Religion would be worthless without such essentials. No true church, community or order of society can be founded and maintained, without making these essentials the standard of righteousness and fellowship.

To a certain extent, then, I do set up a test of faith and practice, and justify excommunication, as well as exclusion, from my proposed Communion. I am sure that this will be a serious objection to my system of Socialism among liberal minds. There are many such minds who detest all creeds, tests and exclusiveness. The creeds, covenants, tests, bigotries, exclusiveness, and above all, the excommunications of the old Sects, are a stench in the nostrils of nearly all the liberals and progressives of my acquaintance. And I fancy most of them will suspect my scheme of society to be only a revised edition of the old book.

I have a very short method of settling all such questions. I ask, What is True, what is Right? Make me sure of these, and I will risk all issues. Are there any fundamental principles of truth, righteousness and social order, which mankind must acknowledge and conform to, or be miserable? If any man says *No*, he is not a guide or companion for me. If a man says *Yes*, then I ask, Are those principles anywhere declared, or made knowable to mankind? If no, then it is useless to talk of truth and error, right and wrong. If yes, What are those principles, and where are they declared? If any man assumes to state them, he states a creed, a confession of faith, a standard of righteousness. If any Society attempts to be governed by them, it has a religious and moral test of fellowship. If that Society takes in members, or knowingly retains members, who persistently set at naught its fundamental principles, it is false to its own standard, and will suffer accordingly. If it excludes such members, then, to that extent, it is exclusive and excommunicative.

I suppose most liberals and progressives would disclaim Nothingarianism. They hold to fundamental principles of truth and duty – right and wrong. If so, they know what those fundamentals are, and in common honesty ought to hold them up as such to the rest of mankind. And if so, have they not a creed, and a test? They may agree that they have, in some sense; but they dislike *written, formal* creeds, and tests of fellowship. In that case, is it the thing itself that they dislike, or only an open, unmistakable written statement of it?

My liberal friends say that they want to preserve freedom of faith, opinion and action. They are afraid of insisting on principles as essential which may not turn out to be really such. They differ among themselves very much as to what are settled fundamental principles; and being devotees of progress, as well as of liberty of thought, they dread tying themselves down to a declaration of faith and practice, which future light may show to have been mistaken. And so they are only modestly waiting the march of progress, and the light of futurity, to find out what their fundamental principles are! And then, when they are sure they have not mistaken error for truth, nor wrong for right, they expect to have a *perfect* creed, standard and test of fellowship! I much admire their chameleonship, as a game of hide and seek, but not at all for the sober work of regenerating the human race. A whole continent of such minds would accomplish very little towards establishing a true order of society. They aim at *nothing*, and will be sure to hit it. Their mission is *noise* – not constructive action.

I have often considered their reasons for dreading creeds, standards, and tests of fellowship, and found them superficial. The exclusiveness, despotism, and persecutions of the past were not caused by having uncompromising standards of religious truth and moral obligation; for without something of this nature one step of human progress was never made, and never can be. But the errors were these: making that *essential* which is *non*-essential; omitting that which really *was* essential; and most important of all, resorting to violence and injurious force for the maintenance of their standards. I am quite sure that I have transcended those errors; absolutely sure as to the third error mentioned. And with regard to the other two, if I were less sure than I am, it would be no reason for giving up my attempt to establish the highest standard of fundamentals I can conceive of; since it is one that eschews all injurious force, and must rest on its own intrinsic merits. Therefore if it needs amendment, it will be sure to receive it in due time. And certainly I do *not* bar out progress; for progress is one fundamental article in the standard itself.

I am sure that no intentional, and no vital injury will be done to evildoers by applying my principles to practice. Incidental weaknesses and mistakes may occur, as in every case of human action. Such will be comparatively slight and correctable. In the main, good, and only good, will be done to the reproved, or disfellowshipped individuals, to all parties immediately concerned, and to the whole human brotherhood. "Whom the Lord loveth he chasteneth."[9] Whom his true children love they also will reprove, admonish, and if necessary faithfully disfellowship, as God does, till the time of reformation; which they will ever seek. Love of the sinner's real *being* must involve proportionate abhorrence of his sins, and of course the just rebuke of them. To flatter the sinner in his sins by approval, or by fellowship, or by acting towards him as if he needed no correction, would not only ruin him, but greatly undermine the community of which he was an acknowledged member.

I anticipate that many may object to the holding and treating of persons as evildoers, who are only theoretically or opinionally so. For instance, suppose a man should honestly avow that he did not accept as true some one, or two, or ten, or even the whole twenty-four essential Divine Principles; but that he believed in doing what appeared to be best for him from moment to moment, and could profess nothing more definite; yet this man should be unexceptionably upright, moral and congenial in the externals of life. Would it be right to hold such a person in disfellowship as an evildoer?

One of two conclusions must be adopted in this case. Either the Principles in question are not essential, or the man is a very dangerous evildoer. Therefore the Principles must stand aside, or the man must. So the question is simply this: Shall the basis of fellowship be one of acknowledged immutable Principles, or shall it be one of mere external *morality* for the time being, without any acknowledged essential Divine Principles? Without hesitation I say, acknowledged, immutable Principles must be the basis. I would not trust mere morality out of sight. It would be like a bank of quicksand in the midst of rolling floods.

Perhaps the man trusts to the instincts and intuitions of his own nature, which he believes to be unerring, and which to him supersede all necessity for definitely acknowledged Principles. Then he has a creed and a standard: *the unerring instincts of his own unrestrained nature.* This is either a true and sufficient standard, or a false one. If a true one, it ought to be proclaimed as such, and made the basis of social fellowship; for all others must be false and injurious to human nature. If this man honestly believes this, he will act accordingly. And in that case, he will not desire to be in our fellowship; neither can he consistently offer us his fellowship, except under his own standard. So both parties will honestly disfellowship each other, until one of them shall have been converted to the standard of the other. And if we stick to our principles of justice and love, it is certain that we shall never intentionally injure your man, whatever his unerring instincts may lead him to do. Besides, the world will afford both parties room to solve their respective problems, without any serious interference of the other. And thus in due time each tree will be known by its own fruits. Until then, he would be an evildoer in our esteem, and we should be evildoers in his; both mutually reproving, disfellowshipping and trying to reform each other.

Let us suppose a good man who accepts all of the acknowledged essential Principles, excepting one or two. For instance, he may say, I do not believe in the mediatorial manifestation of God through Christ, but I believe in God's direct manifestation as a Spirit to each true soul. I believe nothing and care nothing about Christ as a mediator between God and men. In that case I should be instantly certain in my own mind, that such a man would make an uncomfortable member of our fraternity, if admitted into it, and that his influence on the whole would be demoralizing. The interior causes which would make any man say he believed nothing and cared nothing about Christ as a mediator between God and men, while pretending to have manifestations of God within himself, would be causes inevitably operating to demoralize, in a greater or less degree, the man himself, and all his adherents.

Christ was characterized by Divine Love and Wisdom. As a man he was an embodiment and illustration of them, so pre-eminent that no one who ever knew anything of his history could possess the same divine Spirit, and be indifferent to his excellence. As a focalization of the eternal Christ-Spirit in a glorious personality, Christ is Love and Wisdom – is God communicable; and no good man, inspired of God, i.e. possessing the Christ-Spirit, can contemn him. Now here is this supposedly good man sneering at Christ, at faith in Christ, at the manifestation of God through Christ, at the very name of Christ. He believes nothing and cares nothing about Christ as a mediator between God and men. But he believes in One All-Perfect God, and claims that this God is manifested in and through his own soul. Indeed he believes in all the great cardinal principles taught and exemplified by Jesus Christ, yet believes not in Christ himself as being what he claimed to be. A wondrous good man is this, who surely ought not to be disfellowshipped as an evildoer – a demoralizer! Alas! there is a screw loose somewhere in this man's moral nature. There is an evil cause for his believing nothing and caring nothing about Christ as a divine mediator. He has the vanity and self-conceit to set up for a Christ himself. Or, he has too much pride to acknowledge that he is indebted for divine manifestations to any mediation except that of his own internal faculties. Or, there is some peculiar object of personal ambition which he has in view, which makes it convenient to get rid of the New Testament Christ. Or, he is swayed by old disgusts, prejudices and antipathies excited by people who in the name of Christ have become abominable to him. In either case, his bias of mind, and his egotism, will prove to be mischievous. He will not build up, but undermine and pull down the true social fabric. If he can do any good, let him have an open field to work out his ideal, with his own tools, or in cooperation with kindred spirits. Let him not be injured. Let him have a fair opportunity to illustrate his real character. But let not those who honor Jesus Christ as the highest manifestation of God to mankind approve and fellowship him. His career will ultimately prove a failure, though in some respects and for a time he may flourish like the green bay tree. He will diffuse a leaven of evil in the long run, which cannot fail to prove as mischievous to human welfare as it shall be anti-Christian. These are my firm convictions.*

I think all difficulties, under this head, must arise from doubt as to whether my twenty-four fundamental divine principles are *all* really essential to human salvation, progress and happiness. If so, I am perfectly ready to have each of them thoroughly discussed, and if found to be false, or *non*-essential, then discarded. Or, if I have left out any *essential* I desire it may be added. But so long as I honestly and firmly believe that Table to contain all these divine essentials, and no *non*-essentials, I am obliged to make it a test of fellowship. And, if I and my fellow adherents act to our acknowledged obligations under it, where is the evildoer, or the heretic, on whom we can inflict any absolute injury?

Christian Non-Resistance

This is my seventh Principle of Social Order: *the required non-resistance of evildoers with evil.* This great prohibitory principle is exceedingly radical and sweeping. It forbids us to carry our reproof, rebuke, disfellowship, restraint, opposition and resistance of evildoers beyond the bounds dictated by Charity, which seeks every neighbor's good as our own. We have already seen that the evildoer must be reproved, disfellowshipped, resisted and restrained. Now here is another principle which confines us within the limits of the second great commandment: "Thou shalt love thy neighbor as thyself." It restrains us from hating and injuring any one of our neighbors,

---

* Inquirer: "I cannot say I am fully convinced that you are right in this particular, for I can imagine cases of partial dissent from your Standard, in which it would seem very hard for the dissenter to be disfellowshipped by your people as an evildoer, or a heretic."

This did actually occur at Hopedale, contributing to the 1847 crisis that led to the complete re-thinking of the community's constitution. The question was how to respond to "undisciplined recruits in our industrial army" whose work fell short of community standards. "The difficulty was not in [their] intention or purpose ... Else we could have summoned them to answer for their faults before the Community tribunal and, if need be, cut them off from our fellowship. But their virtue saved them from such a fate ... And so the difficulty remained." [Adin Ballou, *History of the Hopedale Community*, 160-161.]

under pretext that such neighbor is an evildoer and may rightfully be injured for the sake of others.

Such hitherto has been the selfishness and darkness of the human mind, that nearly all mankind, form the lowest to the highest classes, have held it perfectly justifiable to resist evildoers with evil, especially in extreme cases. Hence the common doctrine of self-defense, that an individual may rightfully preserve his own life, etc., by killing, or to any necessary extent, *partially* killing, his assailant; provided he cannot place himself under the protection of the civil authorities. Hence the assumed right of civil society to maintain its authority and laws by the halter, and other less deadly penal injuries, when disturbed by outrageous evildoers. And hence also the assumed right of nations to make war against each other for the maintenance of independence, territorial claims, honor, etc.

War, capital punishment, all injurious penal inflictions and all authorized resistance of deadly force with deadly force, rest on this one universal assumption, that evildoers may rightfully be killed or injured when necessary to the protection of the injured party, or the safety of society, or the maintenance of national integrity. This is the predominant private feeling and the public opinion of the civilized, as well as uncivilized world. It is the chief cornerstone of the present order of human society. Nevertheless it is anti-Christian and evil. It must and will be transcended. The new order of society which I am endeavoring to recommend excludes it utterly. It installs, in lieu of the old bloody, injurious principle, the holy injunction of Jesus Christ, which prohibits all resistance of evildoers with evil. This I call an essential divine principle of Social Order. I call it so, because I am certain it must be one of the fundamentals of the new and true social state.

It presupposes that every human being is neighbor, in the comprehensive sense of the term, to every other human being; that every neighbor is bound to love every other neighbor as himself; that this love of neighbor to neighbor is not one of mere personal affection, fondness or attraction, but one of absolute benevolence, which seeks the highest good of every human being as *such*, with equal regard to that of all others. This love necessarily embraces evil-doing neighbors, as truly as it does well-doing ones, and never permits the highest good of either to be disregarded or sacrificed under any pretext whatsoever. The infliction of any absolute injury on an evildoer's person, whether physical or moral, knowing it to be such, is absolutely evil. To render evil for evil, or to resist evildoers with evil, is a radical violation of the divine law committed under a false pretext; which violation not only injures the evildoer, but indirectly many well-doers, and tends to the perpetuation of all evil. To oppose, resist, restrain, reprove, disfellowship and endeavor to reform evildoers *benevolently*, without resorting to any absolute injury, tends to the highest good of all parties concerned, to maintain the authority of the divine law, and to do away with all evil from the human race. Such is the nature and scope of this principle. (I wrote a work, some years since, entitled *Christian Non-Resistance*, in which this principle will be found to have been thoroughly illustrated and defended. I refer you to that Work, as conclusive of all I need to offer on this subject.)

"He that saith he abideth in him, ought also to walk even as he walked." How Jesus himself walked, as the great exemplar of Christian Non-Resistance, the Record very explicitly sets forth up to the dreadful crisis of the crucifixion, the wormwood and gall of his dying hour, when he prayed for his enemies, saying, "Father, forgive them, for they know not what they do."[10] I regard the following texts as unequivocally teaching this principle:

> Ye have heard that it hath been said, An eye for an eye, and a tooth for a tooth. But I say unto you, That ye resist not evil; but whosoever shall smite thee on thy right cheek, turn to him the other also. And if any man will sue thee at the law, and take away thy coat, let him have thy cloak also ... Ye have heard that it hath been said, Thou shalt love thy neighbor, and hate thine enemy. But I say unto you, Love your enemies, bless them that curse you, do good to them that hate you, and pray for them who despitefully use you and persecute you; that ye may be the children of your Father which is in heaven ... Be ye therefore perfect, even as your Father which is in heaven is perfect. [11]

> Bless them which persecute you; bless, and curse not ... Recompense no man evil for evil ... Dearly beloved, avenge not yourselves, but rather give place unto wrath; for it is written, Vengeance is mine, I will repay, saith the Lord. Therefore, if thine enemy hunger, feed him; if he thirst, give him drink; for in doing so thou shalt heap coals of fire on his head. Be not overcome of evil, but overcome evil with good.[12]

> See that none render evil for evil unto any man; but ever follow that which is good, both among yourselves and to all men.[13]

How can such a principle be carried out into practice, in the present state of this selfish, and often outrageously wicked world? We may acknowledge the principle to be Christian and most excellent, yet fear the trial of it under evil circumstances. Yet if we had a firm faith in two truths respecting this principle, we would have no further anxiety about its practicability. These are, that this principle will cost vastly less of human suffering in practice than its opposite does; and that it will certainly make this wicked world better, and ultimately do away with all evil aggression.

The Unity of the Righteous

The last Principle of Social Order in my Table is: *the designed unity of the righteous.* This I need not affirm to be a most important principle. Discord, contention and confusion are the infallible fruits of wickedness – its legitimate manifestations – its inseparable hell. The more sensual, selfish, cruel, hateful, vindictive and devilish mankind are, the more war, violence, strife, quarreling, confusion and misery must they have. So, on the other hand, concord, unity and order are the infallible fruits of righteousness – its legitimate manifestations – its inseparable heaven. The more spiritual, benevolent, humble, truthful, forgiving and Godlike mankind are, the more peace, harmony and happiness will they possess.

If righteousness necessarily tends to concord, harmony and order among those who possess it, then what of this Ishmaelitish Christendom of ours? Its principal business is war. It is a boiling whirlpool of contention. Every part of it throws up the dregs and scum of wrathful selfishness. You can find scarcely a church, or even a choir of singers, that has not a quarrel on foot. And in property matters nearly all our saints are as greedy to get, as snug to keep and as selfish in expending, as were the money-changing sharpsters whom Christ expelled from the temple. The old maxim of Cain has become christened into a sacred precept, "Am I my brother's keeper?"[14] And the almost universal watchword in the market place is, Look out for number one. Is all this the infallible indication of righteousness in Christendom? No; these are the fruits of wickedness. They demonstrate how low even so-called Christendom is in genuine Christian righteousness. Its *few*, (oh how few!), not its professing *multitude*, are the exemplars of that righteousness. As a *whole*, Christendom must be born again, or it cannot see the kingdom of God.

Unity is the necessary fruit, proof and demonstration of righteousness among men; and *discord* of the opposite. A family, a community, a church, a state or a nation, may be correctly gauged, as to their goodness, by the degree of their internal harmony. Devils and wicked men must be in a quarrel among themselves, except when they have a war outside of their clan, or are restrained by fear, or by some strong selfish motive. War is the breath of their life. Heavenly angels, and holy human beings, must love, do good, and be united in the bonds of peace, just in proportion to the measure of their absolute righteousness. Harmony is the breath of their life. Where war, wrath and discord prevail, in a family, a community, a church, or a state, there Hatred and Folly reign, and Wickedness is at home. And where peace, good will and unity prevail, there Love and Wisdom reign, and righteousness is established.

Could I convert twenty minds, or twenty thousand, or twenty millions to the essential divine principles of my Table, those minds would be drawn into proportionate concord, unity and order with each other. But if you should see them still isolated, selfish, contentious, and ready to thrive by devouring each other, you would doubt whether my so called Practical Christianity was better than the nominal Christianity which it denounced. You would know that our fine professions were as "sounding brass, and a tinkling cymbal,"[15] solely because we brought not forth the good fruits of love and wisdom!

When I see two members of the same church, as unlike in condition as Dives and Lazarus, the one faring sumptuously every day, the other a breadless beggar, with dogs only to soothe his sores,[16] I have a strong suspicion that such a church has not the spirit of Christ; that it is far from the unity of heaven. So when I see two professedly regenerate beings spitting venom at each other in a personal quarrel, or expending their resources in a lawsuit, before a worldly Court, about a few dollars' worth of property; when I see one saint shooting another dead because Caesar, Herod, Pilate, or some mere human authority commands it; when I see one member sell another on the auction block, though it be even to raise money for the conversion of foreign heathen; when I see hosts of Christians more zealous as sectarians and politicians, than they are to unite themselves in establishing a higher order of society; and above all, when I hear them sneering at the mere idea of a Practical Christian Community; I wonder how they ever happened to imagine themselves disciples of Jesus Christ! And I turn round to look for a people concerning whom I may exclaim, in the language of the Psalmist, "Behold how good and how pleasant it is for brethren to dwell together in unity!"[17]

The designed unity of the righteous is set forth as a cardinal principle of the Christian Religion in many impressive testimonies. I give you a sample of the Socialistic texts:

Then there arose a reasoning among them, which of them should be greatest. And Jesus, perceiving the thought of their heart, took a child, and set him by him, and said unto them, "Whosoever shall receive this child in my name, receiveth me; and whosoever shall receive me, receiveth him that sent me; for he that is least among you all, the same shall be great."[18]

Ye call me Master, and Lord; and ye say well; for so I am. If I then, your Lord and Master, have washed your feet, ye also ought to wash one another's feet. For I have given you an example, that ye should do as I have done to you. Verily, verily, I say unto you, The servant is not greater than his Lord; neither he that is sent greater than he that sent him. If ye know these things, happy are ye if ye do them ... A new commandment I give unto you, That ye love one another. By this shall all men know that ye are my disciples, if ye have love one to another.[19]

And all that believed were together and had all things common; and sold their possessions and goods, and parted them to all, as every man had need ... And the multitude of them that believed were of one heart and one soul; neither said any of them that aught of the things which he possessed was his own; but they had all things in common ... Neither was there any among them that lacked.[20]

For as we have many members in one body, and all members have not the same office; so we, being many, are one body in Christ, and every one members one of another ... Be kindly affectioned one to another with brotherly love; in honor preferring one another ... Rejoice with them that do rejoice, and weep with them that weep. Be of the same mind one toward another. Mind not high things, but condescend to men of low estate. Be not wise in your own conceits.[21]

For as the body is one, and hath many members, and all the members of that one body, being many, are one body, so also is Christ. For by one Spirit are we all baptized into one body, whether Jews or Gentiles, whether bond or free; and have all been made to drink into one Spirit. For the body is not one member, but many. If the foot shall say, Because I am not the hand, I am not of the body: is it therefore not of the body? And if the ear shall say, Because I am not the eye, I am not of the body; is it therefore not of the body? ... But now hath God set the members every one of them in the body, as it hath pleased him ... And the eye cannot say unto the hand, I have no need of thee; nor again the head to the feet, I have no need of you. Nay, much more those members of the body which seem to be more feeble, are necessary ... That there should be no schism in the body; but that the members should have the same care one for another. And whether one member suffer, all the members suffer with it; or one member be honored, all the members rejoice with it. Now ye are the body of Christ, and members in particular.[22]

Why has the nominal Church so overlooked, ignored, misunderstood, or trampled under foot this great doctrine of fraternal and communal unity? I cannot answer for all this delinquency in others. But I am resolved to correct my own, and to induce as many others to correct theirs as I may be able. The remainder of my earthly life, with its best powers, stands consecrated to this cause of Practical Christian Socialism.

PART II

The Practical Christian Republic

Introduction

In order to realize the vast and complex good contemplated, we have actually commenced the establishment of a universal Practical Christian Republic; within which an indefinite number of local Communities may be formed, all acknowledging the sovereignty of divine principles, and all intimately confederated together, yet differing in many respects from each other as to domestic arrangements and matters of mere local concern.

The outlines of a vast social superstructure, from foundation to dome, are presented in design, that all the builders may know what they are about while constructing its component parts, and do nothing which shall require undoing. But the cooperatives are required only to labor faithfully in that constituent portion of the Confederacy which immediately concerns their respective communal companies. None need leave his proper sphere to assume the responsibilities of a wider one. None need be anxious for anything but the faithful performance of his own duty at the post he engages to maintain. Each needs only to feel that he belongs to a grand army of human regenerators, all devoted to a common glorious cause, under a Supreme Commander who will certainly lead his invincible hosts to complete victory. With such motives and such a faith the humblest soldier will be mighty, and will find his least honorable services ennobled and sanctified by their relation to illustrious final results.

We chose the name, *Practical Christian Republic*, because it seemed most indicative and significant of the real nature of the thing designed. It is proposed to establish by voluntary association a new, grand and comprehensive body politic, such as has never heretofore existed on earth. It is not to be a mere church or ecclesiastical communion. Nor is it to be a mere civil government or political state. Nor yet a duplicate organization of church and state in mutual alliance. But it is to be a perfectly homogeneous organization, at once religious, social and civil in its inherent structural characteristics. It is intended to combine all the useful attributes of a true Christian church and a true civil state, to the utter exclusion of those malign forces which in past time have vitiated both church and state. It is to be preeminently a religious, social and civil Commonwealth, declaratively based on the essential divine principles taught and exemplified by Jesus Christ, and completely subordinate to the sovereignty of those principles.

We call it a *Republic*, because its governmental functions are to be exercised for the common good of the people confederated in it through their chosen official servants. We call it a *Christian* Republic, because its acknowledged fundamental and sovereign principles are distinctively Christian. We call it a *Practical* Christian Republic, because it magnifies and insists on that personal, social and political righteousness which is absolutely *practical,* but treats as non-essential that mere external righteousness which consists in professions, forms, ceremonies and observances. We call it *the* Practical Christian Republic, because there is no other of the kind on earth.

If others can improve on my objects, or my plan, by presenting better ones, I am willing. But for my own part I must have sublime objects in view, and a distinct outline of the operations depended on for accomplishing those objects. I cannot work vigorously with feeble motives, or at random. Permit me then to place in your hands for critical and deliberate examination the Constitution of the Practical Christian Republic.

The Constitution of the
Practical Christian Republic

A new order of human society is hereby founded, to be called THE PRAC-
TICAL CHRISTIAN REPUBLIC. It shall be constituted, organized and governed in accordance with the following fundamental articles, to wit:

ARTICLE 1. OBJECTS.

The cardinal objects of this Republic are and shall be the following, viz.:

To institute and consolidate a true order of human society, which shall
harmonize all individual interests in the common good, and be governed
by divine principles as its supreme law.

To establish local Communities of various grades and peculiarities, all
acknowledging the sovereignty of divine principles, and so constituted as to
promote the highest happiness of their respective associates.

To confederate all such local Communities, wheresoever existing
throughout the earth, by an ascending series of combination, in one common
social Republic.

To ensure to every orderly citizen of this Republic a comfortable home,
suitable employment, adequate subsistence, congenial associates, a good
education, proper stimulants to personal righteousness, sympathetic aid in
distress, and due protection in the exercise of all natural rights.

To give mankind a practical illustration of civil government maintained
in just subordination to divine principles; which shall be powerful without
tyranny, benignant without weakness, dignified without ostentation, independent without defiance, invincible without resorting to injurious force,
and preeminently useful without being burdensome.

To institute and sustain every suitable instrumentality for removing
the causes of human misery, and promoting the conversion of the world to
true righteousness.

To multiply, economize, distribute and apply beneficently, wisely and successfully, all the means necessary to harmonize the human race, with each other, with the heavenly world, and with the universal Father; that in one grand communion of angels and men the will of God may be done on earth as it is in heaven.

ARTICLE 2. PRINCIPLES.

We proclaim the absolute sovereignty of divine principles over all human beings, combinations, associations, governments, institutions, laws, customs, habits, practices, actions, opinions, intentions and affections. We recognize in the Religion of Jesus Christ, as he taught and exemplified it, a complete annunciation and attestation of essential divine principles.

We accept and acknowledge the following as divine Principles of Theological Truth, Personal Righteousness, and Social Order.*

We hold ourselves imperatively bound by the sovereignty of these acknowledged divine principles, never, under any pretext whatsoever, to kill, injure, envy or hate any human being, even our worst enemy.

Never to sanction chattel slavery, or any obvious oppression of man by man.

Never to countenance war, or capital punishment, or the infliction of injurious penalties, or the resistance of evil with evil in any form.

Never to violate the dictates of chastity, by adultery, polygamy, concubinage, fornication, self-pollution, lasciviousness, amative abuse, impure language or cherished lust.

Never to manufacture, buy, sell, deal out or use any intoxicating liquor *as a beverage.*

Never to take or administer an oath.

Never to participate in a sword-sustained human government, either as voters, office-holders, or subordinate assistants, in any case prescriptively involving the infliction of death, or any absolute injury whatsoever by man on man; nor to invoke governmental interposition in any such case, even for the accomplishment of good objects.

Never to indulge self-will, bigotry, love of preeminence, covetousness, deceit, profanity, idleness or an unruly tongue.

Never to participate in lotteries, gambling, betting or pernicious amusements.

---

*Here follow the twenty-four "Essential Divine Principles of the Christian Religion." See part I, chapter 1.

Never to resent reproof, or justify ourselves in a known wrong. Never to aid, abet or approve others in any thing sinful; but through divine assistance always to recommend and promote, with our entire influence, the holiness and happiness of all.

ARTICLE 3. RIGHTS.

No member of this Republic, nor Association of its members, can have a right to violate any of its acknowledged divine principles; but all the members, however peculiarized by sex, age, color, native country, rank, calling, wealth or station, have equal and indefeasible rights, as human beings, to do, to be and to enjoy whatever they are capable of, that is not in violation of those Principles. Within these just limits no person shall be restricted or interfered with by this Republic, nor by any constituent Association thereof, in the exercise of the following declared rights, viz.:

The right to worship God, with or without external ceremonies and devotional observances, according to the dictates of his or her own conscience.

The right to exercise reason, investigate questions, form opinions and declare convictions, by speech, by the pen and by the press, on all subjects within the range of human thought.

The right to hold any official station to which he or she may be elected, to pursue any avocation, or follow any course in life, according to genius, attraction and taste.

The right to be stewards under God of his or her own talents, property, skill and personal endowments.

The right to form and enjoy particular friendships, with congenial minds.

The right to contract marriage, and sustain the sacred relationships of family.

The right to unite with, and also to withdraw from any Community or Association, on reciprocal terms at discretion.

In fine, the right to seek happiness in all rightful ways, by all innocent means.

ARTICLE 4. MEMBERSHIP.

Section 1. Membership in this Republic shall exist in seven Circles, viz. the Adoptive, the Unitive, the Preceptive, the Communitive, the Expansive, the Charitive, and the Parentive.

The Adoptive Circle shall include all members living in isolation, or not yet admitted into the membership of an Integral Community.

The Unitive Circle shall include all members of Rural and Joint Stock Communities.

The Preceptive Circle shall include all members specially and perseveringly devoted to teaching; whether it be teaching religion, morality, or any branch of useful knowledge, and whether their teaching be done with the living voice, or with the pen, or through the press, or in educative institutions. All such teachers, after having proved themselves competent, devoted and acceptable in the Communities to which they belong, shall be considered in the Preceptive Circle.

The Communitive Circle shall include all members of Integral Common Stock Communities, and Families, whose internal economy excludes individual profits on capital, wages for labor, and separate interests.

The Expansive Circle shall include all members who are especially devoted to the expansion of this Republic, by founding and strengthening new Integral Communities; who have associated in companies for that express purpose, and are employing the principal portion of their time, talents or property in that work.

The Charitive Circle shall include all members who are especially devoted to the reformation, elevation, improvement and welfare of the world's suffering classes, by furnishing them homes, employment, instruction and all the requisite helps to a better condition; who are associated in companies for that express purpose, and are employing the principal portion of their time, talents or property in such works.

The Parentive Circle shall include all members who, on account of their mature age, faithful services, great experience, sound judgment or unquestionable reliability, are competent to advise, arbitrate and recommend measures in cases of great importance. They shall be declared worthy of a place in the Parentive Circle by their respective Integral Communities in a regular meeting notified for that purpose by a unanimous vote.

Section 2. The members of no Circle shall ever assume to exercise any other than purely moral or advisory power; nor claim any exclusive prerogatives, privileges, honors or distinctions whatsoever, over the members of other Circles; but shall be entitled to respect and influence in consideration of intrinsic worth alone. Nor shall there be any permanent general organization of these Circles *as such*. But the members of either may unite in cooperative associations, companies and partnerships for the more efficient prosecution of their peculiar objects; and may also hold public meetings, conferences and conventions at pleasure in promotion of those objects.

Section 3. Any person may be admitted a member of this Republic by any constituent Community, or other authorized public body thereof in regular meeting assembled. And any twelve or more persons, adopting this Constitution from conviction, may render themselves members of the Republic by uniting to form a constituent and confederate Community thereof.

Section 4. Any person may resign or withdraw membership at discretion, or may recede from either of the other Circles to the Adoptive Circle, by giving written notice to the body or principal persons concerned. Any person uniting with a Society of any description, radically opposed in principle, practice or spirit to this Republic, shall be deemed to have relinquished membership; likewise any person who shall have ceased to manifest any interest in its affairs for the space of three years.

Section 5. Any constituent Community, or other organized body of this Republic, competent to admit members, shall have power to dismiss or discharge them for justifiable reasons. And no person shall be retained a member after persistently violating or setting at naught any one of the sovereign divine principles declared in Article 2 of this Constitution.

ARTICLE 5. ORGANIZATION.

Section 1. The constituent and confederate bodies of this social Republic shall be the following, viz.: Parochial Communities, Integral Communities, Communal Municipalities, Communal States, and Communal Nations.

Section 2. Parochial Communities shall consist each of twelve or more members belonging chiefly to the Adoptive Circle, residing promiscuously in a general neighborhood, associated for religious and moral improvement, and to secure such other social advantages as may be found practicable.

Section 3. Integral Communities shall consist each of twelve or more members, inhabiting an integral territorial domain so held in possession and guaranteed that no part thereof can be owned in fee simple by any person not a member of this Republic.

There shall be three different kinds of Integral Communities, viz.: Rural, Joint Stock, and Common Stock Communities.

Rural Communities shall hold and manage the major portion of their respective domains in separate homesteads, adapted to the wants of families and to small associations, under a system of Individual Proprietorship.

Joint Stock Communities shall hold and manage the major portion of their respective domains in Joint Stock Proprietorship, with various unitary economies, under a system of associative cooperation; laying off the minor portion into village house lots, to be sold to individual members under necessary restrictions.

Common Stock Communities shall hold and manage their respective domains and property in Common Stock, without paying individual members profits on capital, or stipulated wages for labor. Common Stock Families may also be formed within Rural and Joint Stock Communities, when deemed desirable and practicable; in which case such families shall not be considered Integral Communities, but as constituent portions of the Communities on whose domains they respectively reside.

Section 4. Communal Municipalities shall consist each of two or more Communities, whether Parochial or Integral, combined, as in a town or city, for municipal purposes necessary to their common welfare and impracticable or extremely difficult of accomplishment without such a union.

Section 5. Communal States shall consist of two or more Communal Municipalities, combined for general purposes necessary to their common welfare and impracticable or extremely difficult of accomplishment without such a union.

Section 6. Communal Nations shall consist each of two or more Communal States, combined for national purposes necessary to their common welfare and impracticable or extremely difficult of accomplishment without such a union.

Section 7. When there shall be two or more Communal Nations, they shall be represented equitably, according to population, in a Supreme Unitary Council, by Senators elected for the term of – years.

Section 8. The several constituent bodies of this social Republic, herein before named, shall all be organized under written Constitutions, Compacts or Fundamental Laws, not inconsistent with this general Constitution, and shall exercise the governmental prerogatives and responsibilities defined in the next ensuing Article.

ARTICLE 6. GOVERNMENT.

Section 1. Self-government in the Individual, the Family, and the primary congenial Association, under the immediate sovereignty of divine principles, being the basis of moral and social order in this Republic, shall be constantly cherished as indispensable to its prosperity. Therefore all governmental powers vested in the confederate bodies of this Republic shall be such as are obviously beneficent, and such as cannot be conveniently exercised by the primary Communities, or their component circles. And such confederate bodies shall never assume to exercise governmental powers not clearly delegated to them by their constituents.

Section 2. Each Parochial, and each Integral Community, shall exert its utmost ability to insure all its members and dependents a full realization of the guarantees specified in Object 4, Article 1 of this Constitution, viz.: a comfortable home, suitable employment, adequate subsistence, congenial associates, a good education, proper stimulants to personal righteousness, sympathetic aid in distress and due protection in the exercise of all natural rights. And whereinsoever it shall find itself unable to realize the said guarantees, it may unite with other Communities to insure them, by such means as shall be mutually agreed on for that purpose. Each Community shall have the right to frame, adopt and alter its own Constitution and laws; to elect its own officers, teachers and representatives; and to manage its own domestic affairs of every description, without interference from any other constituent body or authority of this Republic; excepting, always, the prerogatives which it shall have specifically delegated, or referred to others.

Section 3. Each Communal Municipality shall be formed by a Convention of delegates, chosen for that purpose by the Communities proposing to unite in such a Municipality. The delegates shall be chosen equitably on the basis of population. These delegates shall form a Constitution or Fundamental Compact, clearly defining the governmental powers to be exercised by the Municipal authorities; which, having been submitted to the voting members of the Communities concerned, and adopted, the Municipality shall be considered established, and shall go into organized operation accordingly. But either of the Communities composing such Municipality shall have the right to secede therefrom, after giving one year's notice, paying all assessments due the corporation at the time of such notice, and relinquishing its share of the public property therein. Or the union of two or more Communities, constituting a Municipality, may be dissolved at any time by mutual agreement of the federative parties.

Section 4. Each Communal State shall be formed by a Convention of delegates from the Municipalities proposing to unite in the same, through a process substantially similar to the one prescribed in the preceding Section, but without the right of secession therein reserved. And each Communal Nation shall be formed by the States proposing to unite therein, in general accordance with the same process.

Section 5. The duties and powers of the Supreme Unitary Council shall be determined in a Fundamental Compact, to be framed by delegates from all the Communal Nations then existing, and adopted by at least two-thirds of the citizen members of this Republic present and acting in their respective primary Communities, at meetings duly notified for that purpose. And all questions throughout this Republic, excepting the election of officers, shall be determined by a two-thirds vote.

Section 6. No official servant of any grade in this Republic shall ever assume to distinguish himself or herself by external display of dress, equipage or other artificial appliances, above the common members; nor shall receive compensation for official services beyond the average paid to the first class of operatives at large, with a reasonable allowance for incidental expenses; but every official servant shall be considered bound to exemplify the humility, modesty and benevolence inculcated in the Christian precept, "Whosoever will be chief among you, let him be the servant of all."[1] Nor shall it be allowable for any of the constitutional bodies of this Republic to burthen the people with governmental expenses for mere worldly show, or for any other than purposes of unquestionable public utility.

ARTICLE 7. RELIGION.

Section 1. Acknowledging the Christian Religion as one of fundamental divine principles, to be practically carried out in all human conduct, this Republic insists only on the essentials of faith and practice affirmed in Article 2 of its Constitution. Therefore no uniform religious or ecclesiastical system of externals shall be established; nor shall any rituals, forms, ceremonies or observances whatsoever be either instituted, or interdicted; but each Community shall determine for itself, with due regard to the conscientious scruples of its own members, all matters of this nature.

Section 2. Believing that the Holy Christ-Spirit will raise up competent religious and moral teachers, and commend them, by substantial demonstrations of their fitness, to the confidence of those to whom they minister, this Republic shall not assume to commission, authorize or forbid any person to preach, or to teach religion; nor shall any constituent body thereof assume to do so. But each Community may invite any person deemed worthy of confidence, to be their religious teacher on terms reciprocally satisfactory to the parties concerned.

Section 3. It shall be the privilege and duty of the members of this Republic to hold general meetings, at least once in three months, for religious improvement and the promulgation of their acknowledged divine principles. In order to this, Quarterly Conferences shall be established in every general region of country inhabited by any considerable number of members. Any twenty-five or more members, wheresoever resident, shall be competent to establish a Quarterly Conference, whenever they may deem the same necessary to their convenience. In so doing, they shall adopt a written Constitution, subsidiary to this general Constitution, and no wise incompatible therewith; under which they may establish such regulations as they shall deem promotive of their legitimate objects. All such Conferences shall have power to admit members into the Adoptive Circle of this Republic; and also, for sufficient reasons, to discharge them. And each Quarterly Conference shall keep reliable records of its proceedings, with an authentic copy of this general Constitution prefixed.

ARTICLE 8. MARRIAGE.

Section 1. Marriage, being one of the most important and sacred of human relationships, ought to be guarded against caprice and abuse by the highest wisdom which is available. Therefore, within the membership of this Republic and the dependencies thereof, Marriage is specially commended to the care of the Preceptive and Parentive Circles. They are hereby designated as the confidential counselors of all members and dependents who may desire their mediation in cases of matrimonial negotiation, contract or controversy; and shall be held preeminently responsible for the prudent and faithful discharge of their duties. But no person decidedly averse to their interposition shall be considered under imperative obligation to solicit or accept it. And it shall be considered the perpetual duty of the Preceptive and Parentive Circles to enlighten the public mind relative to the requisites of true matrimony, and to elevate the marriage institution within this Republic to the highest possible plane of purity and happiness.

Section 2. Marriage shall always be solemnized in the presence of two or more witnesses, by the distinct acknowledgment of the parties before some member of the Preceptive, or of the Parentive Circles, selected to preside on the occasion. And it shall be the imperative duty of the member so presiding, to see that every such marriage be recorded, within ten days thereafter, in the Registry of the Community to which one or both of them shall at the time belong.

Section 3. Divorce from the bonds of matrimony shall never be allowable within the membership of this Republic, except for adultery conclusively proved against the accused party. But separations for other sufficient reasons may be sanctioned, with the distinct understanding that neither party shall be at liberty to marry again during the natural lifetime of the other.

ARTICLE 9. EDUCATION.

Section 1. The proper education of the rising generation being indispensable to the prosperity and glory of this Republic, it shall be amply provided for as a cardinal want; and no child shall be allowed to grow up any where under the control of its membership, without good educational opportunities.

Section 2. Education shall be as comprehensive and thorough as circumstances in each case will allow. It shall aim, in all cases, to develop harmoniously the physical, intellectual, moral and social faculties of the young. To give them, if possible, a high-toned moral character, based on scrupulous conscientiousness and radical Christian principles – a sound mind, well stored with useful knowledge, and capable of inquiring, reasoning and judging for itself – a healthful, vigorous body, suitably fed, exercised, clothed, lodged and recreated – good domestic habits, including personal cleanliness, order, propriety, agreeableness and generous social qualities – industrial executiveness and skill, in one or more of the avocations necessary to a comfortable subsistence – and, withal, practical economy in pecuniary matters. In fine, to qualify them for solid usefulness and happiness in all the rightful pursuits and relations of life.

Section 3. The Preceptive Circle of members shall be expected to distinguish themselves by a zealous, wise and noble devotion to this great interest of education. And every individual, family private association and constituent body of this Republic, in their respective spheres, shall cooperate, by every reasonable effort, to render its educational institutions, from the nursery to the University, preeminently excellent.

ARTICLE 10. PROPERTY.

Section 1. All property, being primarily the Creator's and provided by Him for the use of mankind during their life on earth, ought to be acquired, aided and disposed of in strict accordance with the dictates of justice and charity. Therefore the members of this Republic shall consider themselves stewards in trust, under God, of all property coming into their possession, and, as such, imperatively bound not to consume it in the gratification of their own inordinate lusts, nor to hoard it up as a mere treasure, nor to employ it to the injury of any human being, nor to withhold it from the relief of distressed fellow creatures, but always to use it as not abusing it, for strictly just, benevolent and commendable purposes.

Section 2. It shall not be deemed compatible with justice for the people of this Republic, in their pecuniary commerce with each other, to demand, in any case, as a compensation for their mere personal service, labor or attendance, a higher price per cent, per piece, per day, week, month or year, than the average paid to the first class of operatives in the Community, or general vicinity, where the service is rendered. Nor shall it be deemed compatible with justice for the members, in such commerce, to demand, as a price for anything sold or exchanged, more than the fair cost value thereof, as nearly as the same can be estimated, reckoning prime cost, labor or attention, incidental expenses, contingent waste, depreciation and average risks of sale; nor to demand for the mere use of capital, except as partners in the risk of its management, any clear interest or profit whatsoever exceeding four per cent. per annum.

Section 3. It shall not be deemed compatible with the welfare and honor of this Republic, for the people thereof to owe debts outside of the same exceeding three-fourths of their available property, rated at a moderate valuation by disinterested persons; nor to give or receive long credits, except on real estate security; nor to manufacture, fabricate or sell shammy and unreliable productions; nor to make business engagements, or hold out expectations, which are of doubtful fulfillment

Section 4. Whenever the population and resources of this Republic shall warrant the formation of the first Communal Nation, and the government thereof shall have been organized, a uniform system of Mutual Banking shall be established, based mainly on real estate securities, which shall afford loans at the mere cost of operations. Also, a uniform system of Mutual Insurance, which shall reduce all kinds of insurance to the lowest terms. Also, a uniform system of reciprocal Commercial Exchange, which shall preclude all needless interventions between producers and consumers, all extra risks of property, all extortionate speculations, all inequitable profits on exchange, and all demoralizing expedients of trade. Also, Regulations providing for the just encouragement of useful industry, and the practical equalization of all social advantages, so far as the same can be done without infracting individual rights. And all the members shall be considered under sacred moral obligations to cooperate adhesively and persistently in every righteous measure for the accomplishment of these objects.

ARTICLE 11. POLICY.

It shall be the fundamental, uniform and established policy of this Republic:

To govern, succor and protect its own people, to the utmost of its ability, in all matters and cases whatsoever, not involving anti-Christian conflict with the sword-sustained governments of the world under which its members live.

To avoid all unnecessary conflicts whatsoever with these governments, by conforming to all their laws and requirements which are not repugnant to the sovereignty of divine principles.

To abstain from all participation in the working of their political machinery, and to be connected as little as possible with their systems of governmental operation.

To protest, remonstrate and testify conscientiously against their sins on moral grounds alone; but never to plot schemes of revolutionary agitation, intrigue or violence against them, nor be implicated in countenancing the least resistance to their authority by injurious force.

If compelled in any case, by divine principles, to disobey their requirements, or passively to withstand their unrighteous exactions, and thus incur their penal vengeance, to act openly, and suffer with true moral heroism.

Never to ask their protection, even in favor of injured innocence, or threatened rights, when it can be interposed only by means which are condemned by divine principles.

To live in peace, so far as can innocently be done, with all mankind outside of this Republic, whether individuals, associations, corporations, sects, classes, parties, states or nations; also to accredit and encourage whatever is truly good in all; yet to fellowship iniquity in none, be enslaved by none, be amalgamated with none, be morally responsible for none, but ever be distinctly, unequivocally and uncompromisingly the Practical Christian Republic, until the complete regeneration of the world.

ARTICLE 12. AMENDMENT.

Whenever one-fourth of all the members of this Republic shall subscribe and publish a written proposition to alter, amend or revise this Constitution, such proposition, of whatsoever nature, shall be submitted to each Community for consideration. Returns shall then be made of all the votes cast in every Community, to the highest organized body of the Republic for the time being. And the concurrence of two-thirds of all the votes shall determine the question or questions at issue. If the proposition shall have been a specific alteration or amendment of the Constitution, it shall thenceforth be established as such. If a Convention shall have been proposed to revise the Constitution, a Convention shall be summoned and held accordingly. But no alteration, amendment or revision of this Constitution shall take effect until sanctioned by two-thirds of all the members present and acting thereon in their respective Communities, at regular meetings duly notified for that purpose.

Chapter 5

Objects, Principles, and Policies

Building the True Social System

Having laid the foundation for my proposed new order of Society, I am now to erect the superstructure. The twenty-four essential divine principles of the Christian Religion have been set forth as the foundation. The whole edifice must be framed and completed in just correspondence with that basis.

The principal objection I have heard made to my Social System is, the gigantic magnitude of its propositions. Some have exclaimed, Here are objects vast as the habitable globe, which require ages for their attainment, and can hardly be grasped by the most expansive imagination! Why does this handful of beginners presume to look so far into the future, and to aim at results at present so impracticable, if ever possible? Why lay out more than Herculean labors for great nations, and for generations unborn? Why not content themselves with undertakings suited to their present actual capabilities? Are they not reaching out to embrace a huge shadow, at the imminent risk of losing the little substance they already hold?

To such cautionary exclamations I respond:

1. The objects proposed are in accordance with the revealed will of God and the divinely predicted destiny of the human race.

2. They are in accordance with the mission of Jesus Christ into our world, with the genius of his Religion, and with the dictates of its essential divine principles.

3. They are such as should be the animating and controlling motives of minds engaged in founding a new state of human society, in order to their making even a fair beginning.

4. Grand and comprehensive objects aimed at as ultimate results do not relax exertions to maintain present possessions, but strengthen and stimulate them.

5. Nothing is proposed to be done towards building up the Practical Christian Republic but what will be practicable from stage to stage of its growth.

I am perfectly aware that the work proposed must be a difficult and a protracted one. I am painfully sensible of the present unfitness of the majority of mankind to maintain a much better order of society than the one in which they live. Many are so undeveloped, so low minded, so ill educated, so blind to their real interests, so selfish, envious, contentious and vindictive, so much more disposed to thrust each other down than to lift up, so full of violence and war, so proud and ambitious, so willing to prey on one another, and to flourish at each other's expense. Few, perhaps, could be worked into an order of society in which nearly all government would be self-government within the individual, or in communal public opinion; in which all injurious force, even against the most outrageous criminal, is prohibited; and wherein selfishness must be checked at every corner and angle of life's intercourse.

But if human imperfection should necessitate a long and somewhat tedious process of actualization, that ought not to discredit my theory; since the most meritorious and magnificent plans may be slow of consummation, merely by reason of men's reluctance to conform to their conditions of success. If people will not do their duty towards providing the necessaries of physical, intellectual and moral enjoyment, then they must suffer, more or less, the lack of them. But give me the concurrence of those whose happiness is sought – only a tolerable concurrence – and the result is to me certain. God wills it; Angels minister towards its consummation; and Creation groans in the travail of progress for deliverance from the bondage of existing selfishness. Nothing else is necessary but the fraternal cooperation of mankind in realizing their destiny. If they help themselves and help each other, this glorious work of their redemption will be accomplished in due time. I wish you to consider three important facts, which I rely upon for my encouragement.

1. My proposed order of society is purely voluntary. None will be compelled to enter into it, or to remain in it against their will.

2. There are a few, perhaps a respectable minority of mankind, high enough to form and maintain voluntarily something like my proposed social order. We have many millions of professedly experimental Christians, who hope they have become regenerate, have renounced their sins, and laid up their treasure in heaven. How many of these are unselfish and heavenly minded enough to dwell together in unity, under the sovereignty of divine

principles, without the sword for their dernier resort, I cannot calculate. It would be a shame if there were not enough to form several Communities. We have hosts of educated people, too, philosophers, refined in mind and manners, besides zealous philanthropists and reformers not a few. I think I have reason to calculate on mustering volunteers enough to make a respectable beginning. It would be deplorable if so many Churches, Theological Seminaries and Sunday Schools; Universities, Colleges, Academies and Common Schools; printing presses, books and publications; literary, humane, philanthropic and reform Associations; and the ten thousand other instrumentalities of the civilized world for regenerating, elevating and refining people, should all be insufficient to furnish a goodly number wherewith to carry forward the experiment.* I will content myself that I may calculate on volunteers enough to make a commencement. Give me this fulcrum for my lever, and I will ultimately move the world.

3. The few who are prepared for this higher order of society will not only accelerate their own progress in Love, Wisdom and Happiness by ascending into it, but will thereby do more than they otherwise could to elevate all below them. For the common and almost universal doubt is, whether the principles of my Social System can be made the basis of any practicable form of society. "Show us your new order of Society in actual, steady operation, and we will then believe," say most of these skeptics. If therefore the thing can be thus shown, the moral effect must be great and salutary, both within and without the new Social State.

Suppose, then, I find twenty souls, or one hundred, or one thousand, or ten thousand, with the distant prospect of millions, who heartily accept my fundamental principles, and who say to me, Please show us how we can communitize and establish an order of society in accordance with your principles. This is precisely what I now propose to do; and thereby I shall present the Constitutional Polity of what, in my judgment, is the true Social System.

---

* Inquirer: "I yield you this point; but remember this prediction: You will find a great many who say they have been born of God, or have become philosophers, or have been elevated by education to great refinement, or are profoundly interested in philanthropy, or are devoted reformers, or have become sincere spiritualists, who nevertheless need high and strong fences to keep them from devouring each other, and the mighty arbitration of a military and penal government to determine their strifes. Not all who can utter fine words on set occasions are good enough to live together in peace on your principles."
Expositor: "I thank you for your words of truth and caution."

The Harmony of Individual and Common Interests

The true Social System has for its grand aim the promotion and harmonization of all human interests. I do not propose to annihilate individual interests, nor sacrifice them to societary interests in the least degree; nor, on the other hand, to sacrifice the common good to individual good.

We have been accustomed to regard it as impossible to institute Society without compromising conflicting interests, and sacrificing those of individuals to the public good. And you may think my Social System would carry this compromise of individual interests much farther than is done in the existing order of society. By no means. I take for granted that all *real* human interests, could we but see them in the true light of nature and the divine order, are perfectly consonant with each other; the highest good of *each* and *all* being identical in every possible case.

As a Practical Christian Socialist, I propose a System of Society which keeps distinctly in view the preservation and promotion of all *real* human interests. It must not destroy, override or impair one of them. It must recognize, promote, secure and harmonize them all. Neither individual nor social good must be sacrificed. Both must stand together on a common foundation, upheld by common bonds. If I do not present such a Social System, my work will be a failure.

First then, let us inquire what the real interests of human nature are. They must all be involved in wants, rights and duties. If man's real wants are well supplied, his real rights well secured, and his real duties well performed, it follows that all his real interests are promoted, and happiness must be the result.

What then are man's wants, rights and duties? I think we may look for them in the seven spheres of his activity and relationship:

1. *Individuality.* He is a unit, an individual identity, a man. This is the central reality of his existence. Should he cease to be an individual, sentient, intellectual, rational, moral being he would be no man. Nothing then could be predicated of him. As an individual being he has wants, rights and duties – consequently real interests. This is the sphere of his Individuality.

2. *Connubiality.* Man was created male and female. Thence comes the union of two individuals in marriage. This is the sphere of Connubiality.

3. *Consanguinity.* From marriage results offspring and blood relationship, which comprehends ordinarily, besides the immediate family, a larger or smaller circle of kindred. This is the sphere of Consanguinity.

4. *Congeniality*. Next comes the sphere of Congeniality, embracing a larger or smaller circle of persons, who, by reason of similar tastes and pursuits, or on account of strong interior sympathies, become strongly attached friends.

5. *Federality*. Beyond the sphere of Congeniality man confederates with his fellows in the Community, the Municipality, the Nationality, etc., to maintain an orderly Social and Political System of relationship. This is his sphere of Federality.

6. *Humanity*. Outside of all federal compacts lies our common humanity, to which we stand in a certain relationship, and must act accordingly. This is man's sphere of Humanity.

7. *Universality*. But still outside of this human sphere, man holds relationship to all beings and things in the whole conceivable Infinitarium, from the invisible atom to the sun, and from the lowest insect to the highest angel – above all to the Infinite Spirit-Father. This is his sphere of Universality.

Each successive sphere, you perceive, is wider than the preceding. But nothing in a narrower sphere is necessarily destroyed or impaired by the peculiarities of the more expanded one. Rather, everything ought to be conserved. None of man's real interests in the sphere of Individuality should be injured by entering into marriage. There must be something wrong in a marriage which makes either husband or wife a more diminutive being than before, which impairs the real interests of either, or renders either on the whole less happy. True Connubiality must therefore be conservative of true Individuality. The same may be said of each widening sphere. All should be harmony in the motion of these "wheels within a wheel."[1] And if man could be brought to act truly in all these spheres, he would be greater and happier in each, for acting well his part in every other. His proper Individuality would then realize its greatest importance, integrity and happiness.

I will now endeavor to set forth the great interests of man's Individuality which must be recognized, preserved and promoted by the true Social System. What then are man's wants, rights and duties in the sphere of his Individuality?

What is man? He is a physical, affectional, intellectual and moral being. The Scriptures represent him as consisting of body, soul and spirit. We are accustomed to speak of his physical, intellectual and moral nature. So he has physical, intellectual and moral interests to be promoted.

Let us look at his physical interests. He needs food, clothing, shelter, exercise, rest, recreation, and, when distressed from any cause, relief; that is, he needs a comfortable home and subsistence, in which we may include whatever is necessary to the physical enjoyment of life. The interests involved in securing these necessaries are so pressing on mankind, that all are sensible of them.

Look at man's intellectual interests. He needs food, clothing, shelter, exercise, rest, recreation and relief for the mind. I mean, he needs knowledge, instruction, use of language, mental training, opportunities for intellectual activity, with the requisite rest and recreation. He needs teachers, books, educational institutions, and all the necessaries of proper mental culture, improvement and usefulness; in fine, all that affords true intellectual enjoyment.

Once more, look at man's moral interests. Here we contemplate him as an affectional, passional, sentimental being, and of course a social one. The true passional loves of the soul, I mean the normal and legitimate ones, yearn for gratifications, which ought to be as promptly and adequately provided as those demanded by the physical and intellectual departments of his nature. Among these I include his Connubial, Consanguinal, Congenial, Federal, Humanital, and highest religious loves. The affectional and sentimental soul is a living fountain of loves – all innocent when normal, legitimate, unperverted and harmoniously exercised. They do not all manifest themselves with equal intensity in all individuals. But I may safely affirm that they exist in human nature; that they involve man's profoundest interests; that they include his highest wants, rights and responsibilities; and that they must not be disregarded. Ample provision must be made for the innocent gratification of these wants, for the just exercise of these rights, and for the faithful discharge of these responsibilities.

I sum up man's interests in the sphere of Individuality thus: Physically, intellectually and morally he wants all the necessaries of happiness; he has the right to all those necessaries; and he is in duty bound to do all he is fairly able towards providing them for himself. The true Social System should guarantee, to the utmost extent, all these necessaries of Individual culture and enjoyment. Any system which should propose less would be unworthy of respect. And the same is true in respect to Connubiality, Consanguinity, Congeniality, Federality, Humanity and Universality – with all the wants, rights, duties and interests appertaining to human nature in those several spheres.

Divine Sovereignty

I affirm that whatever is plainly repugnant to the divine principles stated in Part I is absolutely wrong and of no rightful authority whatever.

I have met with two exactly opposite minds who demurred to the doctrine of the sovereignty of divine principles. One of them said it struck a fatal blow at the sovereignty of all established human governments, whether Monarchical, Aristocratic or Democratic, whether Despotic or Constitutional. He acknowledged it was right in the *abstract*; but, said he, Human Government must be sustained in its assumed sovereignty for the present, right or wrong.

He was right to this extent, that no one man, nor class of men, nor national people, can rightfully do or require to be done any thing whatsoever which is plainly contrary to divine principles. Man is ever a bounden subject of the divine law. He cannot repeal it, nor annul it to the least extent, nor violate it with impunity. If any man, or combination of men, claims a sovereignty of this nature, they are rebels against God, and in a state of insurrection to his authority.

If autocrats, monarchs or constitutional governments set up and enforce laws which they deem just, and which I deem wicked, as being plainly contrary to divine principles, I shall protest against all such laws, as morally null and void. I shall deny that their enactors have any sovereignty or right to make such requirements. I shall refuse to obey such laws, and stand upon my conscience before God. If they enforce the penalties of those laws upon me, then I shall try to suffer their inflictions meekly, patiently and heroically, without physical resistance, but with a solemn moral protest, even unto death, against the wrong done.

My other friend was entirely devoted to the modern notion of *individual sovereignty*. He denounced all monarchical, aristocratic, democratic, ecclesiastical, theocratic, communal and associational sovereignty of man over man as usurpation and tyranny. Every individual of the race, he contended, was a sovereign over him or herself alone. He declared himself totally opposed to all creeds, covenants, standards, declarations, compacts and constitutions whereby individuals relinquish any part of their own sovereignty. And he insisted that it was impossible to have any such without abridging individual sovereignty.

He did not deny the existence and supreme sovereignty of God, but he said every individual must settle all questions of faith, religion and morals for himself, and had no right to meddle with another's judgment of what was true or right. He himself believed in the God of nature, and that this God had made every human being an individual sovereign. He believed also in natural laws or principles, which eternally executed themselves by a regular succession of cause and effect. But what those principles were, and how they were to be regarded, no man could assume to say for another. Each must investigate, judge and act for himself. He deemed it altogether absurd, as well as wrong, for a company of individuals to draw up a formal declaration of so-called divine principles, and acknowledge themselves under the absolute sovereignty thereof. Who could be sure today, whether tomorrow he would or would not regard a principle as divine? One of these same sovereign divine principles might next week become, in the mind's judgment, no principle at all, or perhaps an infernal principle. Everyone was bound by the dignity of his own natural individual sovereignty to keep his mind unfettered from moment to moment, that he might always think, feel, speak and act spontaneously, as seemed to him proper.

I should not deem it worth my while to contend with such a thinker. If sincere in his notion of individual sovereignty, of course he cannot assent to our doctrine of the absolute sovereignty of divine principles, nor approve of our Constitution, nor do otherwise than protest against the Practical Christian Republic. We must follow our convictions of truth and duty, and leave him to follow his. There can be no unity between him and us. He has no faith in our fundamentals. We have none in his. He is positive that every human being is an individual sovereign over him or herself. We are positive that no human being is his own lawgiver, judge or sovereign, or has the least right to contravene the sovereignty of divine principles. Why then dispute about the matter? Let him go his way, while we go ours. Every tree shall be known by its fruits. Time will give practical and conclusive demonstrations of the truth on this, as on all other questions at issue. "Wisdom is justified of all her children."[2]

Adherence to Divine Principles

In relation to the twenty-four acknowledged divine principles, I have been asked if I expect all who accept them to agree exactly in their explicatory ideas. To this I reply, Certainly not. *That* would be expecting what is quite impossible in the nature of things, during the present imperfect development of the human mind. I expect only that the grand central truth of each proposition will be recognized, revered and cherished by all.

You must know that every fundamental principle has a spiritual essence of its own, which cannot be seen with equal clearness and comprehensiveness by all who embrace it as a divine reality, and which cannot be perfectly expressed in any external human language. It is very necessary to express spiritual truths as clearly as possible in external human language, because thereby most minds are inducted, as they otherwise could not be, into juster conceptions of them. But after all, the highest master of language cannot state a fundamental truth in words which perfectly express the spiritual reality. He may approximate such an expression very closely, to his own satisfaction; but other minds will view his grand truth from different standpoints, through more or less lucid atmospheres, and will form peculiar explicatory ideas of it, which they will express in their own way. This latitude of conception and explication must be allowed among the adherents of all fundamentals. It is just, innocent and harmless. So long as the differences among common acknowledgers of declared fundamentals do not affect their spiritual vitality, the necessary unity of the associates remains unimpaired.

To make my meaning unmistakable in the present case, suppose one of my brethren, who perfectly agrees with me in acknowledging *the existence of one all-perfect, infinite God*, differs from me in certain conceptions of His personality, mode of existence, or causative activity in the universe. Why need such differences disturb our harmony? Again. Another agrees cordially with me in acknowledging *the mediatorial manifestation of God through Christ*, which to him is a cardinal truth in his own ideas of it, yet he differs from me respecting the pre-existence of Jesus, or his miraculous conception, or respecting the precise mode whereby the divine nature dwelt in him, spoke through him and made him the Christ. Why need such differences disturb our fraternal harmony; since we both believe that God actually made a sublime, authoritative and world-redeeming manifestation of his will, attributes and moral perfections through that same Jesus Christ?

Again, a brother cordially agrees with me in believing in *the final universal triumph of good over evil*, which to him, as well as to me, is a cheering and hope-sustaining truth. Yet, he is not, like me, confident that there will come a period on earth when all people shall be holy and happy. Nor like me is he confident that all human beings in some future eternity will be perfectly holy and happy. He thinks it possible, and even probable, that some of the race will cease to exist, or will remain to all eternity in a condition of restraint and inferior happiness. He would be glad to hope for as glorious a triumph of good over evil as I do. He feels no repugnance to me on account of the extent to which my faith carries me. He himself rejoices in the assurance that evil will be reduced to its lowest possible minimum and so restrained as to become comparatively inappreciable in the condition of our race. If he thought otherwise, he would have too little hope to work in this great enterprise of human regeneration.

Need such differences disturb our fraternal harmony? Surely not. I might take up all my fundamentals in the same way, and show that unity of faith in and love for each may consist with many differences of explicatory ideas respecting it.

It is true that these *explicatory* differences might sometimes insensibly run into *radical* differences. That is something which cannot be prevented by straining upon words. We have to bear with gray cases till they grow dark enough to be unmistakable. But I have no serious apprehensions on this point. The vital essence of our declared sovereign divine principles is so obvious that no one of them can easily be confounded with its radical opposite. No man can go far towards atheism, pantheism or polytheism without setting at naught the radical truth that there is *one all-perfect, infinite God.* Nor far towards anti-Christian theism without trampling on the radical truth that God has manifested himself *mediatorially through Christ.* Nor far towards naturalism and rationalism without contemning the radical truth that God has given *divine revelations and inspirations to mankind,* as set forth in the Bible, and as asserted with strong attestations by individuals in all ages down to our own times. Nor far towards mere materialism without doubting the *existence of immortal spirits* outside the realm of flesh and blood. Nor far towards mere materialism or fatalism without denying *the moral agency and religious obligation of mankind.* Nor far towards Calvinism without rejecting the grand idea that good is finally to triumph over evil in our universe. In fine, I am confident no person could cherish a radically contrary idea to either of our acknowledged sovereign divine principles without soon flying off in a tangent from the whole movement. Consequently I cannot apprehend any serious mischief to come from the thousand and one explicatory and opinional differences which always inevitably arise on minor points, even in the most united of human associations.

I fell in with one friend, who strenuously insisted that it was all folly to acknowledge any precise statement of fundamental principles as the basis of a compact; because human beings are progressive and cannot absolutely *know* that what they *now* confidently deem a fundamental principle will not turn out to be a fundamental error, and then there must be a great ado made about the change which truth would dictate. He belongs to a class which has many worthy people in it, but who are affected with a kind of *creedophobia,* which has made them fearful of everything in religion and morals which assumes to be a definite assertion of fundamental principle.

All I can say to them is, that they have fallen into an indefensible extreme, of which experience will cure them, or which will forever prevent their accomplishing much for human progress. Little can be done for individual and social improvement without well-settled fundamental principles of religion and morals. Even erroneous ones, if cherished in the deepest convictions of mankind, will accomplish results which mere philosophizing, sentimentalizing, temporizing moralists may be powerless either to rival or to countervail. How much more then truthful ones?

Now it is ever the desideratum of really honest souls to get rid of all false principles in religion and morals. But it would be pitiful in them to treat their present highest convictions of essential truth and righteousness as too doubtful to proclaim and act upon, merely because at some future period they may possibly be obliged to change convictions. No man ought to bind himself never to change his convictions. We ask no one thus to bind himself. But every human being ought to act upon his or her highest religious and moral convictions for the time being, and to be willing to acknowledge them. So long as a certain proposition fairly expresses what to me, for the time being, is a sovereign divine principle, I ought to acknowledge and act upon it as such. If next year new light impels me to renounce what until then I have honestly held to be a divine fundamental, let me renounce it with equal uprightness, without shame, and with a noble willingness to suffer whatever reproach it shall cost me to be a true man.

Am I ashamed or afraid to do this? Do I wish to play hide and seek in such a matter? Do I wish to say, "O I have not changed my mind; I never had any settled religious and moral convictions; I have none now; I dare not profess any; nothing is very certain to me; I am going to keep on learning; and if I never come to the knowledge of the truth I cannot help it!" What are such minds likely to accomplish towards bettering the condition of humanity? Like moth millers they will flutter through their aimless career, from flower to flower by day, and from lamp to lamp by night, till at length drawn by irresistible attraction into the blaze of some much admired light, their wings shall be fatally singed, and they expire. The Practical Christian Republic has little to hope from minds of this stamp. We will do them no harm, and must take care that they do us none.

Policy toward Sword-Sustained Governments

By "sword-sustained governments of the world" I mean all human governments which hold to the rightfulness of resorting to war, capital punishment and penal injury for the maintenance of their own existence and authority. I know of no human governments not sword-sustained, excepting our incipient Republic. And here is a great moral gulf which separates us from the old order of society. We renounce the sword and all manner of penal injury as a dernier resort for self-preservation, whether individually, socially or governmentally.

What if we should gain the ascendancy in any country, so that the responsibility were thrown upon us by the common wish of the people to exercise the government thereof? In such an event they would adopt our government in all its length and breadth, and our course would be straightforward. Our moral power would then have become so strong and consolidated in that country, that we should have no need of the sword or any kind of injurious penalties to sustain our government. We might have our turbulent individuals at home and some foreign aggressions, yet our policy founded on our principles would be equal to all emergencies. We should be under no necessity to kill or injure our offenders. We should have a more excellent way of getting through our difficulties; I mean that of overcoming evil with good. Anyhow, it is useless to borrow trouble from so far off a future. We expect that the members of our Republic are to live for years, perhaps centuries, under these sword-sustained governments; we can anticipate nothing else.

Assuming that our members live under a sword-sustained government, they must not come into anti-Christian conflict with it. What is anti-Christian conflict? A conflict of arms, a conflict by deadly or injurious force, a conflict by resisting any kind of evil with moral evil. Should we resist or attempt to thwart a government by means contrary to our principles, we should carry on an anti-Christian conflict with such government. This we cannot do. We may maintain a righteous moral conflict in a good cause, but cannot resort to immoral expedients of any kind. We may *suffer* wrong, but we must not *do* wrong. In this lies the secret of our strength.

Succor and Protection of Members

We intend to govern, succor and protect our own people, to the utmost of our ability, so far as we can go without coming into anti-Christian conflict with "the powers that be."[3] We all stand solemnly pledged to succor and protect such of our members as may need sympathy, counsel, money or moral influence, by reason of misfortunes, oppressions, persecutions and tribulations which from any cause or quarter may befall them. We are bound to do so. They are "bone of our bone, and flesh of our flesh,"[4] in the best social sense of those terms. So long as our members' demeanor is worthy of the Republic, it would be shameful in us not to succor and protect them to the utmost extent of our ability. I mean ability compatible with our principles. We cannot fight with carnal weapons, even in self-defense. Nor is our revolution one to be promoted by violence. It is a peaceful one altogether, though so radical.

In legislating, adjudicating and executing we can go very far; because we are a voluntary body politic, and may do what we are agreed among ourselves is right. You would not expect such a people to look up to a sword-sustained human government to teach them what was right, nor to settle their controversies, nor to regulate their domestic police. They will govern themselves, and government outside will do little but impose taxes and subject them to its general laws. Now the policy prescribed is, to do everything for ourselves in the way of government that we can do without coming into anti-Christian conflict with the sword-sustained government of the old order of society.

Therefore, if we have talent, wealth, influence, we must pour them out like water for the succor and protection of our suffering members. The pure white flag of our Republic must proclaim to all the world, that its humblest citizen will receive all the sympathy and protection which an undivided people can righteously render. Our poor are not to be thrown upon the old order of society for support. Our widows and orphans are not to go abroad begging relief and protection. And if any of our citizens are fined, imprisoned or in any manner oppressed by "the powers that be" for acting conscientiously according to our standard of Practical Christianity, they are to be aided and befriended by us to the utmost extent of our power, i.e. within the limits of innocence. We are to suffer with them – to make common cause with them. So, if our feebler members are crowded upon, injured and taken advantage of by unprincipled men of the world, the stronger members in talent, wealth and weight of character are to interpose a shield of protection over them, without money and without price; that it may be known by all in due time, that what they do unto the least of us they do unto the mightiest and unto the whole Practical Christian Republic. We could do no less without shame and contempt, in view of our professions.

Avoiding Unnecessary Conflict

The second point of our fundamental, uniform and established policy is, to avoid all unnecessary conflicts with sword-sustained governments, by conforming to all their laws and requirements which are not repugnant to the sovereignty of divine principles. It would be easy to differ with and oppose them for the sake of keeping up a broad line of distinction between them and ourselves. It would be easy for many well-meaning members of our Republic to magnify their disfellowship of the old order of society and government by non-conformity to requirements which were right in themselves, or indifferent, merely because those requirements made a part and parcel of a wrong whole. All such non-conformity would be foolish and pernicious.

Why stickle and make a great ado about non-essentials? The existing order of society and government has many good things in it, good laws, customs and usages – such as with slight modifications would befit our Republic. It has also a great many formal niceties which have a technical and legal importance, which time will sweep away as mere cobwebs of vanity, but which are of no consequence to us. It would be folly for our people to stand out and contend with government functionaries about these indifferent things. Our thunder should be reserved for worthy occasions.

There are essentials enough to stand out for. Let trifles go. We are to differ with no human being or beings for the sake of differing. We are not to be singular for the sake of being singular. We are not to be whimish, mulish and crotchety, merely to let the world know that we are not "*of it.*" We are to choose conformity in preference to non-conformity always when we can do so without violating our divine principles. This should be our policy. Then noble souls and wise minds will see that our dissent, singularity and nonconformity are determined by principle, and not by egotism, clannishness, or wrongheadedness. Unnecessary conflicts are therefore always to be avoided, that necessary ones may be maintained the more courageously, dignifiedly and triumphantly.

Non-participation in Government, Politics, and Law

The third specification of our Policy is to abstain from all participation in the working of the political machinery of sword-sustained governments, and to be connected as little as possible with their system of operations. This is the fundamental love-principle itself, which forbids man to kill or injure man. Those who object to it either do not accept that principle as forbidding all injury between man and man, or they will not allow its application to government, or they plead that the time has not come for insisting on it. Indeed, they seem to be quite indisposed to recognize, appreciate and reason from fundamental religious and moral principles at all. They take everything up by pieces, and look at it in the light of expediency. And their expediency is like the child's world, bounded by the sensible horizon, which terminates in all directions where the sky seems to shut down upon the earth. It is a very short-sighted expediency. But they are none the less confident it comprehends all things. Such is their mole-eyed wisdom.

With this sensible horizon of expediency for their universe, and the self-confidence which is its concomitant, these objectors generally begin thus:* "What, not vote, not take office, not participate in the government of the country, stand off by themselves as a separate people or nation! *That* is preposterous! That spoils the whole thing! I should think something of the scheme, were it not for this silly non-resistance and no-governmentism. I admire the larger part of their Constitution; but such weak, absurd and impracticable notions damn it for me."

I should ask such an objector: "Is the old order of human society right? Are you satisfied with it?"

He would answer promptly, "O no, no; it is very bad – full of selfishness, antagonism, hatred, violence and misery."

"Do you want a better order of society established in the earth?"

He would answer, "Yes, yes, certainly."

"How do you expect that better order of society is to be established?"

He would reply, "By Association, unselfish, peaceful Association."

"By Association on any radically different principles from the now prevailing order of Association?"

"Yes, certainly, more just, fraternal and unselfish principles, and more scientific too – more unitary."

"Would you exclude war and vindictive punishments from the new order?"

"Most assuredly. Stop; *exclude?* no, not *formally*, perhaps; but in true attractive Association all these evils would be transcended. They would cease with the cessation of their causes and occasions, which would not exist in the true order of society. So they would need no other preclusion."

"But you would have the new order of society in close fellowship with the old, so that your members might vote, hold office, litigate, fight and do everything else in the governments thereof just like the rest of its citizens?"

"Yes; only they should be more virtuous and honorable than ordinary, and should do everything constitutionally, legally and properly."

---

* This imaginary conversation between the Expositor and the Objector is found *within* the overall dialogue between the Expositor and the Inquirer in the original.

"You would have them soldiers, generals, hangmen, sheriffs, etc., etc., etc. – all bound by solemn oath to sustain the old order of society and its government, by force of arms if necessary?"

"Certainly; leave all these things to take their course. Only I would have our Associationists and Communists aim continually to improve the old order of society, to favor the new order as much as possible, and to make their influence felt for the general good. *That* is the beauty of the thing. Just think how much good we could do by exercising our political rights in the old order of society and government!"

"But what would become of your new order of society, and who would take care of its growth, while its most talented and enterprising minds were taking such beautiful care of the bad old order of society and government; and while, too, they were in a scramble with each other for the rich loaves and fishes of office, as partisans of rival leaders?"

"O, I would not have our Socialists neglect their own work, nor be mere office seekers, or salary hunters, nor get divided among themselves into rival squads of politicians. Not at all."

You would have them attend to their own business, and other people's too! Expend their best energies in improving the old order of society, and at the same time show all the world the excellences of the new order! Be devoted to the politics of rival parties in sword-sustained governments, and still be united at home in the bonds of peace! Serve two masters with equal fidelity! Sit on two stools, and not come to the ground between them! All this may be very beautiful, but is not very likely to come to pass in such a world as ours. I venture to suggest that it would savor more of common sense, if not of honesty, to confess at once, that the only road to a new order of society is through the old one by gradual improvement, whereof politics is the indispensable "staff of accomplishment." In that case, let the objector cease to amuse himself and others by talking of a new order. Let him stick to the old like a pertinacious tinker till he shall have patched it into a new kettle. I can excuse him from joining the Practical Christian Republic till he takes a few more lessons in the school of experience. It is ridiculous, as well as utterly impracticable, to ride two such different horses, on two such different roads, at the same time.

It is objected that our policy seems to be to leave government wholly in the hands of bad men, by withdrawing all good men from it. What is to become of the world if bad men are to be left to wield all the power of government? Why not vote for State and National officers, to aid in keeping out bad men, and getting in good men? For seven reasons:

1. We seldom know which of the candidates is best.

2. The best as a man is not always the best as a partisan officer.

3. The best man of the best party must bind himself by oath or affirmation to do some things which are in plain violation of our sovereign divine principles.

4. By voting we become complicated with the political party whose general course we most approve, which nevertheless we must radically differ from.

5. We invite discord into our own circles, where there can hardly fail to be honest differences of opinion about the merits of opposing parties, or the propriety of taking sides in such contests.

6. Or, if our people all voted one way, we should provoke public suspicion against ourselves as an ambitious, consolidated clan, ripening for political mischief.

7. We should neglect our own sacred enterprise to help govern an order of society from which we profess to have separated ourselves for conscience' sake; and thus we should not only open the door for all our members to meddle continually with the political, seditious and revolutionary turmoils of the world, but actually involve our whole movement in the uncertain issues of those commotions.

For these reasons it would be folly, madness and suicide, for Practical Christian Republicans to participate in such elections. Our cause would have nothing to gain, but everything to lose, from such meddling. "Let the potsherds of the earth contend with the potsherds of the earth."[5] Let each order of society be managed by its own adherents, on its own professed principles. Then by their fruits good men will know which is most worthy of support. The two cannot be amalgamated. Nor can the new wine of love and peace be put into the old war-bottles.[6] And there would be nearly the same objection to our members voting in municipal affairs – so nearly that it would hardly be worth while to pick out the possible cases which might be exceptions.

I have no fear that I shall succeed in withdrawing all good men from the support of the world's sword-sustained governments. I do not doubt that good men are much needed to countervail bad ones in most governments; but I am afraid they are more *needed* than *welcome*, generally. At any rate, I am sure the Practical Christian Republic will not rob any government of the ability or the will to do good in its own sphere and way.

1. The kind of good men thereby withdrawn from sword-sustained governments will be precisely those who would not be wanted if they could be had, and would not be allowed to lead if they were introduced into government. They might be acceptable as appendages of moral respectability, to make well-meaning people think favorably of the government as a whole; but they would be allowed no real influence in shaping important public measures, or in working its powerful machinery. This kind of good men are always deemed impracticables, or visionaries, by the world's leading politicians and statesmen.

2. All the people brought into our Republic will be of real service to the governments under which they may live. They will govern themselves and their dependents in the best possible manner almost entirely at their own expense. They will exert a healthful moral influence on all around them, and do as much at least as ordinary peace officers to preserve good order. They will be a check on vice, crime and violence wherever they are known. They will dispense alms and relieve much surrounding want. They will make no criminals nor paupers among themselves to be a charge on government. They will breed no lawsuits, and require no police nor military interpositions, either to restrain or to protect them. They will be good customers of the Post Office, being far more than ordinarily addicted to correspondence and to reading public intelligence. At the same time they will be liberal, peaceable and prompt tax-payers to government. If more than all this is wanted of them, to demonstrate that they are the very best subjects any government can have, I should like to know *what!*

3. There are several grades of very respectable good men who will still adhere to all these sword-sustained governments; who will be glad to hold any office of honor or emolument to be had; and who will not be troubled with scruples about doing anything required by the established Constitution or laws of the land. So there will be no lack, on that score, for generations to come.

4. There are always plenty of bad men and rogues ready to serve these governments for money, in hunting down and punishing their own like; and it is well known that such are always remarkably expert and efficient on the police, among the prisons, at the gallows and in the military department. There is nothing like setting a rogue to catch a rogue, or a ruffian to kill a ruffian. Thus our secession from the old order of society will still leave sufficient help in the punishing and fighting line.

5. If by possibility it should ever so happen that any sword-sustained government in any country is obliged to dissolve, on account of the growth of our Republic, we pledge ourselves to take its subjects under our care, and see that nobody in the world is a loser by the change.

I think these reasons conclusively show that no serious calamity is likely to happen from the establishment of our Republic, or from its rigid adherence to the policy under consideration.

Granting that it is totally inconsistent for the members of our Republic to profess allegiance to the sovereignty of divine principles and yet participate in war, preparations for war, capital punishment and penal injuries, either as officers or subordinates of sword-sustained governments, still, why may they not seek redress at law for injuries done them?

It is possible they might innocently resort to judicial assistance in some cases. They are not precluded from doing so, except in cases involving the infliction of death, or some other absolute injury, by man on man. Yet our policy is to stand aloof as much as possible from participation in the machinery of these sword-sustained governments, even in cases where our principles might permit it. This would so seldom happen, and would be so little in unison with the usual course to be pursued, that it would be safest to make no calculation on such a resort at all.

In all sword-sustained governments, the sword, or some other instrument of penal vengeance, is necessarily always behind the civil authorities as their dernier resort. To sue a man for debt, or for the purpose of compelling him to conform to our will, is to call on the government to use their sword-sustained power in our behalf. If it is right for us to sue to them for the use of such power for our convenience, why have we any scruples against doing the same thing ourselves? If wrong for us to use the sword ourselves, is it not also wrong to ask others to do so for us? Would it not be adding meanness to our inconsistency? We should do more harm than good, both to ourselves and the world, by departing from our general course. In some cases, few and far between, it might be best for us to use our rights and innocent liberties in the particulars referred to; but such exceptions will take care of themselves, without disturbing the general tenor of our Policy.

Our principles will not preclude our appearing in the Courts of sword-sustained governments to plead in our own defense, when wrongfully prosecuted or accused by others. The difference between being defendants and plaintiffs in those Courts, is the difference between dragging a man into

Court with the strong arm of power backed by the sword, and being dragged thither unjustly by such an arm against our choice. I am not absolutely obliged to plead in my own defense; but I have a natural right to defend myself by truthful testimony and speech against false accusations and unjust allegations. Most human Courts concede this right. I may therefore use it, as Paul did before Felix and Festus, or waive it, as Jesus did before Pilate.[7] If I use it, I violate none of my principles. If I waive it, I do so at my own option. I am arraigned before "the powers that be" at the prosecuting instigation of another. I did not ask the government to bring me into Court, nor to compel him to come. I am the coerced party; and if I defend myself there, it is not by injurious force, nor by invoking the injurious force of government to help me. I stand up as a man, with the common consent, to plead my cause by the force of truth. And when I have done so, I am in the hands of that authority before which my prosecutor compelled me to appear.

We shall doubtless be wronged more or less in person and estate, both by individuals and governments. But all we shall lose and suffer will not be a tithe of what the same number of people with the same amount of property in the old order of society will lose and suffer during the same period of time.

Faithful Adherence to Principles and Policy

We have all made up our minds to bear true allegiance in our Republic to the sovereignty of divine principles, and to adhere uncompromisingly to the fundamental Policy dictated by these Principles, be the consequences what they may. We have faith in God, in our principles and our policy.

We ask no human being to join us in ignorance of our Principles or Policy, nor against his honest convictions of duty, nor without being fully persuaded in his own mind that he ought to sacrifice all worldly ambition, honor and emolument. We have no bribes, no flatteries, no compromises of principle to offer. We want no talents, skill or enterprise which shall not voluntarily respond to our sublime moral and religious appeal from the living souls of their possessors. God through his holy angels will provide help for us. We have faith that our Republic will not lack for talent, skill and enterprise.

Chapter 6

Rights and Property

Equal Rights of All Members

In our Republic all members have coequal rights. No one has any individual superiority, right or liberty to violate divine principles with impunity. No one has the least right to do wrong – in other words, to do, to be, or to enjoy anything which is plainly contrary to any of the principles acknowledged as divine in Article 2.

All members have equal rights and privileges within the limits of innocence. Female members or citizens of our Republic are to exercise all the rights of males, and members under twenty-one years of age the same rights as those over twenty-one, and colored members the same rights as white ones, and foreign born members the same rights as native born ones, and the poorest members the same rights as the highest born and wealthiest ones.

The Right to Seek Happiness through Freedom of Choice

There are high pretending socialists who denounce all particular friendships and intimacies as contemptuous towards those not included in the congenial circle, and who insist that all the members of a Community are bound to congenialize indiscriminately with all the others.*

We believe such notions to be contrary to the order of nature, irrational and mischievous. Therefore we desire to preclude them from our Republic, by a distinct assertion of the right of every individual member to form and enjoy particular friendships.

I have affirmed that there is a sphere of Congeniality within the sphere of Federality. I have no doubt of this fact. If so, the individual has rights

---

* Ballou was probably thinking here of the Oneida Community.

116

peculiar to that sphere. Now membership in our Republic, and in each of the local Communities, belongs to the sphere of Federality. Its wants, rights and duties must therefore be discriminated accordingly. But within the sphere of Federality are included numerous spheres of Congeniality which likewise have their appropriate wants, rights and duties. Now if your attractions, sympathies, tastes and pursuits connect you with one of these spheres, and mine connect me with a different one, what harm can come of our differences? No matter how much variety exists, it is a variety in unity. We are in unity as to our sphere of Federality, but differ in our spheres of Congeniality. Our difference is not one which brings either of us into conflict with the common sovereignty of divine principles. Neither of us claims the right to violate a single one of those principles. Our differences are harmless, are innocent, are even useful. To break down these differences, by any arbitrary, artificial, forced uniformity of personal and social congenialities, would be as impolitic and mischievous as it would be unjust. If we broke down the boundaries of Congeniality, we might break down those of Consanguinity, then those of Connubiality, and finally those of Individuality itself. Then, instead of a social body fitly composed of multifarious parts and faculties, we should have one made altogether of a single lifeless substance, a wooden automaton, large enough perhaps to conceal inside of it one real man, possibly several men, who might give it motion to suit his or their own fancy. The Practical Christian Republic is not designed to be such an automaton; nor are any of its local Communities intended to have that sort of existence.

The Right of Individual Stewardship

All members have "the right to be stewards under God of one's own talents, property, skill and personal endowments." This is acknowledging that every individual has or may have talents, property, skill and personal endowments which are as rightfully his or her own as any faculty of body or mind; for the use and disposal of which he or she is responsible to God only; and which no other person or body of persons can rightfully make use of without the true owner's consent. Let it be distinctly understood that each individual is always God's steward, bound by divine principles to make no evil use of talents, property, skill &c.; that each may consent at pleasure to let others make use of his or her talents, property &c., with or without an equivalent; but that the real owner's right of control, as steward under God, is always absolute and sacred. I have no right to take what is yours without your consent, nor you what is mine without my consent.

I fell in with one man who contended strenuously that the very idea of individual property was false, and that so long as it shall be tolerated selfishness must reign. He said that the notion of individual property was the root of human selfishness, and the prolific source of nearly all the mischiefs prevalent in civilized society. He insisted on laying the ax at the root of this evil tree, and ridiculed as a cheat the old pretense, as he called it, of man's stewardship under God. The true doctrine, he affirmed, was, that every human being has an absolute right to what he or she really needs, and no one has a particle of right to anything more. All talent, skill, property &c., wheresoever and with whomsoever existing, is really *common,* to be used by anybody and everybody who truly needs it.

And did that wise man say who should be judge in each case what and how much the individual really needed? No; he did not descend into details; and he was so inflated with his own opinions, that I thought it useless to argue the matter with him. So I merely recommended that he and such as agreed with him should make trial of his theory in practice. He said he *should,* when he could get enough talented and wealthy people to join him. I asked him why he waited for such an improbable contingency; since, if his principle was a sound one, it ought to work between people of small talents and property just as well as between them and those above them. He said he had nothing to spare, nor even as much as he really needed; and that it was so with nearly all the humbler classes; but that the talented, skillful and rich had a great deal more than they needed; so that unless they could be brought over to his theory, it was useless to attempt putting it in practice. All which plainly revealed that he himself was quite as selfish as those he denounced.

I have fallen in with such minds now and then, all the way through my socialistic life; and I must honestly declare that, with very rare exceptions, they appeared to me as destitute of high moral principle as of enlightened reason. I have a sincere respect for people who, while acknowledging individual rights in talent, skill, property &c., propose to institute common property Communities on the great LOVE PRINCIPLE; i.e. by voluntary reciprocal abandonment of separate interests, and a mutual waiver of their rights for the time being. But for the class of persons who begin by asserting that there is no such thing as individual property, and who are forever howling like hungry wolves on the trail of prey to be devoured – in other words, forever greedy to better their own condition at the expense of others – I have only the respect due to human nature when perverted, deluded and stultified by vicious ideas. All socialism of this stamp is essentially atheistic, selfish, unprincipled, anarchical and rife with physical violence. Such minds are morally incapable of living together for any considerable length of time in community with each other, and would be discordant elements in any society. Let them go their way to and fro through the earth till the time of reformation.

It is just such restless, selfish revelers as these that have rendered the word socialism a stench and a terror to thousands. These thousands in their ignorance have been frightened into the apprehension that they were to be overwhelmed and despoiled of their individual rights by force, under the plea of social justice. Hence socialism, robbery, anarchy and ruffianism, with *them*, have become synonymous terms. I want they should be undeceived.

Property Righteousness

Article 10 opens with an acknowledgment that all property is primarily the Creator's, provided by him for the use of mankind during their lifetime on earth, and therefore ought to be acquired, used and disposed of in strict accordance with the dictates of justice and charity. The leading ideas of this Article have been affirmed by our best religious teachers in all ages of the Christian Dispensation; perhaps to a certain extent by the best ethical writers of all religions and times. But the great majority of the Christian Church have sadly ignored and contravened this doctrine in practice. Is the Practical Christian Republic likely to be conscientiously strict in carrying it out?

It would be wonderful if many of our members should not come short on this point, as on many others made prominent in their Constitution. But I will mention some reasons for believing that they will pay a far more scrupulous respect to the doctrine than it has received in the old order of society, either in Church or State.

1. Our whole movement has a marked and multiform reference to the right use of property. Our eyes are open to the anti-Christian uses of property, and cannot easily be closed to the ever-recurrent question, What does true righteousness require respecting property?

2. We have acknowledged the sovereignty of divine principles as supreme. These are so explicitly stated, and require so thorough an application to all human affairs, that obvious abuses of property cannot long escape rebuke.

3. Our specific guarantees and Communal arrangements must necessarily fix the general attention almost constantly on the workings of property, especially its accumulation and distribution.

4. Our strong moral prohibitions relative to intemperance, war, slavery and other notoriously prolific evil customs, will operate as strong safeguards against the abuse of property.

The solemn, explicit and prominent declaratory prescriptions, as well as prospective provisions of the Article before us, render it quite impossible that property abuses should go long unchecked in our Republic. The whole genius of my Social System is in favor of *property righteousness,* and against *property iniquity.* For those reasons I am confident that the Practical Christian Republic, notwithstanding many incidental shortcomings, will do honor to its professions relative to this important point.

It will occupy very different ground from the Church and State of the past. Its fundamental objects, principles and polity include all the good of the past, with little, we trust none, of the evil. Its sublime principles were never before set forth in their wholeness with so much clearness and thoroughness of application. Much less were they ever before so organized, as operative forces, to act on all human relations. Many of them, perhaps all, have been solemnly inculcated, reiterated and written down, with more or less distinctness, by the great religious and moral teachers of the past. But never before, I repeat, have they been so recognized, acknowledged and organized into a social body politic, as by ours in this Constitution.

Adverse and evil principles have been organized and inwrought into all the predominant social and political institutions of mankind hitherto extant. And what chance does the fragmentary, unorganized annunciation of great principles stand for success against the organic, popular and wholesale sins of the world? Principles must be organized constructively into the framework of society, before they can finally prevail. It is not enough that they be preached and written by individuals. They must be carried into practice, first by individuals and then organically by society. This is what is proposed by the Practical Christian Republic; and I see no good reason to apprehend a failure in its noble undertaking.

Still, much will depend on the faithful application of our doctrine to individual cases as they rise. I have seen some very fair seeming Christians, who acknowledged themselves stewards under God of all the property in their possession, but who contrived to be extremely selfish, both in accumulating and bestowing this world's goods. Their stewardship was wonderfully warped towards their own gratification. I have seen some such, who lacked little of being shavers, sharpers, extortioners and misers. Doubtless they would tell me that they were only prudent and careful of the Lord's money. So they left large inventories to rapacious and quarrelsome heirs, or perhaps generous legacies to popular institutions. Others have drawn profusely on their Lord's deposits, and consumed the major portion of them in costly mansions, costly furnishings, costly raiment, costly equipage and costly living of every description, whilst Lazarus begged at their gates and had his sores licked by the dogs.[1]

Knowing how many unworthy stewards the Lord has of his earthly goods, I dare not be very positive that none of our Practical Christians will turn out misers or spendthrifts. "Sufficient unto the day is the evil thereof."[2] Be results what they may, we will make a good beginning, and hedge out all the abuses of property we can by placing them under prohibitory laws. At present we shall not be likely to violate our principles in that direction; as not many mighty, not many noble, not many of this world's great ones will feel called into our Republic. The kind of people who ardently love money, either to hoard up in large piles, or to expend in luxurious and showy living, will be pretty sure, most of them, to creep through the eye of a needle, sooner than seek the kingdom of God through the strait and narrow way of Practical Christian Socialism.

A Just Price for Services Rendered

Article 10, Section 2 establishes a maximum compensation between all persons belonging to the Practical Christian Republic, for all kinds of personal service. The minimum is left to adjust itself. This clause is meant to prevent injustice between members, relative to the price demanded of each other for personal services of any description; and to abolish and preclude all high salaries, professional exorbitance and unreasonable exactions, whereby one class may enrich themselves by the impoverishment and degradation of another.

I have been asked why we made a distinction between the pecuniary commerce of members with members, and members with outsiders? Why is it just to deal with outsiders according to the caprice of the market, yet unjust so to deal among ourselves?

I should set limits to the caprice of the market everywhere, *outside* as well as *inside* of our Republic. The rule of trade which makes it justifiable to ask all we can get, and pay the least that others will take, ought to be restricted by the dictates of justice everywhere; because cases often occur in which that rule allows one to make another's absolute necessity an opportunity for extortion. Unmistakable cases of this nature would leave no excuse to one who should take advantage of them. Nor is it intended, by making a distinction between internal and external commerce, to pronounce that just to outsiders which we pronounce unjust as between insiders. Justice would not dictate nor tolerate injustice in dealings even with Shylock himself. It would set bounds to price, even with the most unprincipled and selfish of men.

We do not undertake to fix a maximum with outsiders; because we are not certain what that maximum ought to be. When we can determine what it should be, we will declare and abide by it. Till then we presume not to draw the line. It is not so clear what would be just in outside commerce. That must depend partly on conventional reciprocity and mutual obligations. In dealing with an order of society, or a class of people, or an individual, whose fundamental maxims are *No one his brother's keeper; Every man for himself; Get all you can and keep all you get*; justice would dictate a different scale of prices from one required in commerce with people associated, like those of our Practical Christian Republic, as coequals under pledges and guarantees of mutual support.

In our own Brotherhood, we are sure that justice prescribes a maximum of price to be demanded, at least a general maximum such as we have indicated. Below that maximum line there is still a broad space of pecuniary commerce, which we do not presume to map out by definite lines of latitude and longitude; leaving justice to pronounce extemporaneously its own decisions, case by case, as occasion may require. We only mark one plain boundary, beyond which we are confident it would be unjust for our people to go, in determining compensation for personal service of any kind.

I come then to what seems a practical pinching point. It is hardly to be expected that the average prices paid to the best class of operatives for their services, as matters now stand in the United States, should exceed from four to five hundred dollars per annum. What then is to become of our overseers, superintendents, agents, professionals, etc., whose incomes range all the way up from $600 and $1000 to $20,000 or more each per annum? Are they going to come down by the force of moral principle, or great socialistic ideas, to the level we have prescribed? Will persons whom the world readily pays $600, $1000, $3000, $5000, $10,000, etc., undertake to live on $450 or $500 per annum?

We should ask rather, what is to become of the people whose hard earnings are taxed to pay all these overseers, superintendents, agents and professionals? *That* is the question which justice asks, which humanity asks.

Our Savior declared that all things were possible with God, even the induction of a rich man through the eye of a needle into the kingdom of God. I do not undertake to underrate or deny the difficulty. It must be looked boldly in the face. We do greatly need the talent, skill and prowess of these now highly paid people to help forward our enterprise. But it would ruin the cause to purchase them with money. If we cannot enlist them by a fair conversion to our principles and polity, we must go without them, though it should take a thousand years longer to reach our grand consummation. Of what use would it be to go through the long process of founding a new order of society, if when founded it should be radically like the present order; which impoverishes, degrades and imbrutes five hundred families in order to enrich, elevate and refine one family? I would abandon the whole undertaking, sooner than worry onward to such barren, or rather abominable results.

I can make great allowance for those circumstances which will render it a temporary hardship to enter into our Republic on the terms prescribed. I can excuse them for delaying to unite with us, and even dying in the comfortable places of Egypt and Babylon. I will not denounce them as sinners above all others. To their own masters let them stand or fall. To their consciences and their God let them answer. But I cannot compromise with their ill-formed habits, tastes and customs. They cannot fight this battle of "the Lord and Gideon" without hearts of humility and self-sacrifice. And if they have *these*, they will get down low enough on their hands and knees to lap the running waters of fraternal justice.[3]

I have faith in the power of divine principles over the moral susceptibilities of the managing and professional classes, as well as over other classes. I have no doubt that we shall obtain a fair quota of recruits from that quarter; if not from the highest ranks, yet from the lower, who will be quite as useful to our cause, and probably as worthy in every essential quality. At the same time we hope to have enough born and educated among us to do something towards officering our forces. Thus will we either overcome, or at least render our difficulty endurable. The changes of time and the progress of events will enable us to triumph. So though we have such very formidable obstacles before us, we have no reason to dread them as insurmountable.

Interest and Appreciation of Property

The next clause of this section carries the same principle into trade and interest on capital loaned. As a citizen member of our Republic, if I have any thing to sell or exchange, I must fairly estimate the value thereof, by setting down 1. its prime cost; 2. labor or attention bestowed upon it, not exceeding the prior specified maximum of price; 3. incidental expenses; 4. contingent waste or depreciation; 5. average risks of sale. Thus I am to make myself whole and get nothing more than handsome pay for my labor. I am not allowed to set the highest price I can get in the general market. I am not allowed to gain any more by trading, averaging one thing and one time with another, than may be earned by the first class of operatives, unless I can get it by trading honorably with outsiders.

And what if I make a much humbler living than this, or run completely out? That would be nothing strange. It is just what happens to a majority of those who in the old social order undertake to live by trading. Nine fail where one succeeds in getting rich.

Ought I not to have some guarantees from my purchasing brethren, to insure me against losses? Not if I go on my own hook, and price my articles with reference to the contingencies and risks of trade. Why should I? But we intend to kill out this trading of individuals on their own hook, (I mean trading thus as a business), before long, by socializing, unionizing and systematizing the whole range of commercial transactions. Then individuals will be in no danger of failing, in the common meaning of that term. Associate bodies will employ and pay all the persons needed to conduct trade, and the supernumeraries may go to useful pursuits. Meantime the common people will rise to the enjoyment of their rights; paying no more than they ought to pay for goods bought, and receiving what they ought for goods sold. If we should prosper in our scheme, there would be no more fortunes to make, or to lose, by commercial pursuits. We go against all kinds of gambling; and we trust all the winners, as well as losers by such games, will rejoice with us when the last of their "hells" is cleared of its enticements.

You may wonder why we tolerate four per cent interest; why we sanction the taking of interest at all. Is it right to take interest on money? I answer that question with another: Is it right for any individual, or association of individuals, distinct from the rest of mankind, to take net increase on property of any description whatsoever, except a fair compensation for labor and care bestowed thereon? Apply the question to lands, houses, orchards, cattle, etc. For instance, I own one hundred acres of land, which, in consequence of God's rain, air and sunshine superadded to my labor and skill, or in consequence of some railroad built near it, or in consequence of something else taking place without expense to me, has become twice as valuable as its actual cost. I may mention the rearing of an orchard, or a flock of sheep, or a yoke of oxen, or a horse, no matter what. Now here is a net increase beyond actual cost, and a handsome payment of all labor bestowed on the property in hand; to whom does the increase rightfully belong? To make the case a little stronger, suppose I discover a rich mine of gold, silver, or other valuable metal, which has cost me absolutely nothing; whose is it? Would it not belong to him or them who held the capital on which the increase accrued? I do not see but it would, so long as we allow property to be held in severalty. If we could resolve the whole world into common property, the individual inheritance of our entire race, we might change the issue. But as this is out of the question, we must take things as they are.

Let us see how we would apply our rule of price and sale to one of these net-increase cases. Would I feel bound to sell my farm, lately doubled in value by the new railroad, or rendered perhaps a thousand times more valuable by the discovery of that mine, as "the fair cost value thereof" to one of our Practical Christian Republicans? I should not feel bound to sell such an estate at all. But I should feel bound to place the net increase where it would, in my judgment, do most towards sustaining the instrumentalities necessary to regenerate the world. Or if wanted to relieve suffering humanity, I should feel bound as God's steward to dispense it gratuitously. Or if I had needy brethren who wanted it on loan, to let them have it without usury. But I should not feel bound to sell it at cost, even to a brother, for the sake of transferring the net increase from my control to his. Not under our rule would he have a right to insist on such a transfer of my ownership to him.

There are exceptions to all general rules. But in nine hundred and ninety-nine cases out of a thousand, the ups and downs of appraisal under our rule would only cover the contingencies and risks to which all property is subject. Thus the net increase of a large amount of property in any country, during ten, twenty or thirty years, would be exceedingly uncertain. But in modern times such all increase, greater or less, has been supposed to accrue in all civilized countries. This has grown chiefly out of commerce and the innumerable improvements in all the material interests of mankind. Hence, as money is the immediate representative equivalent of all kinds of property, interest has come to be considered justly due on it, within certain limits. And within those limits interest is not now considered *usury* in the ancient Bible sense. All this, because property in general is presumed to have a certain absolute net increase annually on the average of the nation. The theory is, that the lender of money has as good a right to a certain per cent per annum net increase on his capital, as the borrower has to his net gains thereon.

This theory is just enough under the existing commercial system; but there has been a general tendency to rate interest too high, especially since lenders have reduced their risks by demanding strong securities. The inevitable consequence has been excessive banking, trading and speculation, all tending to the enrichment of the few and the impoverishment of the many. Interest is too high, especially in our own country. It cannot be paid without oppressing the common people. It exceeds the average net increase of property, and so must increase the moneylender's wealth at the expense of the borrowing and working classes. In a true Social System, where commercial exchanges were wisely regulated, it is clear to my mind, money would be loaned at cost, under the general rule we have been criticizing. Accordingly, the fourth Section of the Property Article in our Constitution contemplates such an ultimate state of things. At present, however, we are obliged to make a compromise with the existing commercial system. Hence we make a protest against exorbitant rates of interest, and indicate our drift for the future, by naming four per cent per annum, as the maximum rate of interest which our members shall demand of each other.

We allow our members, when combining their capital under joint management as partners in the risk of it, to divide higher profits, if they can. This is not intended to allow them a greater general average than four per cent, but only to enable them to offset one term of years with another in respect to the risks of their general business. Such arrangements will be likely to take care of themselves. This is a complex and knotty matter to settle in its details at present. We have done what seemed practically best under the existing state of things; hoping for great improvements in the future.

Ethical Business Practices

The third section of this Article is directed against contracting improper debts; giving and receiving long credits without real estate security; manufacturing and selling shammy and unreliable productions; and making business engagements etc. of uncertain fulfillment. All these are evils which prevail in the existing social state, and are pronounced incompatible with the welfare, prosperity and honor of the new Republic.

By not allowing any of our members to run in debt, outside of the Republic, beyond three-fourths of the worth of his property, we will get no bitter curses nor reproaches for failing, and cheating our neighbors out of their dues. As to long credits, they are bad enough at best; but if they must be given or received, let good real estate security make them safe. Neither leave them at loose ends, nor ask one man to be bound for another.

Shammy and unreliable productions glut the markets, and are every where a fraud. Any honest man ought to be ashamed of them, and Practical Christians had better lay aside their professions, if they cannot take a higher stand in this matter than the world in general. I do not suppose any class of manufacturers or mechanics can work up raw materials so as to turn out only first quality productions. But they ought to turn out a reasonable quantity of such productions, and then mark the rest at their true value as of interior quality, to be represented and marketed accordingly. *Work* preaches louder than *words*, and a people whose fabricated or cultivated productions should *lie* would deserve to be set down for liars themselves. The other prohibition, against making business engagements and promises which there is no certainty of being able to fulfill, ought to be superfluous in its application to a people professing high morality. The making of such engagements and promises is very common in the world, I know; but it is a kind of lying so mean and inexcusable, that any decent person ought to be utterly ashamed of it.

Economic Institutions of the Communal Nation

The objects set forth in the fourth section of the Property Article are at once grand, and fraught with the highest importance to the welfare of the common people. I have made no definite calculation as to the number of members necessary to the formation of the first Communal Nation. Not less than ten thousand, probably; and one hundred thousand would be few enough. Half a million would make things come into the new course much more easily. We must leave all that to God and the future. A beginning has already been made in respect to most of the particulars named, and all the objects in view may be approximated long before the national organization can be inaugurated. But it is not to be expected that more than preparative and incipient advances will be made during the early infancy of the Republic.

Of the contemplated system of Mutual Banking, which is to furnish loans at the mere cost of operations, I will not attempt to enter into many of the details, but barely indicate some of the outlines. Suppose then we have five hundred owners of real estate, or five thousand, or fifty thousand if you please, or twenty Communities or more with valuable Domains. A Mutual Bank is proposed with a Capital of $100,000, or $250,000, or $500,000. One-tenth of the capital stock shall be specie or its equivalent. The other nine-tenths consist of real estate securities; that is, mortgages of real estate running to the Trustees of the Bank, so conditioned as to be available to the Bank in certain contingencies, but otherwise harmless to the mortgagors. For instance, I subscribe $500 towards the stock in one of these Mutual Banks, of which I pay $50, in specie or its equivalent never to draw interest. The other $450 I pay in by a mortgage on real estate worth a least $1000 at a tolerate valuation, and clear of all prior encumbrances. I receive scrip for $500. One thousand other persons do the same. We have now a capital of $500,000, of which $50,000 is specie or its equivalent. Each stockholder by the terms of the Institution shall be entitled to a loan from the Bank of at least thirty per cent on his stock, or the average thereof through the year, and as much more occasionally as the Directors may deem safe on the part of the Bank, never exceeding the amount of his stock. He may obtain these loans as principal, or as endorser for some friend. And only such a per cent is to be charged by the Bank on its loans as shall be sufficient to pay its cashiers etc. the maximum compensation heretofore stipulated for services, and to defray all the other incidental charges of banking operations. This might be *one*, certainly not *two* per cent per annum. At the same time the stockholders all stand pledged never to loan at second hand to their fellow members any of this money at a higher per cent than cost, according to the rule of trade stipulated in Section 2 of the Article under examination. And all the people of the Republic stand pledged to favor its circulation among themselves and their friends, by preventing it passing into the hands of persons likely to draw upon the Bank for specie, or its equivalent, and by assisting its directors to all the money of other banking institutions which it may lie in their power to command. In this way a numerous population would be continually well supplied with a reliable circulating currency on most easy terms, enterprise would be fostered, fraternity promoted and Shylockism effectually counteracted. Let there be as many such Banks as the Republic may need.

Such a Bank needs only people who are able, willing and committed to it. I do not see why such a Bank could not be instituted by the honest farmers, mechanics and manufacturers in any County of the existing order of society. But most of them want to get large interest or profits on their own capital. They have too little confidence in each other to work such a system smoothly. They are too antagonistic in their other interests, and withal too much enslaved to the old customs of business. It will therefore be almost impossible for them to come into such a system, without first coming into a new social order. Yet if they had the will, they would soon find the way; which I should much rejoice to see take place. But in our Republic the thing will be perfectly natural and feasible. And what a deliverance will it work from the covetousness and growing extortion of the existing Mammonitish order!

Suppose they should combine to crush our Mutual Banks, I am sure they will never be able to do it. With solid capital for our basis, moral unity of action, tolerable financial skill, and the good will of the working, honest, friendly outsiders, we should be impregnable.

I suppose the other great objects proposed, Mutual Insurance and reciprocal Commercial Exchange, will come about gradually on the same equitable and fraternal principles. The path lies open, and ample inducements beckon our people on. Indeed, their sovereign divine principles will not let them stop short of planning and executing the measures necessary to accomplish all these objects. The genius of our enterprise will not be satisfied with less.

Chapter 7

Membership, Organization, and Government

The Seven Circles of Membership

Our Constitution prescribes that membership shall exist in seven Circles: the Adoptive, the Unitive, the Preceptive, the Communitive, the Expansive, the Charitive and the Parentive. These distinctions are made because they must exist to a considerable extent in the very nature of the Association which we denominate the Practical Christian Republic; because such a classification of the members will be exceedingly convenient for the orderly organization and regulation of the Republic; and because this classification will suggest, incite, encourage and invigorate a great deal of spontaneous effort, both individual and congenially associative, in various branches of the common cause.

In the first place there must be a considerable number of persons who will adopt our principles and approve of our polity, whose circumstances will not admit of their uniting immediately, if ever, with any Integral Community. By receiving such into the Adoptive Circle of our membership, we shall attach them to the general movement, facilitate their progress, afford them needful encouragement, enlist them effectually in the dissemination of our doctrines among people otherwise unapproachable, bring their children into our educational institutions, and induct many of them by an easy transition into the more interior Circles of the Republic.

Next comes the Unitive Circle. Those who unite in building up Rural Communities, or Joint Stock Communities, plant themselves on an integral territorial domain which is thenceforth consecrated to the perpetual ownership of the Republic. It is redeemed and guaranteed against the evil uses to which other portions of the earth are every where exposed. The vices and abominations which elsewhere have a foothold on the soil are effectually yet peaceably excluded from every square rod of these redeemed domains. The land and whatever shall be placed thereon becomes subordinate to the sovereignty of divine principles. This is a great step taken. Some will take it from the Adoptive Circle, and others directly out of the old order of society. But all who take it enter the Unitive Circle. They unite to dwell together on an integral domain, forever annexed to the grand Social Republic.

The third Circle includes all members specially and perseveringly devoted to Teaching; whether it be teaching religion, morality or any branch of useful knowledge, and whether their teaching be done with the living voice, or with the pen, or through the press, or in educative institutions. All such teachers, after having proved themselves competent, devoted and acceptable in the Communities to which they belong, shall be considered in the Preceptive Circle. This is designed to call out, consecrate, and combine all really meritorious and devoted teachers in the Republic, as a class thoroughly committed to the great work of enlightening, disciplining and perfecting mind.

The prosperity and glory of such a Republic demand that its population be exceedingly intelligent and moral. All branches of useful knowledge, of true religion and of solid virtue must therefore be promoted with a zeal and energy unparalleled in the history of any previous people. If so, there must be numerous competent teachers inspired with an unconquerable ambition to effect such a consummation. They must love their work, and feel that they are consecrated to it by the highest of motives. They must be spontaneously united, too, as a congenial phalanx, all engaged in various departments of a common enterprise. They must consult and cooperate together, as a highly responsible class of whom great things are expected and will be required. They are all ranked together, because they really belong together, and ought not to be separated into learned professions, as in the old order or society; because religious, moral, intellectual and physical improvement ought to go forward together harmoniously; and because we mean to have the whole Circle consist of persons who are intelligent and conscientious enough to preach the gospel in its proper connection with all useful sciences and arts. Thus we shall secure all the real benefits which the several learned professions and preceptors of the old order of society honestly aim to render, without the superstition, craft, mischief and evils of which they have often been prolific generators.

No teacher can gain a foothold in this Circle without being specially and perseveringly devoted to teaching. Each must also have proved him or herself competent, devoted and acceptable in some Community, as a member thereof engaged in teaching. Teachers cannot be manufactured by a mere course of study, a license, a diploma or an ordination ceremony. They must go to work and prove their competency to the acceptance of those who need their labors. If they attempt the thing and cannot succeed to the general satisfaction, they will be obliged to betake themselves to a less responsible calling; and as all extra pecuniary temptations are abolished in our Republic, I think its Preceptive Circle must consist chiefly of worthy men and women.

Next comes the Communitive Circle. This is to consist of persons belonging to Integral Common Stock Communities, or Families; whose internal economy excludes individual profits on capital, wages for labor, and separate interests. This class of members may be presumed to have attained a somewhat higher development of their moral and social nature than the generality of their fellow members in the Adoptive and Unitive Circles; inasmuch as they are willing to place their capital and labor in common stock together, to be content with the proper necessaries of life, and to share these by mutual agreement equally as brothers and sisters of the same household. They may provide in their Communal Covenant for the withdrawal and discharge of members, and for assigning to such a just dividend of property to retire with.

These Communities are presupposed to live more unselfishly and in greater unity together than their brethren and sisters, who either dwell in isolation, or in Communities carefully recognizing individual claims to property and compensation for labor. Yet it would not follow that all who lived in isolation, or in Communities where the dollar was carefully credited to its individual owner, were inferior to the Communitives in moral and social development. Because some of them might actually be preeminently disinterested and generous in all their feelings and dealings, but, by reason of circumstances wholly beyond their control, would be obliged to dwell among associates highly individualistic in their property interests. I have no doubt that *some* of our nominal Adoptives and Unitives will be better Communitives in *spirit*, than *some* who may be connected with Common Stock organizations. Nor am I at all disposed to lay a foundation for self-righteousness on the part of the Communitive Circle. They will have nothing to boast of, should they be ever so faithful to their convictions; for they will have done no more than their duty, and will enjoy happiness in proportion; while the Adoptives and Unitives, if faithful to their highest convictions, under their different circumstances, will enjoy proportionate good, and be entitled to respect accordingly.

The next named Circle is to include all members especially devoted to the enlargement of the Republic, by founding and strengthening new Integral Communities. There is no distinguishing characteristic about this class of members, except zeal and devotion in the work of establishing new Communities, and so expanding the Republic. They are to be associated in companies for this express purpose, and to employ the major portion of their time, talents or property in the work. It is assumed that there will be a class of members who will have just such an ambition as this; who will delight in this particular work; whose glory it will be to push forward the common cause by selecting and purchasing suitable territorial domains for new Communities, enlisting recruits to settle on those domains, and helping them through the struggles of their associative infancy.

The Expansives would not be speculators in land, nor self-seeking money makers, but patrons and protectors of young Communities. They would be in close affinity with each other, and would not be hindered in their schemes by having to consult reluctant fellow members belonging to other Circles. They would be of one heart and one mind among themselves, and consequently would operate much more efficiently than could be done by any organization not congenially and intensely interested in a common object. It will often be in the power of a few members of this Circle to combine their capital and energies for the purchase of lands in various places, especially in the great West, if not in the older settled parts of the country: which lands they may hold without loss to themselves until fairly occupied by a Community gathered for that purpose. Meantime, with prudence and judgment they may do much to give their young Community a fair start. Afterwards they can resume up their resources and apply them to new enterprises elsewhere.

The Charitive Circle is the sixth named. This Circle includes all members who are especially devoted to the reformation, elevation, improvement and welfare of the world's suffering classes, by furnishing them homes, employment, instruction and all the requisite helps to a better condition. Here is a most laudable work for the class of members whose sympathies and consciences draw them towards it. A wide field of charity and usefulness opens before them.

But if I might be permitted to suggest a word of advice to them, it would be this: Expend most of your energies on those whom you can induce to *help themselves*. It is of little use to feed idleness and vice. There must be employment, education and reformation. Where the very stamina of moral principle has been choked to death by persistent licentiousness, reformation is all but impossible in this state of flesh and blood. I have seen such unfortunate transgressors. While sick, hungry, naked, in prison, in trouble, or in a fit of sheer exhaustion, the evil spirit would seem to have quite departed from them; but when cured up, well fed and clothed, and no longer in dread of impending punishment, the same foul demon would return with seven-fold greediness of lust, and be welcomed into a swept and garnished house; so that the last state of the obsessed victim became worse than the first. Actual distress ought to be relieved, at least in its crises; but I have seen so much of that sort of charity which pumps itself out of breath to keep filthy ships from sinking, all their leaks still left unstopped, that I sincerely hope the Charitive Circle will not exhaust its energies in such fruitless labors.

Finally, we have the Parentive Circle. This is to comprise our most worthy and reliable counselors in cases of great importance, the fathers and mothers of our Israel. We shall need such, and shall have them. They will be known by their fruits through a long course of experience, and in due time be publicly acknowledged worthy of confidence by a unanimous vote of their respective Communities. Their responsibilities will then be mature, and they must deserve accordingly, or sink into obscurity.

There will be no base inducement for anyone to aspire to membership in the Parentive Circle, nor for any Community to bestow such a mark of confidence on persons unworthy of it. Section 2 of this Article prescribes that the members of each Circle shall be entitled to respect and influence in consideration of intrinsic worth alone. Nor is there to be any permanent general organization of the Circles *as such*. This precludes all evils of caste and useless organic machinery, which some might fear would grow out of seven such distinctions.

The Parochial Community

Article 5, entitled Organization, designates the various constituent and confederate bodies which are to compose our Republic. The first of these is the Parochial Community, which will consist of twelve or more members belonging chiefly to the Adoptive Circle, residing promiscuously in the same general neighborhood, and associating as a kind of Parish. They will guarantee to each other all the social advantages possible in their circumstances. But it is hardly to be expected that they will be able to carry out these guarantees to their full extent.

A Parochial Community can be formed wherever there are twelve or more members of the Adoptive Circle. This will be an easy step for many to make towards the upper plane of the Republic, who might be quite unable at the time to take a longer one. They will enter the vestibule of the new Social Temple, and commit themselves decidedly to our grand movement. There will probably be many Parochial Communities formed during the early stages of the Republic; and it will be in their power to render the cause great service, as well as to derive important advantages from their connection with more advanced Communities.

I cannot assume to give you the precise form of the Constitution of a Parochial Community, *verbatim et literatim*, because each Community, when actually formed, will adopt its own Constitution according to its own taste and judgment. I can give you such a draft as will serve the purpose with incidental alterations.*

The Rural Community

The next constituent body of our Republic is the Rural Community. This is one of the three kinds of Integral Communities. It differs from the Parochial, in respect to its having an integral territorial Domain so held in possession and guaranteed that no part thereof can be owned in fee simple by any person not a member of the Practical Christian Republic. Perhaps I shall best explain the peculiarities of a Rural Community by proposing a Constitution for one.**

I have no doubt many Rural Communities will be formed in our Republic, by persons unprepared to enter into more intimate social relations. It is a very natural and easy step to take, from the Parochial Community to the Rural, or even directly out of the old social state itself. It would be a laudable enterprise to form a nucleus of a Rural Community with congenial members, say in New England, and then locate on a healthful, convenient, ample domain at the West. The combined emigrants would be able to carry their neighborhood and many of its advantages with them to their new home;

---

* Appendix B
** Appendix C

instead of scattering off, family by family, among strangers, and subjecting themselves to all manner of social privations, as has heretofore been almost unavoidable. And after becoming well settled as a Rural Community, they could, if they pleased, gradually unite more and more closely in congenial associations among themselves, and, finally, perhaps, resolve themselves into a Joint Stock, or even a Common Stock Community.

The formation of a Rural Community might be practicable in any part of the country for persons adopting our principles and polity, whose farms, already in a flourishing state, should lie contiguous or nearly so. Half a dozen land owners, by purchasing estates intervening between them, could resolve the whole into an integral territorial domain. They could form their Community, raise their subscription loan, elect their trustees, pass their real estate into the hands of those trustees, lay off their village site, house lots and homesteads, and thus consummate all the arrangements necessary to their new social state. At present this is not likely to occur very often; because converts will be comparatively few and far between. However, there is no harm in looking ahead, and forestalling probable future contingencies.

The Hopedale Community: A Joint Stock Community

The most unexceptionable and beautiful theories involve this drawback, that they have not yet been tried, and may not work well in practice. As the next constituent and confederate body of our Republic is a Joint Stock Community, I refer you to the Constitution and Enactments of the Hopedale Community. That Community is of the Joint Stock class. It is an established actuality of many years' standing. By reading its Constitution and Enactments you will obtain an insight into its polity, and receive many suggestions applicable to all our contemplated Communities, such as it would be almost impossible to give you in the most elaborate statements.

The Hopedale Community commenced its existence under great worldly disadvantages, struggled through many trying experiences, and has overcome all obstacles; so that now, after more than twelve years of persevering effort, it presents itself to beholders an established and prosperous institution. No stranger to such an undertaking, and no mere theorist, can justly estimate the difficulties to be overcome. Those who have had responsible positions in attempts to establish Communities or Associations of this general nature, know what it costs, in money, labor, mental energy and moral power, to gain even a permanent foothold for successful operations.

The Hopedale Community is not yet out of its childhood, and has only made a decent beginning. There has been a remarkable guardianship of Divine Providence attending the formation, location, upbuilding and progress of that Community. At its birth most friends of Association in the country deemed it as insignificant as it was harmless. It was regarded as a root out of dry ground, without form, comeliness or strength.[1] Not so, however, its devoted friends. They had faith that it was a Social Bethlehem, which, though least among the Communities of Israel, would ultimately become one of the most illustrious.[2] It took root in obscurity. It learned wisdom by experience, and gained strength in the midst of adversity. It saw Associations and Communities one after another laid in their graves, which at their outset would have disdained its own poor chance in the world. Thus it lived on and prospered in its humility, till now it promises to be the parent of a numerous progeny. Still it is but a child, and, of course, an imperfect sample of what a multitude of Joint Stock Communities in the Practical Christian Republic are designed to be.

In the matter of unitary economics it has hardly made a commencement. It has no Unitary Mansion, Bakery, Refectory, Baths or Laundry. All these were contemplated by its founders; and the friends of the Community will continue to demand them with increasing urgency until supplied.

The Common Stock Community

There are persons already belonging to our Republic, and will doubtless be a constantly increasing number in the future, who aspire to live in Community with kindred minds free from the corrosive cares and conflicts of separate interests – the continual vigilance, calculation, reckoning and trafficking which necessarily prevail to a greater or less extent where individuals manage their property affairs in severalty. This class of minds would not be satisfied with membership in a Parochial, nor in a Rural, nor in a Joint Stock Community. They want to go up higher. Let them do so. At least let them make the attempt, even though they should fail. I have no doubt that some of them will learn that they are not exactly the unselfish, wise beings they take themselves to be. And in this particular they will only learn what is likely to be learned in all the other Communities.

Whoever joins a Common Stock Community ought to have great confidence in his or her fellow members generally, as to their moral purity, intelligence and real benevolence of heart. Also, great frankness of expression, and a perfect willingness to share equally with the humblest member of the Community. So long as he or she shall remain a member, no claim is to be made for profit on capital invested, nor for compensation of labor performed, nor for extra allowances of a pecuniary nature. All property interests are reduced to a common level. And whoever cannot contentedly stand on that level has no remedy but to retire from the Community. Provision is made for this; but as it is due to the Community that seceders should not endanger its existence by withdrawing from its funds the full amount credited to them on its books, I have stipulated that ten per cent of all such credits should inure to the Community in every case of withdrawal.

I submit my draft of a Common Stock Compact without further introduction.* It may be imperfect in some particulars and need amendment, but it will serve as an approximation at least to the true one required. It will also suggest the form of Covenant suitable for a Common Stock Family of any size, gathered within the limits of a Rural, or of a Joint Stock Community. It might happen that a few persons in such Communities would desire thus to associate, and could do so, not only without detriment to others, but with great advantage to themselves. Such a Family in one of those Communities would stand in the same relation to the Community as an ordinary family, and would differ only in numbers and internal arrangements. Outside of itself it would enjoy all the advantages afforded by the Community to which it belonged, and within itself it might make all the improvement which its Common Stock arrangements were calculated to secure. Besides, if any of its initiates should find they had undertaken more than they were capable of carrying through, they could easily recede into the ordinary social positions of their Community associates. The Common Stock plan could be tried with great ease and little risk under such circumstances. If it worked well, the Family formed within a Rural or a Joint Stock Community would become a nursery for a Common Stock Community, and might at any time unite with kindred Families elsewhere in purchasing a Domain and establishing a Community of their own kind. And if the experiment failed in any case, there would be no serious loss or inconvenience attending its failure.**

---

* Appendix D

** Inquirer: "There is something so unselfish, noble, loving and harmonious in it, that I confess I should greatly prefer your Common Stock Community to either of the other kinds, if I had confidence enough in my own virtue and that of my proposed Communal associates. But that, I fear, would prove fatal. Poor human nature has so many selfish tendencies besides the mere love of money, so many weak points, so many uncomfortable twistifications, and is so undeveloped in true Wisdom, that I am afraid of myself and of all mankind."

Common Stock Communities have existed here and there in different countries of the earth for thousands of years. There is a natural want of them in a comprehensive Social System, that they are likely to work better in a general confederacy like the Practical Christian Republic than as constituting a uniform and exclusive Communal scheme of their own. If they do not benefit my System they certainly cannot harm it.

Communal Municipalities, States, and Nations

Communal Municipalities come next in the series of organizations contemplated in our Republic. These will consist of two or more Communities, whether Parochial or Integral, combined as in a town or city for municipal purposes necessary to their common welfare; which purposes must be such as would be impracticable or extremely difficult of accomplishment by one Community alone. It is anticipated that in process of time, perhaps at no distant day, Communities will be formed near each other. Their domains may adjoin, or they may be so contiguous as to render a municipal union of two or more Communities exceedingly convenient, if not absolutely necessary.

It will be unwise for any Community to be very large. From five hundred to fifteen hundred people, or two thousand at the extreme, would be as many as ought to be concentrated in a single Community. A large population would impair unity, concert and effectiveness of action. They could neither deliberate nor execute so well in respect to any of their common interests. Besides, it is unnatural for more than about fifteen hundred, or at the outside two thousand persons, to be closely associated in a simple organization. Hence it is common to find them forming new societies, by offshoots, even before numbers reach this maximum. Like bees they must needs swarm and have a new hive. It was necessary, therefore, in the Constitution of our Republic, to provide for the Municipality, as a natural combination of two or more distinct Communities. This will encourage the formation of new ones side by side with the parent hive, or at least in close contiguity with some kindred body. Thus situated they may form a confederate Municipality of any size they please, from that of the smallest of our common townships, to that of a large city or county. The Municipalities will be formed, not to overrule arbitrarily the integral Communities, nor to assume any of their merely local responsibilities, but to promote their common welfare, by doing many things necessary to that welfare, which otherwise could not be done without great difficulty and perhaps not at all.

All this belongs to the future, and cannot be provided for except in the general manner prescribed in the Constitution, until the first occasion for forming a Municipality shall actually arrive. Then the Communities proposing to enter into a municipal union will elect their delegates to form the compact necessary to such union. The convention of delegates so elected will send out the compact agreed upon to their constituents in the several Communities concerned; which, if ratified by the requisite majority, will go into operation; and thus the new Municipality will become an established organization. I have made no draft of a Constitution for a Communal Municipality. I thought it quite unnecessary, and even improper. That matter cannot fail to take good care of itself in its own time and place, if the Integral Communities shall be fairly started.

Next come Communal States, which are to be somewhat analogous to the States composing the American Union. The same principle would be followed out which is to govern the formation of a Municipality, and the process would be similar, only on a wider scale. Next comes the Communal Nation on the same principle. And then follows ultimately the grand Fraternity of Nations, to be represented by Senators in the Supreme Unitary Council. The serial combination, from the Municipality upward, follows a natural order of ascending gradation.

Self-Government the Best Government

Self-government in the Individual, the Family and the primary congenial Association, under the immediate sovereignty of divine principles, is the basis of moral and social order in our republic. Therefore, all governmental powers vested in the Municipality, the State, the Nation, and the Supreme Unitary Council, shall be such as are obviously beneficent, and such as cannot be conveniently exercised by the primary Communities. And the confederate bodies are prohibited from ever assuming to exercise governmental powers not clearly delegated to them by their constituents.

This is true Christian Republicanism. It subjects all human government to the sovereignty of divine principles, magnifies self-government into its just importance, throws back the responsibilities of government where they ought to rest, and prohibits the assumption of all power not delegated by the people themselves. It makes government a natural cone, with a broad base and a narrow apex. The people will govern themselves almost entirely, as individuals, families and Integral Communities.

All Communities shall do their utmost to ensure their respective members and dependents a full realization of the objects specified in Article 1 of our Constitution: "To ensure to every orderly citizen of this Republic a comfortable home, suitable employment, adequate subsistence, congenial associates, a good education, proper stimulants to personal righteousness, sympathetic aid in distress, and due protection in the exercise of all natural rights." If unable to do so single-handed, they may unite with sister Communities to do it. Doubtless this will sometimes be necessary, and often convenient. A strong Municipality may easily ensure some of those guaranties which a single Community cannot.

But the Municipalities will be limited to a well-defined sphere of prerogatives. So will the States. So will the Nations. So will the Supreme Unitary Council. And though each successive sphere widens the diameter of its scope, it will narrow in respect to the discretionary power delegated to it. The interests to be supervised and the authority to govern will be specific. Thus government will grow more and more simple in its ends and machinery as it ascends above its primary sources.

Our Government will of course eschew all official display of dress, pomp, parade, arrogance and needless governmental show. Likewise all compensation for official service beyond the average paid to the first class of operatives at large. This provision speaks for and commends itself to all who abhor the worship of baubles, the pampering of mortal vanity, and the exorbitance of sellers.

Religion and Religious Institutions

Our Republic insists only on the essentials of faith and practice affirmed in Article 2; the Christian Religion being acknowledged as one of fundamental divine principles and preeminently practical. Therefore no uniform religious or ecclesiastical system of externals shall be established, nor shall any rituals, forms, ceremonies or observances whatsoever be either instituted or interdicted; but each Community shall determine for itself, with due regard to the conscientious scruples of its own members, all matters of this nature.

Our Constitution prescribes the holding of general religious meetings once in three months throughout the Republic, and the formation of Quarterly Conferences in every region of country inhabited by any considerable number of members. It indicates the powers and duties of such Conferences, and requires that they shall be organized as religious bodies under a written Constitution. In making converts and admitting them into the Adoptive Circle, I am confident these Conferences will render the general cause an indispensable service. They plant trees which will bring forth much fruit.

The nature of these Quarterly Conferences will fully appear from the Constitution of the only one yet established, the Hopedale Quarterly Conference. This may serve as a model Constitution for all Quarterly Conferences hereafter formed, leaving the door open, of course, for all possible improvements.

Amendment

Our movement includes among its fundamentals the principle of progress; is purely voluntary in its associational compacts; provides for both amendment and secession; and therefore cannot interpose any insurmountable obstacles to improvement. If it should happen in the course of time, that one or more of our now fundamental principles turned out to be an error, then it must be discarded as such. If two-thirds of the citizen members of the Republic should become convinced that errors were being cherished, it would be their duty, as well as their right, to amend their Constitutional declaration. If individuals should change their convictions, it would be their duty and right to secede.

The final Article of our Constitution specifies that the whole thing is left open to revision and amendment – resting on its own intrinsic merits, and unreservedly subjecting itself the deliberate judgment of all coming times. This is right, and implies unswerving confidence in the ever living Spirit of Truth and Righteousness to adjust its external forms to the progressive changes of human nature.

PART III

Education
for Practical
Christianity

Introduction

Without a highly improved and thorough course of education, I could not expect success and permanency for my Social System. Education may be divided into three general processes: development, enlightenment and government. Whatever expands, unfolds and matures the inherent constitutional faculties of a human being, belongs to *development*. Whatever imparts ideas, knowledge, understanding, wisdom, belongs to *enlightenment*. Whatever gives controlling motives, principles of action, regulation, habituation and decided characterization, belongs to *government*.

Education presupposes beings to be educated, educators, and processes or methods of educative operation. Both the educated and their educators are human beings. What then is a human being?

A human being is a compound identity consisting of *matter, soul-spirit,* and *Deific spirit.* The exterior personal identity is composed of mineral, vegetable and aqueous matter – inert, passive substance. Interior to this is an incomparably finer substance which I have called soul-spirit. This soul-spirit pervades, animates and controls the body until after death. Sensation, affection, intellect, sentiment and reason are developed from germs inherent in soul-spirit. Thus we have the soul within the animal body. But interior to the soul is a still finer essence, a little ganglion on one of the innumerable Deific nerves that traverse immensity in all directions throughout the Infinitarium. This divine nerve ganglion is at first so minute and impalpable, that the soul is unconscious of its presence. But it is inherently capable of such expansion and intensification as to gain absolute control over the whole man, and ultimately to absorb his identity as it were into its own divinity, and thus without annihilating that identity to harmonize it perfectly with the

Supreme Deific Volition. This inmost essence is what chiefly distinguishes man from beast, allies him to the angel world, forms within him the divine image, renders him receptive of heavenly inspirations, and finally brings him into perfect union with the Infinite Father.

From this view of the human constitution it is seen that education must be adapted to develop, enlighten and govern man in accordance with the wants, susceptibilities and capabilities of his threefold constitutional being. His physical part must be treated physically. His psychical part must be treated psychically. His divine part must be treated divinely. And every condition and circumstance necessary to these results must receive due consideration.

I fully believe that human beings will progress by development, enlightenment and discipline through all ages until complete reunion with the Infinite Divinity. In that sense education can terminate only when man's identity shall have become perfectly divinitized. But now I am treating of education in a more restricted sense. I mean by the term that compound of development, enlightenment and government which renders men and women what they are at full maturity in *this* life. If this process be well carried out by human agency, we may confide all the rest to higher teachers. Practically the question is, What have *we* to do in the education of the rising generation?

Chapter 8

Education for Health
of Body, Mind, and Spirit

Education Begins in the Womb

The human seed commences its development, for good or evil, in the maternal womb at or soon after impregnation.* Therefore I must begin at this point. When I come to treat of marriage and procreation I shall begin even farther back. But educationally I will start where development is first cognizable. Who now are educators of the embryo man or woman? Primarily, directly and chiefly the mother. Next in degree of influence the father. And next subordinately the mother's intimate associates in the family and neighborhood. All these exert a greater or less influence, designedly or undesignedly, to determine the development of the unborn child. Their influence is variously limited, yet great. Their educational responsibilities are proportionate. The structure, conformation, nervous system, appetites, passional propensities and moral tendencies of the future man or woman will be more or less affected by influences operating in, upon, and through the mother before birth. This may be safely affirmed of ordinary cases, not to mention extraordinary ones in which very dire calamities sometimes occur. Before birth, as well as afterwards, it holds true that "Just as the twig is bent the tree's inclined."[1]

It is a pity that multitudes who are grossly unfit to become parents could not be deterred by some wholesome motive from perpetrating those dreadful generative and gestative wrongs which so grievously afflict their offspring. I cannot indicate all the wrongs to which I allude. "Their name is Legion."[2] They result from great abuses, some of which I will briefly mention.

---

* Inquirer: "You astonish and alarm me. I never dreamed of education before birth. Who will dare to become parents with such responsibilities as these resting upon them!"

1. Frequent and persistent venereal indulgence of the husband, sometimes with, sometimes without, and sometimes against the reciprocal inclinations of his pregnant wife. This is a great and prevalent abuse of nature. Perverted amativeness, unchastened lust and the force of habit, strengthened by the ignorant plea of passional necessity, thus inflict incalculable mischiefs on the helpless fetus. Such indulgence should seldom, if ever, take place during pregnancy, or during lactation. It is contrary to unperverted nature and productive of most blighting consequences.

2. Cruelty, unkindness, indifference, neglect and various kinds of ill-treatment from the husband, or from other persons, towards the pregnant wife. This is sometimes gross and outrageous, sometimes refined and secret, but always injurious to the mother, and through her to the unborn child. There is no period of female life during which a loving, kind, considerate treatment is so necessary – so indispensable. Yet ill-treatment from the husband, or other intimate associates, to the incipient mother is no uncommon occurrence. And the consequences are deplorable. Many a child comes into the world malformed, or *non-compos*, or sickly, or irascible, or ill balanced, by reason of the gall and bitterness amid which it has been gestated.

3. Undue excitement of the passions, especially the more malignant ones – anger, envy, jealousy, hatred, revenge, fear and despair. These exert a blighting and baneful influence on unborn offspring. Mothers thus excited often unintentionally stamp the most fatal impressions on the fruit of their wombs. Abuses of this nature are fearfully prevalent, if not in their extremes, yet to a malign extent. But it is of the highest importance that they should be studiously avoided during both gestation and lactation; indeed, for other reasons, at all times through life.

4. Physiological abuses which in millions of cases poison, pervert and curse human nature before birth. We need not dwell on instances of disgusting drunkenness, gluttony, filthiness and gross intemperance of the animal propensities, which sometimes occur in the degraded classes of society. They are horrible to contemplate in connection with the procreation and gestation of children. Besides these, we may find evils enough to deprecate in more favored circles. Look at the food generally eaten. Think of the quantity, the quality, the cookery, the condiments, the accompaniments, the mastication and the digestion. Is it nutritious, wholesome, simple, digestible? Far otherwise. Look at the exhalations, perspirations and evacu-

ations. Are they open, free, regular and healthful? Far otherwise. Look at clothing, dress. Is it adapted to preserve a just temperature of the body? Is it comfortable and easy at all points? Is there no compression of the lungs, chest, abdominal viscera, blood vessels, muscles of the limbs or pores of the skin? Far and fatally otherwise. Look at sleeping rooms. Are they spacious and well ventilated? Alas, little better often than death cells, where people breathe a most vitiated, gaseous atmosphere from eight to twelve hours in the twenty-four! Look at the exercise taken by women, over the cooking stove and the fervent coal fire, on the treadmill of household drudgery, in the streets with elegant good-for-nothing shoes, or worse yet in the parlor or ballroom, or some frivolous party got up for amusemental dissipation, killing of time and reversing of day and night.

5. Extreme toil, hardship, care and anxiety of the pregnant mother, whereby in many instances she is overtasked, worn down, and her vital energies nearly exhausted. This is no uncommon evil. Sometimes it seems absolutely unavoidable. Sometimes poverty impels it. Sometimes it is enforced by rank covetousness on the part of the husband, or the wife herself, or both. Sometimes pride, fashion and a false hospitality, which oppresses the family with company to be entertained, occasions the drudgery. And not infrequently it is necessitated by too large a family.

A thoughtless husband ignorantly indulges his venereal lusts at every opportunity. Impregnation occurs just as often as poor jaded maternity will admit of it. The good woman perhaps believes it to be the visitation of Divine Providence upon her from year to year, and that she is irrevocably fated to have her "number." So the house swarms with unbidden offspring, and resounds with the clamor of their conflicting wants. There is an utter disproportion of strength, qualification and means to the necessities of the case. They cannot be properly cared for even physically, much less intellectually and morally. The affectionate but worn-down mother drags on through it all as well as she can, meantime adding to the household another and another crying loved one, till age or death terminates the struggle. And long after she shall have paid the debt of nature will her ill-developed, half-lived children re-echo her sighs.

All this is wrong. Such abuses ought not to go uncorrected. In fulfilling functions so momentous, and under circumstances so delicate, the wife should not be overtasked, oppressed with care nor tortured with anxiety.

At least such evils should be avoided to the utmost possible extent. The developing embryo should have the benefit of a calm, cheerful enjoyment of life's needed comforts. Otherwise both mother and child must be more or less injured.

I will not allude to the thousand and one other abuses rife among women, the mothers of each successive generation of our race. When we contemplate the wrongs inflicted before birth on millions of human beings, is it any wonder that the world abounds with so many unfortunate, incompetent, intractable, depraved, vicious, contentious, destructive and unhappy creatures? Is it any wonder that mankind are so low, ill-developed and miserable; especially when we adjoin to the education before birth that which follows after through infancy and youth? Imagine now a million of unborn babes in process of development amid the blight and bitterness of these multiform abuses. Every one of that million comes into outer life more or less perverted in physical, mental and moral capability. Is it very strange that one-third of the race die in infancy? Is it very strange that so many of the survivors spend a wretched life? Is it very strange that only a few of them are really healthful, intelligent, virtuous and happy?

Education for Physical Health

We have traced development from conception to parturition. Let us suppose that thus far all is right. Well formed, healthful, promising infants are born, and now we are to proceed with their education. What have we to do? They are to be developed into men and women – such men and women, physically, intellectually, and morally, as shall be truly happy. We wish them to be, to do, and to enjoy all that is really desirable, to the extent of their natural capabilities. This then is what we have to do, so far as it can be done by education.

Suppose we are now to take charge of a newborn infant, which is to be provided for and trained up to adult age. Our first concern is for the body of this child. Our great desideratum is the child's health. If this can be promoted and preserved, we are sure that the whole body will naturally grow to full size and consistency, experiencing much pleasure and comparatively little pain. What then are the indispensable conditions of physical health? First, proper protection against external injuries by means of suitable care-takers, a suitable habitation, and suitable clothing.

Care and Shelter. The little stranger comes into the world the most helpless of all creatures, yet exposed to multiform dangers. There must be persons to take suitable care of this helpless being until rendered capable of all necessary self-care. Let the midwife, the nurse, the mother, the father and the subsequent assistant educators, be qualified, both by knowledge and good will, to do their duty. Thus will the child fall into good hands, and receive suitable care.

Let the habitation be a safe and quiet shelter – a suitable protection against the inclement elements and all invading annoyances by day and night – a pleasant, healthful home. To be such, it should have a good surrounding atmosphere and pleasant prospects, plenty of natural light, moderate warmth, ample ventilation, very little dampness, very little filth, and very little harsh noise. The wretched abodes in our large cities, and often in our villages and country places, where so many of the human race are born, and for a while vegetate rather than live, are deplorable opposites of the suitable habitations I am recommending.

Clothing. Clothing is an important item of physical protection. What is suitable clothing? That which is absolutely healthful. All other is unsuitable. The following precepts may be safely followed.

1. Let the clothing next the skin be flexible and congenial; of linen or cotton, such as may be easily cleansed; a day suit, and a night suit, often well washed and aired.

2. Let the more exterior apparel be of various material, and adapted to preserve the normal heat of the system, which is about 98 degrees, in just equilibrium from head to foot, by night and day, adding or diminishing the quantity as the varying temperature may require.

3. Protect the feet and other much exposed parts from injury by substantial yet flexible attire. Also, the head and shoulders in hot weather from the scorching sunbeams, by very light, cool coverings.

4. Let not the head be over clothed. It needs little clothing additional to the hair, while that lasts. Keep it cool, and the feet warm.

5. Let all clothing be as light as it can be and afford the necessary protection against cold, moisture and other injury.

6. Let no part of the clothing be so tight as to impede the circulation of the blood, or the free play of the muscles, or the full respiration of the lungs, or the natural action of any internal organ, or the ingress of a portion

of air to the skin. Let it be so loose and easy at every point, from head to foot, as to move readily at all times.*

Nutrition. Another indispensable condition of physical health is proper nutrition, by means of eating, drinking etc. I may sum up my leading ideas on this point in the following precepts:

1. Let the child be nursed at the breast, or fed on similar liquid nutrition, for one year, or until the period of dentition; then on easily digested liquids and solids suited to age until seven years old.

2. Let nutriment be taken often by infants, but never to surfeiting. From seven years of age and upward let three meals be taken per day at regular periods, and seldom anything else eaten, except wholesome fruits.

3. Let all food eaten be of a good quality, not adulterated, damaged or inferior.

4. Let all cooking be cleanly, simple and wholesome, not filthy, not greasy, not compounded of many ingredients, not highly concentrated, not undercooked nor in any wise unfit for comfortable digestion. Eschew nearly all confectionery, pastry etc. as abominable.

5. Eat only one, two or at the most three kinds of food at the same meal. Masticate well, and be careful not to overeat. Intemperance is the common fault in alimentation. There are as many gluttons as there are drunkards.

6. Let the flesh of animals be wholly eschewed if vigorous health can be secured without it; and if used at all, let it never be in large quantities, nor oftener than once a day. Studious, sedentary and excitable people must live on the simpler and more digestible kinds of food. They must be regular and abstemious feeders, yet not starvelings.

7. Intoxicating liquors of all kinds must be eschewed as beverages or ordinary refreshments. Likewise coffee, tea and hot refections in general. Likewise tobacco and narcotics of every description. Some of the more

---

* Inquirer: "I was scarcely ever dressed for company without a tight hat, a tight cravat, a tight coat at certain points, a tight vest, tight pantaloons, tight hose, tight boots or shoes, besides other fashionably uncomfortable things ... My poor sisters are living martyrs to unhealthful dressing, and never suspected it till lately. They are always elegantly dressed when ready to be seen. But such work have they made with their spines, lungs, hearts and internal organs, nay, even with the very frame-work of their chests, that scarcely any thing *natural* is left about them. They breathe unnaturally, in semiquavers. Their hearts are palpitating in contracted cells. Their blood has been driven from their feet to their heads. Vertebrae, stomach, liver and most other parts of their main structure are more or less deranged."

harmless coffees and teas may be occasionally used; but moderate quantities of pure water, or milk, or milk and water or some other unstimulating drinks, are the healthful liquids to be taken into the stomach.

These are good general rules for proper alimentation. Some will think I go too far, and some that I am too latitudinarian. More might be added, and doubtless some exceptionable cases provided for. But with common sense these are sufficient; and without common sense ten thousand rules would be useless.

Exercise. Proper exercise is a condition of health. The physical system is so constituted that every part of it must have more or less motion. Certain vital organs keep up a perpetual motion from birth till death without volition, and to some extent without the mind's consciousness. Thus the heart throbs, the blood circulates, the lungs respire, digestion goes on and the secretions take place, by what we call involuntary action. But the healthy action of even these organs depends much on external exercise; i.e. on the proper activity of the organs which we can voluntarily put in motion. Muscular exercise is quite indispensable to development and strength. I will give my ideas on this point in the preceptive form:

1. Let every kind of exercise be so adapted to the present strength of the organ or muscles exercised as to increase it, but never to overtax any part. Thus the feet, hands, chest, eyes, ears and every part of the system will be invigorated.

2. Let exercise take place daily, and, when at all convenient, in the open air. Let it commerce while the infant is yet young, and be varied in all practicable ways.

3. Let it be gymnastically adapted to exercise daily and harmoniously all the muscular powers of the system. So soon as the child can walk and run, let it be taught to use its limbs in all manner of wholesome ways. Also, to inhale long breaths, and slowly exhale them, that the lungs may be strengthened, the chest expanded, and the blood exhilarated.

4. Let there be multiform graceful and invigorating exercises gradually taught, such as the most unexceptionable calisthenic and gymnastic movements. Also, marching and dancing in the *open air* to music; or if within doors, never in crowded, heated, ill-ventilated rooms.

6. Let not exercise be sought in the wanton killing of harmless creatures, nor in any kind of cruelty to human or brute beings, nor in vulgar demoralizing antics, nor in any pugilistic rencounters, nor in mimicking the arts of

war, nor in burning gunpowder with firearms and annoying playthings, nor in any other vitiating sports. These have prevailed long enough; and there are plenty of innocent unexceptionable methods, which will completely subserve the promotion of health.

Sleep and Rest. The human body must have a due portion of proper sleep, rest, and repose, or become diseased and wear out. Some persons require more and some less. The following rules may be observed to advantage:

1. Let sleep always be natural and abundant – never otherwise except from necessity. Infants, if healthy, will sleep a large part of the time for the first few months. Let them sleep all they will naturally; but do not stupefy them with drugs. The young generally require more sleep than adults. Let them have what they need. It is a much praised folly in many quarters, that the less people sleep the better. Not even the benefits of early rising, though great, will offset the evils of insufficient sleep.

2. Let beds be as soft as they can be without overheating the sleeper, with bedclothes as light as they can be and preserve sufficient warmth. There is no merit in hard beds *per se*. Feather beds are well enough in cold weather, but bad in hot. Mattresses of decent flexibility are generally preferable at all seasons.

3. Let sleeping rooms be large, well lighted by day, well aired at all times, and kept thoroughly clean. Let the bedclothes and bedsteads be frequently cleansed and aired. Let bedsteads be well elevated above the floor, and never hung about with curtains. Curtains are an unhealthful nuisance. Let there be no trundle beds for the children. They are too near the floor, where the air is often carbonized. Let there be wide berths, or single ones, that the sleepers may not annoy each other, nor suffer from vitiated air, or fetid exhalations.

4. In securing the requisite ventilation, freshness of air and coolness, let damp vapors and atmospheric currents be carefully avoided.

5. Let sleep be taken regularly and in the night season; when practicable between sunset and sunrise. At other times, of course, according to age, circumstances and necessity.

6. Let there be other repose than that of sleep, whenever the weary and exhausted system requires it, especially about mealtimes, during the heat of summer noon days, in the evening, and on the weekly sabbath.

7. Let the amount of sleep and rest, if possible, always be to the wants of the physical system; and let no one involve him or herself, except from

necessity, or considerations of duty, in cares, anxieties and toils which prevent the taking of needful repose.

Purification. The term purification implies proper attention to all the natural and artificial processes of physical cleanliness. There is a constant effort of the human body to expel from itself all impure and deleterious matter. This is done through the lungs, the skin, the bowels and the other excretory organs. This effort of nature to cleanse itself must be encouraged and assisted from without. Otherwise the natural channels are obstructed, the discharges checked, the rejected matter flows back, and the whole system becomes diseased.

It is said that five-eighths of this impure, poisonous matter is expelled naturally through the lungs and skin, and three-eighths through more obvious channels. What then if the lungs do not expand and contract freely, so as to inhale a full supply of oxygen, and to exhale the carbon and fetor from the circulating blood? Or what if the air breathed is itself vitiated, so as to be unwholesome? Or what if scurf and filth agglutinate the pores of the skin from the crown of the head to the soles of the feet? Or what if uncleanness be absorbed from foul linen about the body, or the bed occupied by night? Or what if there be unfrequent and insufficient discharges through the other excrementary organs? Can there be health? Surely not. Then let the following be carefully observed:

1. Breathe long full breaths of good air habitually. Let the lungs do justice to the blood in purifying it.

2. Cleanse the whole surface of the body with soap and water frequently; every day if you can, but every week without failure. If you cannot bear cold water, use warm. Apply the comb, the towel, the flesh brush, and the scraper if necessary, till the dead scurf and oily impurities are purged away, and the exhalent putridity can freely escape through the pores. "Wash and be clean."[3]

3. See that your clothes are washed and aired often enough not to scent the surrounding atmosphere as you sit down or walk about. Let not the absorbents of the surface be doomed to take in exuded pollution from unclean linen. Never leave the bedroom in the morning till the clothes have been well laid open, and the window has welcomed the fresh air.

4. Promote habitually a regular stool at least once in twenty-four hours, and attend promptly to the other natural purifications, that there may be no unhealthful obstructions, and that the whole machinery of the physical system may run smoothly.

5. Let your habitation and all its appurtenances within and without, share in the general purification.

6. Let children from birth receive all needful purifications, and be so trained that they will cheerfully adhere through life to the law of cleanliness.

Illness and Medication. If due attention were always paid to the five previously named conditions of health, it would not often need recovery. But there are many casualties, unavoidable exposures to disease, and delinquencies through imperfection. Hence there will arise frequent occasions for medication of some sort. Therefore let the following rules be observed:

1. If a surgical operation be requisite, for any sufficient reason, let reliable aid be seasonably called and skillfully applied.

2. In all ordinary cases of disease, rely on dieting, exercising, bathing, journeying, resting, and kind, simple nursing. Be not easily alarmed; be patient, and nature will recuperate. Three-fourths of all the cases wherein doctors are called, and drugs swallowed, or other worrying applications prescribed, would pass off well if treated according to this rule. Perhaps nine-tenths. Perhaps even a greater proportion.

3. In very extraordinary cases, resort to the physician in whose medical skill and judgment you have the greatest confidence; and let his prescriptions be faithfully followed so long as you profess to trust him. But if the medicines prescribed, or the applications urged, are of a violent nature, from whichsoever of the conflicting *Parties* emanating, make up your mind that the chances of your recovery are doubtful, and be ready for death.

4. Abstain from all artificial interferences with the course of nature as much as possible. When. you make use of any, be sure that they will not damage or weaken, but assist and strengthen, the system. As a general thing, eschew the whole chaos of high-pretending medication.

5. Let the sick have a good nurse, plenty of wholesome air, cleanliness, few watchers, and little excitement. There is commonly too much company and too much noise about sick persons. It is a great mistake to fill the house with what is called help, kind callers and night watchers, when one of the family is taken sick. Let there be silence, serenity and order to the utmost extent.

6. In time of health prepare for sickness. Let there be as many conveniences in readiness as can well be provided. The changes of body and bed clothing, the utensils, implements and other requisites should be kept in

readiness by every household; or at least by every group of families, so that when the visitation is made all things necessary and comfortable may be readily available.

7. Finally, let the old rule of health preservation be constantly respected: "Keep the head cool, the feet warm, and the bowels open."[4] Then you may hope for the best, and be prepared for the worst.

This is what I have to offer relative to physical education. In general accordance with this outline, I would have the bodies of the young, in my new social order, treated, trained, habituated, and governed. And if they were thus physically educated from birth to adult age, it seems to me that their average health must be incomparably greater than that of mankind in general as society now is.

Education of the Instincts, Passions, and Affections

I have treated of physical education. I now take a step inward to the soul which animates the material body. It is but a step. I come to the sensational instincts, the animal propensities and the passional forces. All these are variously excitable, normally and abnormally. In their aggregate general character and tendency they give what we call disposition. Hence we say of children, *this* has a good disposition, *that* a bad one. When these sensational instincts, animal propensities and passional powers are strongly excited by external objects or influences, we speak of excited feelings as *passions*. Thus we have the passions of anger, fear, grief, etc.

What we properly call *affection* comes between disposition and passion. It is a determinate love or hate, like or dislike – a settled inclination of feeling in a certain direction. Human nature is so constituted as to become strongly affectional, both carnally and spiritually. The ruling affections make the man. They determine his character to a great extent, also his measure of happiness, and frequently that of others. The propelling power of human nature is affectional; the directing is rational. But the affectional often overrules the rational. Hence the importance of affectional education. It is this which regulates and molds the affections.

Among the principal affections of the human soul:

1. The love of food or gustatory pleasure: Alimentiveness.
2. The love of property: Acquisitiveness.

3. The love of crushing, destroying, or overcoming what is offensive: Destructiveness.

4. The love of contest and debate: Combativeness.

5. The love of secrecy: Secretiveness.

6. The love of the opposite sex: Amativeness.

7. The love of friends: Adhesiveness.

8. The love of display: Approbativeness.

9. The love of command or power: Self-Esteem.

10. The love of justice: Conscientiousness.

11. The love of safety or security: Cautiousness.

12. The love of worship, homage, adoration: Veneration.

13. The love of benefiting and blessing others: Benevolence.

These samples sufficiently explain my meaning. Phrenologists designate organs which serve as the vitalic centers of all the known loves. Some make these organs more and some less numerous. Without discussing the merits of their general philosophy, which I regard as fundamentally sound, we know very well that human nature has these loves in great number and variety. We know that it has what may be called animal affections, intellectual affections, and religious affections.

I propose to educate all these affections. You may ask, do they admit of much education? Do they not naturally and necessarily grow up from their roots? Are not all man's loves and hates, likes and dislikes, phrenologically predetermined before birth by hereditary transmission, or gestatory influences? Not to any such extent as to preclude education. Were I to entertain such a persuasion, I should, of course, abandon all idea of regulating these streams of feeling by means of education.

I have already taken for granted that the physical system is very much affected, for good or evil, by what takes place before birth. The same is undoubtedly true of the affectional constitution, which during the present existence is almost inseparable from the material body. But I maintain that both the material and affectional systems, however predisposed at birth, are capable of education to an immense extent.

I do not assume either that infants are born wholly normal and pure, or wholly depraved. I believe that infants come into the world in all degrees of impurity, from the least to the greatest. Consequently the very first inquiry I should institute, in order to the right affectional education of children, would be, What are their hereditary and gestatorial predispositions?

Because the desideratum is affectional health; just as in physical education the desideratum was physical health. To secure health there must be well balanced activity, order and harmony. Angular, ill balanced, disorderly affections are necessarily incompatible with happiness. This is why there is so little true happiness in our world.

First, let educators understand and duly consider the following truths:

1. That all the natural affectional powers of human beings, rightly exercised, are good.

2. That they are all liable to abuse and perversion.

3. That they have no inherent self-regulation, but are the proper subjects of enlightenment and law.

4. That they are all to be regulated by reason and divine principle.

5. That they are all to be temperately exercised, indulged and gratified in their proper place and season.

6. That the more animal and selfish affections are to be kept in just subordination to the spiritual and unselfish ones.

7. That the whole need to be harmoniously balanced.

Second, let educators take care to be well informed concerning the following particulars in the state of children and youth under their influence:

1. Whether they have any extreme hereditary or gestatorial angularities or affectional proclivities, which require to be corrected; or any important deficiencies of affectional capability which require special remedies.

2. Whether their nervous and affectional systems, as a whole, are too excitable, or too torpid, or of a proper sensibility. Whether *excitive* or *moderative* influences are necessary, what they should be, how they should be applied, and when.

3. Whether they have *refined* or *gross* constitutional affections.

4. Whether their sensual, or their spiritual capabilities are predominant.

5. Whether there be danger of the precocious or unseasonable development of any affectional power.

6. Whether the good effects intended are really produced on their pupils by the course of educative treatment pursued.

Third, let educators earnestly and persistently endeavor to approve themselves competent and well qualified to discharge their responsibilities in dealing with the affections of children and youth. In order to this they ought themselves to be truly and wisely affectionate, truly and wisely intelligent, truly and wisely exemplary, truly and wisely diligent, truly and wisely firm, truly and wisely patient, and truly and wisely progressive.

Fourth, let them always conscientiously aim at the following results:

1. To promote the permanent happiness of the educated in their proper relations to all other beings.

2. To secure their real love, confidence and respect.

3. To render them benevolent, friendly, kind, forgiving and courteous.

4. To render them conscientious and reverent of divine principles.

5. To inspire them with a modest but just self-respect as rational and immortal beings, and a due mutual respect for each other.

6. To give them confirmed habits of self-discipline and self-control.

7. To bring all their loves into healthful, orderly and harmonic activity.

Fifth, let educators understand and wisely make use of the following specific means for accomplishing the aforementioned results:

1. *Example.* Let them take care to be affectionally right themselves; to be what they would have their pupils be; to treat infants and children tenderly, gently, benignly and lovingly; to speak to them and to all around them in like manner; and thus by looks, tones, gestures, and all other indications to give them the best possible impressions. This treatment should commence at birth and never cease. Children are responsive, imitative beings. Let them not be taught by an evil example to be affectionally perverse.

2. *Habituation.* Insist perseveringly on their exercising their affectional powers aright, and on their restraining their wrongly indulged appetites and feelings as they ought. Let them exercise their right loves, and disuse their wrong ones, till habit is confirmed. Habit is well termed "second nature." Once established it is not easily changed. Give the right, the good and the delightful all the advantage of habit. Habituation is indispensable in education, especially affectional education.

3. *Association.* All things familiar belong to association; and all familiar things exert their influence, for good or evil, on the young soul. Scenery, objects, sights, sounds, vegetables, animals, persons, playmates, schoolfellows, industry and amusements all make their impressions. They sweeten or embitter, purify or corrupt, ennoble or degrade the passional nature. Let educators see that they be rendered salutary and beneficent.

4. *Contrast.* When the educated become old enough to appreciate opposites, let them be occasionally, yet judiciously, placed in circumstances to know how abhorrent and dreadful are the evils from which they have been

preserved; and how wretched is the condition of children, youth and people who are suffering those evils. Let them not merely see the gilded exterior of incipient vice and folly, but rather the lower degradations and woes which are the legitimate results of gross and perverse loves. This will indelibly stamp their souls with devotion to affectional righteousness, and also stimulate them to determined efforts for the reformation of the world.

5. *Intimacy*. Parents and all auxiliary educators may act powerfully on the affectional nature of the young by confidential intimacy with them. This must be based on mutual love and truthfulness. Indifference, austerity and despotism on the part of educators, with distrust, fear and slavishness on the part of the educated, work only mischief to the affections. The parent and child, the teacher and learner, should be on such terms of confidential intimacy that their souls may at all times flow into each other congenially. Then the young heart will freely confide all its little hopes, fears, joys, sorrows, desires and difficulties to the older; and the older one will entrust the younger with information, suggestions and counsel of the most delicate and sacred nature, as well as interchange with it the best of sympathies. Thus a sweet reciprocal confidence will mutually expand and genialize their bosoms. And all this may be so conducted as not to destroy but greatly promote true filial reverence. Let sympathetic, confidential intimacy be regarded as an indispensable means of affectional education.

6. *Thought and imagination*. By thought and idealizing, all the human loves, from alimentation to veneration, are powerfully excited, and also moderated. A simple suggestive idea enters the mind relative to some affectional pleasure. If retained and cherished, it generates a series of thoughts which soon inflame the imagination, thence awaken passion, and at length generate a permanent desire for gratification. On the other hand, the most pernicious lusts can be gradually conquered if only the thoughts be effectually turned away from their ideal indulgence and concentrated on some good object of pursuit. If a vicious appetite, or wonted criminal lust, can be thus corrected by the power of thought, or a holy love strengthened, educators should regard it as of great importance in affectional education. They should carefully endeavor that the educated be disciplined to cherish right thoughts, and to avoid evil imaginations. Much may be done to this end by keeping them from witnessing demoralizing exhibitions, from being corrupted by evil conversation, and from being poisoned by vile reading; but the grand preventive of all such mischief will be found in habituating

them to cherish only right thoughts and a pure imagination. Thought, idealization, imagination, is the key of their affectional citadel.

7. *Religion.* This is the last great lever of affectional education; and it is absolutely indispensable. The veneration and love of God, and of his law and righteousness, is the mightiest of all human affections. To this all others must do homage. Let educators develop and perfect it in their pupils by all suitable influences. Let it not be so developed as to be a servile and superstitious fear; but a profound, worshipful, filial love for the universal, all-perfect Father; and not merely for a Deific Person, but also for divine principles, attributes and qualities, as exemplified by God, angels, and good men. If this grand religious power can once be developed and enthroned, its scepter will become a sovereign regulator of the entire affectional nature.

Education of the Intellect

The intellectual powers, faculties or capabilities are comprised in seven classes:

1. With our *perceptive* powers we acquire knowledge of existing facts.

2. With our *retentive* powers we retain more or less of what has come to our knowledge, and are able to remember it.

3. With our *reflective* powers we examine, consider, compare, reason and judge. We inquire into the nature, causes and effects of things.

4. With our *imaginative* powers we form mental images of external realities, or images of things partly real and partly fictitious. We idealize and fictionalize indefinitely.

5. With our *inventive* powers we devise and contrive new things – new combinations of matter, of mechanical power, vegetable or animal nature, or human association and cooperation, and so on through all the departments of external and internal nature.

6. With our *expressive* powers we express, or manifest, by speech, language, signs, gestures, looks and actions, our knowledge, our thoughts, convictions, opinions and mental determinations – as also our emotions, passions and affections.

7. With our *executive* powers we are enabled to actualize our ideals somewhat in the outward world, to reduce theories to practice, to be skillful constructors, elaborators, and performers.

Now what is the desideratum in intellectual education? Health again
– intellectual health. This requires well-balanced activity, order, and
harmony. The intellectual faculties, being all good in their place, ought to
be qualified to perform their appropriate functions. How may this be done?
By suitable intellectual education.

Let parents and all educators of the young consider well their responsibilities and how to handle them. Their children and pupils are in their
hands to be intellectually educated. Let them begin by ascertaining as
nearly as they can:

1. What the hereditary, gestatorial, and actual developments of their
children are; what the capabilities and marked tendencies of their intellectual powers are; and what can or cannot be made of each child intellectually.
For there are radical and almost unalterable differences between children in
these particulars, which require corresponding differences of educational
treatment. There is no such thing as running all through the same mold. It
is wisely ordered that there shall be a variety of gifts, aptitudes, and minis-
trabilities of usefulness among the individualities of human nature.

2. What the activity and strength of each pupil's nervous system are,
whether great, or small, or average. Because otherwise too much haste may
be made, or too little, in urging forward the intellectual powers.

3. Whether, as the process goes on, any of the faculties are getting along
too fast, and others too slow; so that one flourishes greatly at the expense of
another, and the requisite balance is being destroyed. It is not wise to make
a prodigy of a child in one direction, and a simpleton in all others. Let it be
remembered that there is always a limited quantity of vital stamina in each
individual, which if overdrawn at one outlet must leave others deficient.
Peter must not be robbed to pay Paul.

4. Whether the age, physical development and affectional state of
the pupil are sufficiently mature to admit of vigorous intellectual drilling.
Nothing is gained, but much lost, by overtaxing the young intellect, hurry-
ing the child into the man, and breaking down sickly constitutions with
premature or excessive study.

5. What general sphere the pupil is best adapted to occupy, and probably must occupy in mature life, to be successful, useful and happy. If this
point can be rationally settled, let *that* be taught which is indispensable
to all, with the addition of what will probably be needed for actual use in
the anticipated sphere of adult life; but let not time, strength and other

resources be wasted in lumbering the intellect with useless freight. Of what use are the dead languages, for instance, to one who has no taste for them, and who will never be likely to use them, even if able to do so?

6. Whether the child or scholar can be best taught by direct lessons and close application to study, or by more general observation, by free conversation, by illustrations, by association, and by other indirect means. For there are minds that can easily be educated by the latter method, but not by the former, especially in childhood and early youth. Wise educators will choose their methods judiciously.

7. What the opportunities and means are which can be commanded for giving particular individuals an intellectual education; i.e. whether ample or limited. If anything desirable must be omitted, let it be that which is least important. The indispensable, or most necessary, should always take precedence.

These preliminaries being judiciously settled, let the following order of induction and progress be followed. Begin with the child, or pupil, as him or herself first to be studied, and thence, proceed:

1. From that which is nearest in kind, locality or time, to what is most distant.

2. From that which is most noticeable to what is least so.

3. From that which is most exterior to what is most interior.

4. From that which is most simple to what is most complex.

5. From that which is most material to what is most spiritual.

6. From that which is most knowable to what is least so.

7. From the comprehensible finite to the incomprehensible infinite.

According to this order we may see that a person, having a good intellectual education, will know himself and human nature as well or better than any thing else that exists. Though he began with studying his hands and fingers, he has come at length to a good practical knowledge of his body, soul and spirit; he knows himself physically, affectionately, intellectually and religiously. He is well versed in anatomy, physiology and pneumatology. He understands his wants, rights and responsibilities. Hence also he knows mankind within and without; what they are, what they have been and what they are destined to be; their constitution, their relationship and all that is essential to their welfare.

He has a good knowledge of the earth, its animals, vegetables, soils, minerals etc.; but is best informed respecting that part of its contents nearest his own home; because he studied first the geography, zoology, botany, geology, mineralogy etc. of his immediate vicinity, of his own country, and thence outwardly to the remotest parts. So he understands best the climate and atmospheric peculiarities of his own latitude and longitude. So of language; so of history; so of all that can be known in the earth, or in the heavens. His education began, proceeded and was matured in the natural order. From himself he went outward, exploring in all directions the fields of knowledge. Thus he ascended upward through nature to nature's God. First well instructed in the nursery, in the vicinage, in the continent, in the earth, in the skies, he is now qualified to fly on the wings of thought far abroad into the boundless expanse of the Infinitarium.

Compare one thus educated with the thousands of *nominally* well educated, the graduates from high schools, academies, colleges and universities. Behold great numbers of them as profoundly ignorant of themselves, and of what is practically necessary to their physical, affectional, intellectual, industrial, economical, social and religious welfare, as they are learned in mere fashionable lore. They know something of the dead and of foreign languages, but far too little of their own. They are profound in knowledge, useless or worse than useless, but ignorant of a thousand things necessary to their own highest happiness. I will not descend into specifications. Men of sound common sense, acquainted with real life in its practicals, know how defective is much that passes for "liberal education."

I think the dead languages, heathen classics etc., held so important in our old-fashioned educational institutions, are worse than useless in nineteen out of twenty cases. It is high time that this old folly were exploded. It is incompatible with my educational theory, and with the genius of the Practical Christian Republic. Possibly five students in a hundred might be encouraged to master the dead languages, and plod through the so-called classics. These should have a natural predisposition and adaptation to such learning. Let the rest read the compound wisdom and folly of heathen masters in some one of our numerous translations, or, what would generally be better, leave them unread. Let the grand aim be a thorough knowledge of the natural sciences and arts, and of the living languages. An intelligent naturalist, geologist, chemist, physiologist, agriculturist, is worth a thousand adepts in the Greek and Roman classics. Let living knowledge be accumulated and perfected, not the learning of dead pagans.

I propose then that the young be taught:

1. Humanity or anthropology and all that is peculiar in the manifestations of human nature.

2. Geography, geology, botany, zoology and whatever belongs strictly to the earth, as to its substance and productions.

3. Meteorology and everything appertaining to the atmosphere which surrounds our globe.

4. Chemistry, or the science which investigates and explains the composition and changes of all material substances.

5. Electricity, magnetism, and all the more subtle material forces.

6. Astronomy, with all that appertains to it.

7. Theology, with all that is naturally and legitimately connected with it.

Now I do not expect that any possible intellectual education which can be given to men and women previous to maturity is to make them thorough masters of all these sciences, nor of any of them. The best that can be done will be to induct them into such an elementary knowledge of these sciences, as shall supply their rudimental necessities and qualify them for all desirable progress. They will then have learned what there is to learn, and how to prosecute those sciences which most attract them. This, to be sure, is a great work to accomplish in the youthful soul. It fairly launches the intellectual ship, and provides for its long voyage of discovery on the ocean of knowledge.

In effecting all this do I propose to exhaust the student, by confining the attention to one particular, or one topic, or one theme, or one department of science at a time till that be mastered or have received all the attention it demands? By no means. Beginning at the right point I would so apply my rules as to give the child some rudimental ideas in each of the seven great sciences above specified before he was five years old. But I would not overstrain a single one of his faculties, nor tire, not disgust him. But whatever might be the range and variety of my inculcations, each child should then and always have most knowledge of himself and that which most immediately concerned human nature.

Here is a child in the nursery, just old enough to distinguish persons and things, to understand a few words of the tongue spoken by his parents, to toddle about the room, and to remember some familiar names. His mother is now his principal educator. She is teaching him daily the difference between his feet and his hands, his fingers and toes, and sundry other parts of the body; i.e. physiology. She is teaching him the elements of grammar by the pronunciation of names etc.; the elements of music in a sweet melody of sounds frequently changed to soothe him; the elements of geography by acquainting him with the apartments of the house, the door-yard and garden; the elements of mathematics by counting his hands and fingers; the elements of botany by frequently directing his attention to flowers; the elements of zoology by awakening his admiration for the domestic animals; the elements of astronomy by pointing out to him the full moon in her silvery brightness, or the setting sun; or the glowing stars; the elements of theology by the offering of devout prayers, or the first direct inculcation that there is a great Spirit Father. In many ways, simple, pleasing, and impressive, she inducts her loved one into the rudimentals of the seven sciences. And as the capacities of the child unfold and strengthen, she goes on deeper and wider, more and more systematically, more and more thoroughly with her inculcations.

When the young have fairly become teachable in any science or art, educators should endeavor to give them the following habits. Once fairly formed, they will prove of incalculable value.

1. Of close attention and application, for the time being, to the lesson in hand.

2. Of original thinking and questioning about the more important particulars of their lessons.

3. Of reflecting and reasoning on all subjects for themselves.

4. Of freely expressing by speech, or in writing, and in both ways at different times, their own thoughts, views and feelings.

5. Of taking notes, and making memoranda of what seems most important in any lesson, lecture or case considered.

6. Of criticizing their own productions and performances, and correcting defects therein.

7. Of being humble, modest, candid, frank and straightforward in expressing their own minds, and above all in acknowledging mistakes or errors into which they may have fallen.

I would have educators inculcate knowledge and train the young intellect to think and reason by a great variety of means, but chiefly by the following:

1. In early infancy by intellectual toys and amusements, and by living objects talked about.

2. Subsequently, by a higher grade of pleasing contrivances, pictures, books, conversations and simple lessons, making very light requirements of thought or study till at least seven years of age.

3. Later, by regular lessons adapted to capacity and health, by books, pictures, maps, outlines, models, illustrations, practical exercises and demonstrations.

4. Later still, by similar appliances of a higher class and adaptation, by lectures added to conversation, observations in real life, and manifold experimental exercises.

In short, I would have them taught by all the instrumentalities, appliances and contrivances discovered and proved to have been worthy of adoption, whether ancient or modern.

Religious Education

I mean by religious education that which trains the young to be, to do, and to suffer always, in all things, conscientiously; i.e. with a supreme reverence for and love of divine principles. This is recognizing the sovereignty of those principles as supreme and absolute. It is acknowledging and cherishing the very highest obligations which can bind the human soul. It is enthroning in the mind the purest and strongest motives by which it can be controlled. It transcends, overrules and corrects all mere philosophy, expediency and policy, and establishes firmly the conviction, that only what is *right* can be *best*. It brings the creature into true spiritual relations with the Paternal Creator, and with fellow creatures. Human beings thus receive the inspirations of the spiritual world, realize that they are accountable for all their conduct, and learn how vast and far-reaching will be the good or evil consequences of their actions. Thus inspired with faith, hope and charity, they may *be, do* and *endure* all things necessary to the sublimest practical results. Thus religious education becomes the life and perfection of the entire superstructure.

All true morality grows out of true religion, derives its vitality from religion, and would die without its sustaining forces, as a tree does when cut away from its roots. Without religion, morals become mere *manners*, liable to change with the fashions of time and place. What are manners without principles? They are little to be trusted.

I have met with a considerable class of persons who praise morality, and seem to despise religion. These are confident that morality can be maintained independently of religion, and ought to be; because religion, in their minds, is always associated with superstition, bigotry, formality or hypocrisy, or with all four together. Now, false religion may, and often does, involve all these evils. So may and does false morality. But true religion and true morality exclude them. We must be careful, however, not to take every person's assumptions as just, when superstition, bigotry, formality or hypocrisy is charged. Some minds mistake facts, and some misapprehend them, through the perverseness of their own prejudices. Let us be intelligent, discriminating, just and candid. And if others are not so, let them go their way. By their fruits will they be known. One thing I am sure of, that no human being ever did or ever will accomplish anything morally great and good without some strong religious principles.

Religious education must be both theoretical and practical. Theoretically the young should be seasonably, gradually and thoroughly indoctrinated into what I call the essential divine principles of the Christian Religion.

I would have educators make these divine fundamental principles the basis of all theoretical religious teaching; following them out into their legitimate bearings; tracing them back to their divine source; simplifying them to the common understanding; adapting them to the comprehension of each mind; and so ultimately bringing all to a complete knowledge both of their nature and practical requirements. In accomplishing so important and complex a process, much discretion, patience and perseverance will be requisite. A beginning will have to be made in early infancy, and progressively followed out in an orderly and well graduated course to adult age. All this should be done in the most simple, natural and pleasant manner possible. But the persistent design should be to graduate every young man and woman a willing subject of acknowledged, well-understood divine principles; so that each should always be able to judge whether any law, custom, habit, practice, act, expression, idea, feeling, was true, right, good and best, by a ready reference to those great first principles. Thus would the sovereignty of divine principles become supreme and absolute over all mere human assumptions and prescriptions.

In respect to practical religious education, I must be somewhat more particular. This should be carried along concurrently with the theoretical, as its inseparable and necessary complement. It consists in habituating the young to be consistent in practice with their acknowledged principles. Now the genius of the Christian religion is averse to all mere external show made to be seen and admired, and insists uncompromisingly on practical substantial goodness. It is therefore extremely simple and unostentatious in respect to what may be called the ceremonials or externals of religion. It does not prohibit them, yet denounces all human *show* of them. It tolerates and even recommends the simpler forms of them, but constantly urges its disciples to transcend them in spirituality and absolute righteousness. This must be impressed on the young indelibly from the outset. For there is no religious error, perhaps I ought to say *vice,* into which mankind more easily slide, than imagining that forms and ceremonies, observances and solemnities, *are religion*; when in reality they are at best only the husk which protects the ripening kernel of religion, and after its full maturity are separable from it, as chaff is from wheat.

Wherever people fall into this error, they become mere idolaters. They substitute the non-essential for the essential, the shadow for the substance of religion; resisting and despising all appeals in behalf of the plain dictates of divine principle. These are the Scribes, Pharisees and Formalists of all ages. Antipodal to these are those extremists who, through disgust with Formalism and Pharisaism, denounce all external manifestations of religious devotion, even its most harmless observances, and strain themselves into a studied anti-formalism, which itself becomes absurdly formal. I would have the young educated to avoid these and all similar extremes.

Practical religion consists in piety, philanthropy and morality. Consequently religious education must relate especially to the habitual practice of these.

Piety. This is love to God, as required in the first great commandment, "Thou shalt love the Lord thy God with all thy heart, and with all thy mind, and with all thy strength." God is a *person,* in respect to all that spiritually constitutes a person. But being an infinite person, finite beings can form only a general idea of his personality, which must be simple or complex, diminutive or grand, according to age and development. The child can conceive of him only as an exalted and mysteriously constituted man. The Mosaic Religion would not tolerate this natural tendency of the mind, because it *finitized* God, was derogatory to his true nature, and led to idolatry. The Christian Religion follows up the same idea, and insists that God shall be worshipped as the great Father-Spirit, who cannot be *limited,* or *localized,* and is accessible to all true worshipers, in all places alike, at the same moment.

It is plain then, that while it is proper to educate the young into the general idea of God's personality, we must not dwell upon it as something comprehensible by finite minds; but hasten to give them the true conception of God as an Infinite Spirit, who is to be known, reverenced and loved, rather in his attributes, qualities and principles than in his personality. Attributes, qualities and principles are comprehensible, in a high degree, by the human mind; but an *infinite* personality is incomprehensible except as a general idea. Hence each finite mind may fully believe that there is an infinite divine Mind or Spirit possessing all the constituents of personality; but no one can definitely know and comprehend more of that Mind or Spirit than fills the measure of his own limited soul. It must of necessity be so with all children, youth and adults, and even with the angels of heaven.

It is plain that God cannot be truly loved by any creature who does not love his divine attributes, qualities and principles. One who hates Truth cannot love God. One who hates Justice cannot love God. One who hates Mercy cannot love God. One who hates Purity cannot love God. One who hates Charity cannot love God. Many imagine that they love, worship and serve God as a person, while they have no love for divine principles, and are in a state of rebellion against them. I would have the young assiduously educated to love God as a Spirit, in those holy attributes which man can spiritually cherish within himself, which he can exemplify towards his fellow man, and which render him Godlike.

Let the loving and devout mother, the wise and conscientious father, and educators of every grade, impress on each expanding soul such views of God's Love, Wisdom, Power and Perfection as shall exclude every particle of hatred, revenge, partiality, injustice, untruthfulness, cruelty, selfishness and weakness. Let the profound conviction be deeply rooted in each unfolding mind, that the All-Perfect Father is incapable of malevolence or enmity towards any of his offspring, even the most unthankful and perverse of them. That he is the disinterested and unchangeable friend of all. That his highest glory consists in promoting their greatest good. That he commands nothing tyrannically, and forbids nothing which ought to be allowed. That he requires us to do only what is best for us, and prohibits only what is injurious. That he cannot interfere to prevent evildoers from rendering themselves miserable, if they will persist in their evil-doing; nor restore them to goodness and happiness against their own will, nor without their sincere repentance and reformation. But that he desires the repentance of all sinners, that he is ever using the wisest means to induce all to come to repentance, and that all who truly return to him are graciously accepted. That all the good in every universe emanates directly or indirectly from him. That he is present by his Spirit in all good angels, spirits and beings, prompting, inspiring and directing them, and through them ministering continually to the spiritual and temporal wants of the more necessitous. That his providence and government are omnipresent and perfect over all beings. That he is to be loved, trusted, and obeyed in all things, as one who will never leave nor forsake his dutiful children, but cause all things to work together for their highest ultimate good. That no wickedness can permanently prosper, but righteousness and truth will finally triumph. That sinners are their own worst enemies, who though they inflict great sufferings on the innocent, are certain to procure greater ones to themselves; and therefore are always to be pitied rather their hated. That the Infinite Father overrules partial evil for universal good, and in the fullness of time will completely explain the dark mysteries of human experience so as to vindicate all his ways, by demonstrating them to have been dictated by unerring Love and Wisdom. Therefore that God is absolutely worthy to be loved with all the heart, all the understanding and all the strength of all his moral offspring.

Thus let parental and all auxiliary educators gently lead the young to love their Heavenly Father and all that is divine with a perfect love, which they will find to be the highest bliss of the soul. By precept and example let them teach all under their guidance to meditate often in the retirement of the closet, in the field under the starry firmament, and through all nature's walks, with reverence and gratitude, on the divine perfections; to pray daily in secret for divine Love and Wisdom; to confess their sins with true contrition and purpose of heart to forsake them; to resign themselves meekly under affliction in hope that all things will be divinely overruled for good; and to persevere without faltering in all righteousness, under every discouragement and trial, with a full assurance of ultimate victory. Thus will they cherish more and more of the Holy Christ-Spirit in their souls, become more and more subject to the sovereignty of divine principles, grow more and more holy as God is holy, more and more perfect as he is perfect, more and more his true children, and consequently less and less the mere creatures of external control.

This religious teaching and formation of character must not be done artificially, austerely, ostentatiously, sanctimoniously or superstitiously; but it must be done artlessly, familiarly, meekly, unpretentiously and naturally, on every fit occasion which occurs. It should come in everywhere as a natural, simple, sincere recurrence to divine and spiritual principles, and as the application of fundamental religious obligation to all the feelings, expressions, actions and pursuits of life. Otherwise it will degenerate into heartless formality, cant, superstition and hypocrisy. I do not mean that religious education shall be unsystematic, or left at haphazard to take care of itself; I do not mean that there should be no regular public seasons of devotion, that there should be no family worship, that schools should never be opened with religious exercises, that children should never be taught the use of little prayers to God and hymns of praise, and that the young should be brought up as if all frank and definite expression of their highest sentiment were useless or pernicious. I have no fellowship with such extremes. Let piety be natural, free, sincere, all-pervading, persistent and Christlike. Let it be systematically inculcated and practiced by all in their own best way. But let it not be neglected, suppressed, perverted, distorted, abused.

Philanthropy. This is love to man, as expressed in the commandment, "Thou shalt love thy neighbor as thyself." It is pure good will; not the love of our neighbor's personal peculiarities, qualities or appendages, but the disinterested love of his highest good for time and eternity. The young must be carefully and unequivocally impressed with the deep conviction, that they cannot possibly love God and yet hate man; that piety and philanthropy must live, or die, together; that God never accepts any pretended love, worship or praise which is offered to him by an injurer, persecutor, hater of man; that he regards the good or the evil done by man to man as done to himself, and acts accordingly; that he delights in justice and mercy, truth and goodness, purity and charity, shown by man to man, more than in any expressions of piety, any sacrifices, any worship offered directly to himself; and that nothing which man can say or do will be received as a substitute for genuine love to man. This is the plain doctrine of Jesus Christ, and must be insisted on continually throughout the entire religious education of the young. And so much the more assiduously must it be inculcated, as mankind in past ages have shown a general proneness to ignore and practically disregard it. Nothing is more common than to see piety divorced from philanthropy, and multitudes blindly, stupidly worshipping God while trampling humanity under foot as the mire of the streets. Let it not be so in the Practical Christian Republic.

I close on this point with one caution to parents and teachers, which is, to be sure and make the young understand distinctly the difference between loving their fellow creatures with the love of complacency, and loving their internal persons with reference to their absolute highest good. They cannot love enemies, offenders and hateful persons with the love of complacency; this kind of love can exist only between those who are reciprocally congenial or agreeable to each other. It will be utterly useless therefore to urge it in words. It cannot be felt. And if the young think this is the love which they are required to feel for every human being, the requirement will become worse than a nullity; it will induce rebellion, cant or hypocrisy. But if they are enabled to see that the love required to their neighbor, and even to their enemy, is the sublime, disinterested love of benevolence – the pure charity which looks through all external hatefulness and repulsive surroundings to the absolute highest present and eternal good of the real being – its excellency will be felt, its practical possibility admitted, and the divine obligation in some measure obeyed. Then, if nothing more can be gained, there will be a determined purpose formed never to do a known injury to the most unlovable, disagreeable, hateful human being. And this in most cases will be followed, sooner or later, by truly benevolent efforts to do the disliked party positive good. Thus will pure philanthropy take its appropriate place as the inseparable companion of pure piety.

Morality. This implies all kinds of right outward behavior, conduct or manners, whether with respect to one's self, to other individuals, to human society in general, or to God. All true morality must be rooted in religious principle, in order to be reliably permanent. This is already understood. What I now wish to urge is, that the young must be so educated as to attach great importance to *good works* – positive, scrupulous, unequivocal, everyday morality; not as the tree of righteousness, but as its requisite and indispensable fruit. They are not to be taught that morality is the whole of religion, nor the foundation of righteousness, nor the ground of self-merit in the sight of God. But they are to be taught that piety and philanthropy in the heart can demonstrate their existence only by their fruits in the outward conduct; that faith without works is dead or useless; that it is shameless hypocrisy to pretend to love God yet not keep his commandments,[5] or to love man and yet treat him as if he were a brute, or to be personally pure and yet live a life of corruption and crime.

Actions speak louder than words. He who is obviously immoral in word and deed, whether toward himself, his fellows, or his God, ought to be ashamed of all pretensions made to piety or philanthropy. If he do his whole duty, he will have nothing to boast of; but if decidedly immoral, he is an actual violator of his undeniable obligations. I would have the young so educated as never to misunderstand that true morality is the fruit of true piety and philanthropy. Let them be carefully guarded against that hollow religionism which is always belittling morality, and also against that equally hollow moralism which is always belittling religion. The former is sour, solemn and ugly – magnifying mere creed-faith and external forms above downright everyday morality. The latter magnifies mere conventional, superficial morality, such as keeps people passably respectable outside of the House of Correction, above all deep-seated religious principle and scrupulous conscientiousness.

Chapter 9

Education for Community Life

Industrial Education

I mean by industrial education that which trains the young to respect, love, and practice useful industry. Industry is habitual diligence in some employment, either bodily or mental. *Useful* industry is that which aids in supplying real human wants, whether of body or mind, so as to increase the sum of human happiness. Every kind of industry which contributes to the comfortable physical subsistence of man, or to the augmentation of his innocent pleasures, or to enlighten, elevate, purify and angelize his soul – whatever promotes his absolute good of body or mind – is useful industry. And that is *most* useful which supplies the *necessaries* of life.

Many kinds of industry are not useful; some may be termed *useless*; and many are *injurious* to human welfare. Contemplate the industrial energy and skill expended by mankind in war, its preparations, concomitants, and adjuncts; in upholding chattel slavery and the secondary kindred oppressions; in sustaining drunkenness, gluttony, debauchery and the numerous vices, follies and hurtful extravagances which are prevalent in the world. Poor foolish mortals certainly work hard to injure themselves and their fellows, to shorten their days, or fill them with misery, to render earth a bedlam and a hell.

Imagine all this industrial energy and skill turned completely round in the opposite direction, so as to preserve life and promote happiness – physically, intellectually, and morally. Then you have my idea of useful industry. And my Social System requires that the young be educated accordingly. What then are the leading incentives to a good industrial education? What the cardinal ends to be sought?

1. *Justice.* A certain amount of industry, manual and mental, is requisite to carry every human being decently through mortal life. This labor must be performed by somebody. Every human being, who has any ability at all to labor, is in justice bound to perform his equitable share. To consume the fruits of other people's industry without rendering an equivalent, according to industrial ability – i.e. to live upon and at the expense of others – is manifest injustice toward them. It is to defraud, oppress, rob them. We must not educate our young to live by robbery, oppression, fraud and injustice, but to bear their part of the burdens of life.

2. *Health.* The health of the human system, physical, mental, and moral, depends largely on exercise. Every part of the body and mind is strengthened by due activity. Much wholesome exercise of the muscles and brain may be had in useful industry. But idleness, effeminacy, sloth and indolence are the foes of health. We must not educate our young to laziness and imbecility.

3. *Competence.* Each individual and family need a certain amount, greater or less, of the good things which useful industry alone supplies. There is enough for all, if all will but do their part towards producing, preserving, distributing and adjusting. This is true of things material, and of things spiritual; of things indispensable, of things convenient and of things innocently pleasurable. If there is insufficiency anywhere, it results from lack of useful industry, from non-production, or waste, or unjust distribution, or carelessness. Somebody is in fault. Let not the fault be in industrial education. Let all do their part towards securing a competence. And let it be remembered that a competence includes what may be necessary to dispense to the unfortunate, as well as to meet the calls of "a rainy day" at home.

4. *Pleasure.* Useful industry, rightly pursued and properly circumstanced, is really pleasurable, really recreative, really delightful; not all kinds of it, not in all degrees, not at all times; but much of it is when pursued under good conditions. The idle and the misemployed are unhappy. The usefully and wisely employed find substantial pleasure in their industry. If you would defraud the young of a large amount of pleasure, withhold from them a good industrial education. If the contrary, confer on them such an education.

5. *Virtue.* All the virtues are fostered by useful industry; all the vices by idleness, and by pernicious industry. This is so obvious to all right thinking minds, that I need add nothing to the statement by way of illustration. To train up the young without habituating them to useful industry would be to place them in what has been aptly designated as "the devil's workshop."

6. *Dignity.* No man or woman can justly respect him or herself, who is too imbecile, or too lazy, or too mean to earn an honest living. No matter how much property, or rank, or fashionable gentility may be possessed, such a human being stands an object of pity, or contempt, by the side of a self-subsisting industrian. The less a person is able and willing to help him or herself, the lower that person sinks in true dignity; always of course excepting cases of absolute misfortune, of infancy, and of old age. All that false and vicious respectability, which prevails with certain classes of people in the old order of society, is to be held disgraceful under my proposed Social System. To be waited on, served and pampered by menials; to be useless, helpless dolls; to be masters and mistresses; to be mere consumers; to be fattened and decorated paupers, maintained by slaves, is to sink to the lowest rank of humanity. These are the ideas to be inculcated and acted upon in our Practical Christian Republic. True dignity and honor are inseparable from usefulness; and he is greatest who is most usefully industrious.

7. *Charity.* Charity is not in mere word, but in deed; not in effeminate sentimentalism, but in substantial benefits conferred on the needy. But how can we confer these substantial benefits without possessing the ability to do so? And how can we honorably possess that ability without exercising ourselves in useful industry? We may have honorably inherited something from others; but we cannot so honorably and satisfactorily confer benefits on the necessitous as with our own hands, or out of the fruits of our own industry. Then we bestow what God has made ours by the best of titles. Other charities are but giving away what we never earned. Let the young be taught that the most truly charitable benefits they can bestow on others are those devised by their own intellects and wrought out by their own personal industry.

I will now suggest several points to be understood and considered by educators with respect to their pupils. They should, if possible, ascertain and determine:

1. What department of useful industry the young are predisposed to prefer as their principal one. Many give early indications of genius and taste in a certain direction. When this bent of mind can be innocently and practically indulged, it should be. If not, the next best thing must be done. But no one should be exclusively confined to a single industrial calling. There should be a principal one and then two or three subsidiary or contingent ones, so as to secure choice and alternation, if health or success require it.

Yet the idea is not to be acted upon, that the same individual may excel in several different callings, or accomplish much by changing frequently one kind of employment for another. Some few individuals may be adapted to such variety and changes, but not the generality.

2. What those are capable of and most fit for who have no marked predilection, genius, taste or choice. There will be many such. They should be trained, with the young in general, to the common industries proper to all. Then they should be habituated to one, two or three, as primary and subsidiary, which on the whole appear to be most appropriate and useful.

3. How in each case there may be a due and well balanced amount of manual and mental industry, according to age and circumstances; and how good habits may be formed in respect to manual and mental labor. It is not to be expected that all will perform the same amount of these two kinds of industry. There will be great differences. Nor is it to be expected that each individual will excel equally in both kinds, or delight equally in both, or be occupied equal portions of time with both. It will be so with very few. But all should be educated to perform habitually the amount of manual labor requisite to physical health, and the amount of mental labor requisite to intellectual vigor. No faculty of body or mind should be left to suffer from inertia.

4. By what means useful industry can be rendered most subservient to the seven cardinal ends of Justice, Health, Competence, Pleasure, Virtue, Dignity and Charity. All these ends should be sought in every case. If it be impossible to subserve all, then as many of them as possible should be secured. And certainly no one of them should be intentionally contravened. But if, in extreme cases, any one of them must be sacrificed, let it never be Justice, Virtue, or Charity.

5. What perversions and abuses of industrial activity are liable to be committed, and how they may be most effectually guarded against. Children and youth, as well as adults, often make mistakes, even in practicing useful industry. They over-exert themselves in one direction, and under-work in another. They are unseasonable, irregular and intemperate, both in bodily and mental pursuits. Their errors should be carefully corrected at the earliest period after being discovered. It is the business of educators to bring them upon the stage of adult life with good industrial habits, and as free as possible from all those irregularities, perversions and abuses which now so often defeat success.

Economical Education

This is closely connected with industrial education, yet is not identical with it. The young need to be taught economy in all things. They ought to be trained by instruction and habituation to economize their time, their strength, their skill, their money, their talents and all their resources. This is what I mean by economical education.

Reflect for a moment on the waste and loss which the majority of mankind suffer through bad economy. Even the honestly and usefully industrious suffer much. Through ignorance or wrong habit they are great losers in numberless ways. One loses a great deal of time, and is often out of season. Another lays out muscular strength to great disadvantage. Another throws away skill foolishly. Another contrives to enjoy less at a cost of two dollars than might be obtained for one. Another has good talents, but does not know how to employ them effectively. So of all the resources of the human soul. They must be economized aright, or they fail to satisfy our wants. A sound economical education would be almost indispensable to the success of my Social System. I offer these precepts, to be inculcated and practiced. Let educators make such exceptions, qualifications and additions as enlightened reason shall dictate or as peculiar circumstances may necessitate.

1. Depend not on others to do for thee what it is wisely possible to do for thyself. Hire not, beg not, accept not unnecessary assistance.

2. Find out the best method of doing what must be done, and practice it.

3. Do all things in their proper season.

4. Do all things thoroughly in their kind.

5. Do nothing that is useless.

6. Destroy nothing, damage nothing, waste nothing wantonly, recklessly, carelessly.

7. Save, repair and be careful of all things useful; make the most of them.

8. Consume nothing on thy body or mind that is injurious, however tempting.

9. Consume nothing that may wisely be dispensed with, however harmless.

10. Consume nothing which conscience, reason or charity forbids, however fashionable.

11. Reduce all mere artificial wants to the lowest terms of health, decency and innocent indulgence.

12. Purchase nothing which thou really dost not need.

13. Purchase only what is good in its kind – not those cheap things which prove dear.

14. Purchase seasonably and in sufficient quantity.

15. Purchase nothing for which thou art not able to pay according to terms; beg rather.

16. Pay promptly, cheerfully, liberally.

17. Do away with all credits, if possible, both in buying and selling. But if thou must owe, let it be to *one* well secured creditor in a large sum, rather than to *many* clamorous creditors in small sums.

18. As a seller be open, truthful and upright; no jockey, no higgler, no sharpster.

19. Demand an equitable price, and insist on it; let thy words be few in trade. Sell only that which is good in its kind, that which is fit for use, that which sensible people choose; little else, however marketable.

20. Take advantage of no one's necessity to obtain high prices; be not an extortioner.

21. Give ample weight and measure; be accommodating; stand not in thine own light. Penny wisdom is pound folly.

22. Be no gambler, no mere speculator; never seek to enrich thyself by making others poorer. True trade is that which profits both parties. Covet not unearned wealth.

23. So deal with all that the honest, the upright and the liberal will delight to deal with thee.

24. Deal as little as possible with the unprincipled, churlish and quarrelsome.

25. Keep current, orderly and reliable accounts, not only with others, but with thyself, that thou mayest know thy standing at any time.

26. Put in writing all agreements and understanding that are of any considerable importance; it will pay.

27. Preserve all writings which prove or explain transaction long after they seem to be useless; they may be wanted.

28. Study the writings, and treasure up the maxims of sound economists, whether ancient or modern, and reduce all that is unexceptionable to practice.

29. Make and adopt all possible improvements in the various economics of life.

30. Be not ashamed of true economy in the presence of sumptuaries, spendthrifts and simpletons, though genteel, fashionable ones; being careful only not to slide into parsimony and miserism.

In accordance with these precepts would I have the young of both sexes thoroughly trained from infancy to adult years. The motto should ever be before them, *Economy in all things* – in time, strength, skill, money, talent, capability and resources of every description.

In this matter of economy, notorious facts indicate that multitudes have been so educated, or I would say miseducated, as to be adepts in consuming, wasting, perverting and destroying both the spontaneous wealth of Nature and the hard earned products of human industry. I am inclined to think that all the perishing classes might be comfortably subsisted on what is thus lost. My mind even now recurs to families whose children were brought up to waste and destroy more property than would have sufficed to bring up twice their number. And yet several of these families had hard drudging parents, one or both of whom struggled under an almost insupportable burden of toil, scheming and anxiety to supply the wants of their dependents.

There should be a wise and habitual economy in producing and consuming, in acquiring and expending, in planning and executing, in saving and dispensing, in transporting, exchanging and using all things. It should be so in the house and out of the house, with individuals, with families and with associations, in respect to all good things. And if it were so, who can calculate how much of hardship, privation, poverty and misery would be prevented? or how much of convenience, comfort, wealth, virtue and happiness would be secured?

Social Education

By social education I mean that which trains the young to propriety of feeling and conduct towards their fellow human beings in all the intercourse of life. A vast amount of happiness, or of unhappiness, depends on social influences. No individual exists, acts, speaks, thinks or feels wholly uninfluenced by others, nor wholly without an influence on others. We are preeminently social beings. A large portion of our wakeful conscious life is occupied with social concernments. It cannot be otherwise. It follows therefore that the young should be educated to feel, think, speak and act with propriety in all their social relations and intercourse.

Let the young be trained to behave with propriety towards their parents, elders and superiors. Reverence, docility, modesty and kindness are indispensable to this. Order is said to be Heaven's first law.[1] Order forbids that the young should treat their parents, elders and superiors irreverently, self-conceitedly, impudently or unkindly. The Christian religion explicitly and repeatedly enjoins this ancient righteousness of the young in their behavior towards parents and elders. "Honor thy father and thy mother."[2] The experience of all ages has demonstrated that this divine ordinance cannot be violated without the most deplorable consequences to all parties concerned.

There are two evil extremes into which this kind of education may run: training the young to an abject, slavish subjection, or an irrational deference for mere authority; and training them to equality, self-sufficiency, debate and contempt of all authority. In the former extreme there is despotism, austerity and tyranny on the part of the parents, elders and superiors; whilst on the part of the young there is slavish fear, crippling constraint, mental degradation and many demoralizing effects. In the latter extreme there is indifference, impertinence, impudence, contempt, disobedience and all manner of confusion on the part of the young; whilst parents, elders and superiors are degraded, insulted, abused and rendered miserable.

It is hard to say which of these extremes is most abhorrent. At present the tendency, at least in our country, is to the latter error. And it will require the greatest consideration, care and perseverance in the new order of society, to counteract this evil tendency, without running back insensibly into the old extreme. It is lamentable to see so many children and youth of our times precociously old, assuming and contemptuous. They look, speak and act towards their elders, not merely as if they were equals with them, but quite their betters. They are far from that reverence, docility, modesty and respectful kindness which is so becoming and so salutary in the well educated. The fruits of all this are evil and only evil continually.[3] These miseducated beings graduate into adult life and society only to carry out their pernicious immorality in all manner of lawless practices, and, what is still worse, to marry and propagate a new generation of their own like. Such mischiefs *must* and *will* be prevented, under my Social System. Educators must see to this.

Let the young be trained to behave with propriety towards equals, juniors and inferiors. They cannot do this without respecting each other's rights, regarding each other's welfare of body and mind, carefully avoiding to inflict unnecessary pain, frankly yet kindly reproving wrongs, generously forgiving acknowledged offenses, making reasonable allowance for weaknesses and incidental faults, being uniformly courteous, and scrupulously abstaining from all inflictions of injury defensive as well as offensive. Not a blow, a word, a gesture, a look, should be indulged, much less repeated or approved, that is contrary to social propriety. All usurpation, tyranny, brute force, fighting, quarreling, hectoring, contempt and abuse must be rebuked and superseded, in the family, in the school, at work and at play. All base rivalries, jealousies, hatreds and revenges must be put away by the appliances of love and wisdom. The older and stronger must not be allowed to domineer over the younger and weaker, nor the intelligent to despise the simpler minded, nor the more favored to contemn the less favored.

The world is full of such mischief. It must not be tolerated in the new social state. Equals with equals and superiors with inferiors must be educated to live in love, courtesy and peace. And above all it must be held abominable for a superior to insult, trample on or take advantage of one who either is or is imagined to be an inferior. It is a great work to keep all these little socialities right; but it is worth the cost, and educators must not shrink from a vigilant and patient discharge of their duty.

Let the young be trained to behave with propriety towards strangers, foreigners, the poor, the ignorant, the degraded and all the commonly despised classes. How mean and base is it to be uncourteous, inhospitable and neglectful to the stranger, who is exactly in the condition to need the offices of friendship, and to whom the least kindness will seem a great favor! How revolting to see a fellow creature hated, spurned, insulted, or unkindly treated, because born in another country, or speaking another language, or colored with a different skin, or educated in a different religion, or belonging to a lower class, or dressed in a different garb, or unfortunately brought up in ignorance, or marked by some personal deformity, or destitute of money, or crushed under the heel of oppression, or laboring under insanity! All such are to be treated humanely, compassionately, kindly, considerately; never haughtily, contemptuously, cruelly, unfeelingly; never in a manner which either justice, courtesy or charity would condemn.

This is a matter never to be passed over with indifference. Children readily imbibe the prejudices, likes and dislikes of their parents, teachers and associates; and as readily their morals. Hence the universal prevalence of feuds and quarrels among mankind, originating in mere narrow-mindedness and clannishness of education. It is sickening to see the little ways of clanship and caste, as well as the great ones of nationality. Nothing of all this must be encouraged, or even tolerated in the new order. It is incompatible with my

Social System, which rests on the Love and Wisdom of God as gloriously manifested through Jesus Christ.

Let the young be trained to behave with propriety toward enemies, offenders and the vicious classes. It is wrong to injure enemies, offenders, etc. either in body or mind. It is wrong to hate them. It is wrong to withhold any needed good from them because they are unthankful and evil, vicious and perverse, hateful and injurious. It is wrong to feel, speak or act toward them otherwise than as their sincere well-wishers.

The animal instincts and impulses, which are developed in human nature before the spiritual sentiments can be rendered commanding, rise up in wrath, violence and retaliation against enemies and offenders. Resistance of injury with injury, and the punishment of offenders vindictively, will be found common among children, as among adults not Christianized in their upper nature. It will therefore require the best and highest moral culture to place the young on the right track and keep them there. Nevertheless, it must be done. Educators can do it by divine assistance and perpetual diligence. Let them insist on the practical observance of the following precepts:

1. The worst of human beings may be converted into good ones, and God wills that they should be.

2. The good of no human being, however wicked or hateful, must be disregarded. It is wicked to injure even the wicked.

3. God loves his enemies; and we must ours. He reproves and rebukes his offenders, yet always seeks their good; we must do the same with ours. True love worketh no ill to its object. We may reprove, disfellowship and if need be forcibly restrain evildoers; but we must never do them a known injury.

4. Evil cannot be overcome with evil, but only with good.

5. "It is better to suffer wrong than to do wrong."[4]

6. The worst enemy and the vilest offender injures himself more than he can injure the innocent; he cannot escape the evil of his own hands; he will receive a just retribution in harvesting the evil seed he sows.

We ourselves are often sinners against God and our fellow creatures, and need great forbearance; let us act out the goodness toward our enemies and injurers which we hope to have exercised toward us. Why are we less vile, offensive and guilty than our enemies and offenders? Why are they worse than we? If we had been in their circumstances and they in ours, are we sure we should now be less evil, than they? Ought we to boast and be vindictive?

God knoweth all things; he will do justly by all; he will suffer nothing to injure us, if we be followers of that which is good; let him judge and dispose of all our enemies, all our offenders, all the wicked. Therefore we will avoid enemies and offenders when possible, befriend them when in distress, reform them if we can, pity rather than hate them, do them the good which may be in our power, but injure them intentionally never. We will do nothing, say nothing, desire nothing that shall make them worse in character or condition.

Let this be done "line upon line, and precept upon precept,"[5] against all obstacles and discouragements, till ingrained into the whole texture of their character. It will work two grand results: one's own highest happiness, and the constant diminution of evil in others, till there be none left on earth to overcome or endure. The contrary education ever has had and ever must have just the contrary effect. It keeps man a fighting animal, and reproduces all the evils it professes to repress.

Thus let education comprehend and foster true piety, philanthropy and morality. Then will the young be enrolled in the beautiful garments of practical Christian righteousness, crowned with diadems of spiritual excellence, qualified for every kind of earthly usefulness, and made meet at last "for the inheritance of the saints in light."[6]

Educational Institutions

The Family. I know that the family is not commonly regarded as an educational institution. But I deem it a very important one; partly for what it is naturally, and partly for what it ought to be and may be made. It needs little reflection to learn that the family is naturally and necessarily a very influential educational institution. Consider how much of education, for good or evil, almost every human being receives in the family. There generation, gestation, lactation, refection and all the rudimentals of education operate to form the character. If family education be right up to twelve years of age, there is everything to hope for the future man or woman. If very wrong, there is much to fear. All other educational institutions are greatly affected by family influences. If these have been good, how easy to build on the foundation laid! If bad, how exceedingly difficult to overcome and correct their mischief!

The father and mother are principals in this family seminary. All the adults are assistant teachers; so are the older brothers and sisters. What then should be the qualifications of these principal and assistant educators? Alas, what are they in the generality of cases! There is yet little absolutely good family education in the world. Much of it is absolutely bad. Is it any wonder that they turn out such swarms of untoward pupils?

Under my System the family will gradually become a very systematic and thorough educational institution. When the parents themselves shall be persons well educated; when all the domestic and adult members of the family shall also be well educated; and when there shall be no vile distinctions of caste remaining, it is easy to see that children will come into the world and be developed from infancy to early youth amid exemplifications of wisdom and goodness now seldom known even in our most favored families. This consummation, so devoutly to be wished, cannot come soon.[7] But it will come at last, if the Practical Christian Republic be established.

The Nursery and Infant School. It will be found extremely convenient, economical and beneficial in many cases, for several families living in a Community together, to combine their resources for the establishment of a common nursery and infant school. As a general thing these infants will remain only during certain hours of the day. Exceptions might however be provided for by special arrangements of the proprietors.

The establishment must have suitable rooms, playgrounds and conveniences of every description. Great care must be taken to have ample space, good air, good light, and everything healthful as well as pleasant and convenient. There must be separate apartments for the different grades of children, who will be of different ages from nursing babes to children of five years old. There must be open and sheltered places of exercise adapted to all kinds of weather. The nursery must have all the labor-saving accommodations requisite to economy and comfort. The infant school must be furnished with an amplitude of pleasing pictures, intellectual toy apparatus, music, etc., such as experience shall demonstrate to be necessary. And the older children must be inducted into the simpler kinds of useful industry. Of course there must be matrons, superiors and assistants in such an institution.

Such an institution will cost money, time, skill, labor and many experiments for a while. But the expense need not be over-burdensome. Where there is intelligence and a *will* there will be a *way*. If well endowed and well conducted the results can hardly fail to be satisfactory. The proprietors, whether a Community acting together, or a select association formed for that particular purpose, shall incur all the expenses of founding and sustaining this kind of educational institution.

Common Schools and Other Existing Institutions. The common primary school comes next. I would adopt the best existing models of these, with improvements conformable to the seven kinds of education. The modified institution would be a highly improved common school for both sexes. The same in substance may be said of grammar schools, academics and high schools of various adaptation. Thus modified and improved, I would have them liberally sustained as useful educational institutions by the Practical Christian Republic.

As to the Libraries, Reading Rooms, Lyceums and the numerous instrumentalities for mental improvement now in vogue, I hold most of them in high estimation. I should adopt them, with the modifications necessary to conform them to the new order of things.

Educational Homes. I would establish Educational Homes as the most comprehensive and perfect of all the educational institutions to be sustained in the new social order. These should be *Universities*, in the best sense of that often misapplied term. They should afford all the requisite accommodations, facilities and appliances for giving a first-rate education to children and youth, from the infant group to the highest collegiate class. As such, they would nearly supersede most other educational institutions.

Imagine a flourishing Integral Community of several hundred persons. Imagine, within that Community's territorial domain, a pleasant, healthful educational plat of land, containing from ten to one hundred acres, set off and devoted to the Home. The land included in this educational plat is adapted to the erection of all kinds of buildings necessary to accommodate from one hundred to five hundred persons, pupils, students, teachers, supervisors, professors, etc. It is also adapted to the laying off of common grounds for promenade and recreation, ornamental enclosures, walks, gardens, fields, orchards etc. Thus the culture of useful plants, flowers, roots, vines, shrubs, fruit trees and the like will be provided for. Imagine ample unitary buildings, affording a suitable accommodation for all these industrial educationists of every grade, whether at work, at study, at play, at refection, at rest by night, or assembled together on public occasions. Imagine all the work and care, within doors and without, properly attended to by the educationists themselves, together with a reasonable amount of mechanical and manufacturing industry executed in the production of articles for sale. Imagine the institution to be self-subsisting in respect to its current expenses, leaving out of account the original outlays. Imagine the two sexes to be nearly equal in numbers throughout this Educational Home, to have equal rights and privileges in all respects, and to receive the best qualifications which their natural capabilities can acquire, for all the appropriate pursuits of adult life; and all this side by side, with the utmost freedom of intercourse compatible with unequivocal chastity.

Imagine my theory of education carried fully into practice throughout the establishment. Imagine the buildings and apartments so constructed, that every group of twelve students, more or less, with their two, three or four teachers and assistants, should constitute a family for the time being by themselves; eating, sleeping, working, recreating and doing all things as a select educational family – the two sexes in equal numbers as nearly as practicable. The principal teachers are the responsible heads of these families. They and their assistants together are competent to take all necessary care of their respective families, by night and day, physically, affectionally, intellectually, industrially, economically, socially and religiously. They live on intimate, confidential and endearing terms with all under their family care. And they have all the facilities for promoting their highest progress, improvement and happiness. As occasion requires, but not too frequently, changes are made in the heads and members of these educational families, until the infant at the end of eight, ten or twelve years, graduates a ripe adult Master or Mistress of Arts.

The institution is a whole is under the general supervision of a President and Faculty of Directors, and is sustained outside by a strong patronic Association, who liberally contribute their money, talents and influence to render it worthy of universal admiration and confidence. This Educational Home, once fairly in operation, becomes a most perfect Normal School, sending out annually to all the other educational institutions of the Republic and country excellent teachers of every grade. At the same time, imagine the superior fitness and qualifications of its graduates to enter into the estate of matrimony and to become the heads of families. Can you set any bounds to the blessings which must flow forth in living streams from the Educational Homes? Compare them for a moment with the now elegant and popular resorts called colleges and universities, from which females are generally excluded, and in which so many thousands of young men are ruined in health and morals, or transformed into unnatural and impracticable literati. The best of them are often to be pitied, whilst the worst are to be dreaded as leeches and scourges let loose to prey on the unlettered multitude.

And now I should like to imagine some practicable process by which the pecuniary, physical, intellectual and moral resources for an Educational Home are to be collected and wrought into form. Here indeed is the mountain to be removed. Yet if we have "faith as a grain of mustard seed," we may remove even this high mountain.[8] What ought to be done can be done. Now ought Educational Homes to be established? Yes. Then let those who think so go about the work. It is a great work – a difficult one. The first of these institutions will have to begin small and grow up slowly. Money will come hard. Buildings will be insufficient. Facilities will be deficient. Teachers will be scarce, inexperienced and imperfectly qualified to carry out the new system. All things will work disadvantageously. But the triumph will come at last.

First we must proclaim our ideal, that people may know what ought to be done. Then we must make definite propositions for founding an Educational Home on a small scale. The few that are interested must be intimately associated, so as to cooperate actively in judicious measures for promoting their object. Patrons must be enlisted; a location chosen; a few thousand dollars secured; a commencement made on the requisite buildings; teachers put in train of proper qualification; and thus a small beginning made, such as circumstances will allow. Meantime our Republic will be gradually taking root here and there; Communities will be founded; members will be multiplied; wealth will slowly increase; talent, learning, skill and enterprise will be augmented; unity of feeling, ambition and effort will give consolidation to the new social order; and glorious results will be more easily achievable. All this will come in the fullness of time. But it can come only as the legitimate elaboration of our own faith, zeal, fidelity and invincible perseverance.*

A plan of the whole establishment, as intended to exist when completed, might be drawn. This plan might contemplate a continuous range of block to be put up piece by piece, as occasion should require and resources warrant. Or it might contemplate a chain of cottages, with ample accommodations for study, industry and recreation, located between every two of them, so as to

---

* Here the Inquirer suggests that "an Educational Home might be commenced on a small scale, in an economical way, by adopting the suggestions and recommendations in Mr. O. S. Fowler's *Home for All or the Gravel Wall*."
Expositor: "That is an admirable and highly valuable Work. Mr. Fowler has conferred a great favor on humanity in that book. I am sure that the Communities of our Republic will thankfully avail themselves of his labors. I think it would be practicable to commence an Educational Home piecemeal, so to speak, with the Gravel Wall architecture."

form at last a well arranged village. There would be room for great ingenuity, taste and judgment in devising these architectural plans. Special regard ought to be paid to economics, to health, convenience and beauty. The establishment ought at maturity, if not earlier, to have the very best unitary Bakery, Refectory, Baths, Laundry, etc. It ought to be pleasantly situated with respect to prospect, air and light. It ought to be ventilated in the most improved manner; and should be so constructed as to afford each of its educational families all the privacy necessary to a distinct home. This last mentioned feature of the institution is fundamental. It is the essential characteristic of the establishment – Home. Promiscuity and generalism would reduce the whole concern too nearly to the level of our old educational establishments.

I am aware that Manual Labor Schools, so called, have generally failed; and I can tell you why. Nearly all of them have been shams. Manual labor has been virtually treated as derogatory in them. Few of the teachers have ever condescended to perform it. The majority of scholars have eschewed it. Those who could afford to pay their tuition bills with money previously earned, or supplied by their parents, have pushed forward their studies faster than would be convenient for manual labor pupils. A minority of the students, sometimes a lean one, have tried to pay their way, in part at least, by the labor of their hands. Could they do so, and readily keep pace with their non-working associates? No. Could they enjoy the presence, society and example of their teachers in the shop or field? Not at all. What kind of persons must they work under and with? Perhaps respectable people, in respect to general good feeling, and competent to teach hand labor in their craft, but otherwise unintelligent and uncongenial. What sort of accommodations and facilities have commonly been afforded to these manual labor students? Very ordinary and imperfect ones. Could manual labor under such conditions be either attractive, profitable, or respectable? Just the reverse. Is it to be expected that young men and women will go to such Manual Labor Schools, and thus advertise themselves as obliged to submit to such discomfort and degradation? No; they will work till they get money enough to pay their tuition bills, and be respectable like their teachers and fellows. All such pseudo Manual Labor Institutions ought to fail. They are contemptible. But my proposed Educational Homes are not to have teachers who will shirk manual labor, nor a privileged class who may be allowed to dispense with it, nor an inferior caste invited to advertise their poverty, and obliged to work under disreputable, disagreeable conditions.

Textbooks. A great deal of labor will be requisite to prepare manuals and textbooks suitable for the educational institutions of the new social order. But we have an ample variety of good things to select and adopt from, and ought to avail ourselves of all the acceptable works which the past has bequeathed to us.

What can be done in respect to the doctrines and moral tendencies of many school books, which are filled, or at least highly tinctured with war literature and other objectionable peculiarities? Must we exclude all the fine prose and poetry written in glorification of these hoary evils? I would not have the young kept artificially ignorant of old abominations and the panegyrics uttered on them, but rather thoroughly enlightened, and well provided with antidotes against them. I would recommend the following remedies and counteractions for this demoralizing literature:

1. That all our teachers habitually point out its incompatibility with divine principles, wherever it occurs in the books used by their classes.

2. That all our pupils and students be taught to point out of their own accord these incongruities of their textbooks with divine principles.

3. That new textbooks be compiled which shall exhibit in close contrast the best pieces in glorification of these old evils, and the best pieces on the right side, with a few pertinent comments adapted to set the matter in a true light.

4. That new textbooks be multiplied wholly free from objectionable literature.

Amusements

I include under the general designation of *amusements* all kinds of games, sports, diversions and recreations – all contrivances sought after or delighted in mainly for the sake of the diversion, entertainment, sport or recreation which they afford.

All mankind, in all ages and countries, have been more or less addicted to amusements. Even the few who have denounced and opposed them most strenuously have insensibly fallen into some form of amusement. I am therefore obliged to conclude that there is an ineradicable want in the very constitution of human nature, which can never be satisfied without amusements of some kind. Having come to this conclusion, I concede that they are natural and necessary in their place. And I see that my Social System would be radically defective, if it did not make wise and ample provision for them. But here lies the grand difficulty; to determine what is a wise and ample provision.

Knowing how important a place amusements must occupy, for good or evil, in our Practical Christian Republic, I am extremely anxious to guard against abuses, and at the same time to make liberal provision for all possible true enjoyment. To this end I would gladly furnish such limits to parents, educators and Community legislators as should enable them to institute a well-regulated system of unexceptionable amusements, judiciously adapted to all ages, from the earliest infancy to the ripest maturity. In my judgment, such a system should aim at the following principal objects:

1. The physical health of all concerned.
2. Their mental health and improvement.
3. Their social health and improvement.
4. Their moral health and improvement.
5. Their cheerfulness and contentment at home.

All things, however natural, necessary and good in themselves when rightly used, are liable to perversion and abuse. Amusements are no exception. They are preeminently liable to perversion and abuse, on account of the strong affinity our senses have for them. Just in proportion as they charm and captivate our mere animal and intellectual loves are they dangerous. So much the more likely will mankind be to pervert and abuse them. The whole history of our race admonishes us in thunder tones to bridle our appetites, passions and tastes – to beware of excessive, foolish and perverse pleasures – to be governed always by reason, conscience, divine principles and our Creator's best understood Will. Amusements then must be completely subjected to the highest divine law. That law will condemn and prohibit all amusements which may be justly included under either of the following heads:

Wicked amusements. I mean by wicked amusements all such as are positively contrary in their nature and tendency to essential divine principles. This evil world abounds with such. Mankind have consequently devised and delighted in wicked amusements, from the most ancient times down to our own age. And the more brutal and depraved they have been, the more wicked have been their favorite amusements. Hence the abominable gladiatorial shows among the ancients, in which the actors adroitly murdered each other by piecemeal in protracted personal combats, eagerly watched by thousands of eyes and greeted by shouts of applause at every blood-letting blow. Our modern pugilistic fights, in which hardened bullies bruise each other to death with their fists for prize money and the diversion of profligate spectators, are of the same class. Likewise the ancient combats of men with wild beasts, and the bullfights of our own times in Spanish countries. Cock fighting, dog fighting and all such like cruel entertainments of vulgar ruffians belong in the same category. Likewise the cruel hunting, worrying, teasing, maiming and killing of harmless creatures for sport. Every amusement which consists in or requires the shedding of blood, or which causes unnecessary pain to any living creature, is plainly repugnant to the great law of love and must have a demoralizing influence on all who countenance it. All such are malevolent amusements.

But there are other wicked amusements. All obscene, lascivious, lewd, sexually unchaste amusements must be wicked. Likewise all which are contemptuous toward God, divine principles, and religious responsibilities. Likewise all which entice to sensual intemperance, injustice, falsehood, envy, reckless passion, resentment and revenge. The Bacchanalian orgies, licentious carousals and idolatrous feasts of the ancient pagans were of this nature. So are many of our popular modern orgies, carousals, festivals, balls, theatrical entertainments, plays and games, from the enjoyment of which the partici-pators all come out demoralized to a greater or less extent. Amusements of every description which obviously make people ungodly, sensual, drunken, vicious and unprincipled, must be set down as wicked. Behold our dissipated, libertine, gambling, reckless, profligate votaries of corrupt amusements! Every tree is known by its fruit.

Unhealthful, useless, foolish, derogatory and equivocal amusements. There are many such, which it would be improper to call *wicked*; but which the divine law must prohibit as *wrong*. All such should be avoided. We can find amuse-ments enough which are healthful, useful, wise, elevating and unequivocally salutary. We have no excuse therefore on the score of necessity, for resorting to any which impair our health of body or mind, or which are obviously mere time-killers, or which make fools of us, or which reduce us to the mannerism of the monkey tribes, or which are so equivocal that we are at a loss to deter-mine whether they are good or evil. Any amusement, from the enjoyment of which we cannot conscientiously retire with the conviction that on the whole it has done us good, ought to be immediately eschewed. If it promote innocent mirth and cheerfulness, or otherwise conduce to improved health of the physical and intellectual powers, without injuring the moral character, it is an innocent and commendable amusement. If it have the contrary effect, it is at best more or less a pernicious one, however fashionable, specious or captivating.

Excessive amusements. It is not enough that our amusements be unexceptionable in themselves; they must not be carried to excess. Amusement is not rightfully the business of anyone's life. It should be no one's principal occupation. The moment it is made so, it becomes perverted. It should be regarded as the spice of life, not as the staple food. Its use is to relieve and recreate the otherwise too continually worked powers of the human system. It belongs to the incidental and subsidiary occupations of our earthly pilgrimage – not to the fundamental business. But by carrying amusement to excess it soon becomes an *end*, rather than a *means* of good – a labor, rather than a recreation. It exhausts, rather than refreshes us. It enslaves us into dissipated votaries of its intoxicating exhilaration. Here is one of the greatest dangers connected with amusements. We do not know when we have got enough; we hold on too long; we turn pleasure into pain; we overdo and spoil that which would be real enjoyment, if only kept within the bounds of moderation.

Unseasonable amusements fall under the same condemnation. They may be unobjectionable in all other respects, yet if unseasonably appointed or persisted in they become pernicious. Solomon truly said: "To every thing there is a season, and a time to every purpose under heaven: a time to weep and a time to laugh; a time to mourn, and a time to dance."[9] So there is a proper season for all innocent amusements; and if they are put out of their proper season they cease to be innocent. An amusement is seasonable which does not interfere with time due to religious devotion, moral improvement, intellectual culture, the relief of human distress, sympathy with mourners, the burial of the dead, the exercise of justice, the necessary business of life, healthful repose and proper consideration of other people's well being. No amusement is seasonable which disregards these important particulars.

Ill-associated amusements. Amusements in themselves innocent become pernicious when ill associated. Thus they may take place in corrupt localities, abounding with temptations to vice; or in close intimacy with corrupt associates, ever ready to seduce the unsuspecting into sin; or in combination with interludes and after-pieces of an exceptionable nature. Good parents might be perfectly willing that their sons and daughters should enjoy certain amusements at one place, but not at another, with one set of companions, but not with another, and with one combination of adjuncts, but not another. Thus a game, a dance, a concert or a drama might be innocent and salutary with right associates, but would be corrupting and pernicious with wrong ones. All these things are to be considered.

I suggest the following precepts:

1. Abstain from all wicked amusements. Consider all amusements wicked which contemn God, injure man or inflict unnecessary pain on any living creature. Consider all amusements wicked which are obviously repugnant to any divine principle, and especially which contravene humility, justice, benevolence, charity, meekness or sobriety.

2. Eschew all unhealthful, useless, foolish, derogatory and equivocal amusements. Be sure that every amusement you encourage is in accordance with the laws of health, is of some real utility, is justifiable by wisdom, is of an elevating tendency, and is unquestionably innocent.

3. Carry no amusement to excess.

4. Take care that all your amusements occur in their proper season. Let them never interfere with the discharge of any duty which you owe to God, to fellow man, or to your own well-being. Pursue no amusement after 10 o'clock at night.

5. Indulge in no amusement which disregards the sorrow and sadness of afflicted neighbors.

6. Never sacrifice piety, humanity, justice, charity or virtue, in the slightest decree, to amusement.

7. Resort not to the most innocent of amusements in corrupt places, nor with associates likely to lead you astray, nor in connection with demoralizing accompaniments.

8. Remember that you are to do all things to the glory of God in the exemplification of true personal righteousness, even to indulgence in amusements.

There is a vast range of physical, intellectual, social and moral amusements, from which to select and compile an unobjectionable system. And whatever more may be needed can undoubtedly be supplied by contriving new sports, games, exercises and entertainments, all conformable to the genius of our Social System. With a will there must be a way.

Still, great discrimination and judgment will be requisite to determine wisely what ought to be retained, what rejected, and what invented. Every amusement will have to be brought into judgment and tested by our acknowledged sovereign divine principles. If repugnant to any one of these, it must be wholly rejected, or correctively modified. In the existing code of amusements there is a large infusion of demoralizing elements which must be purged away. The worst of these elements are the following:

1. All *amusements of a pro-war character* must of course be excluded, or at least expurgated of that pernicious element.

2. *Games of chance and hazard* have a natural tendency to unsettle the mind, to inspire it with a disorderly ambition for success without merit, and to induce actual gambling. All amusements strongly marked by this evil element ought to be discarded.

3. *Games of rivalry and desire for triumph* include those of chance and those of skill. The latter have some redeeming traits, inasmuch as the triumph is often gained by real merit, and inasmuch also as the emulation engendered may sometimes be a salutary stimulus to necessary exertion. I do not recommend that all amusements of this nature be interdicted, but only such of them as are obviously objectionable. Nevertheless, everything like ignoble emulation, rivalry and triumph should be effectually rebuked.

4. The element of *sexual corruption* inheres chiefly in certain over-familiar house-party sports, in midnight balls, in waltzing, dances, in theatrical exhibitions, and in the lower kinds of musical entertainment. The pruning knife should be unsparingly applied to all these. I do not condemn them *in toto*, but they need a thorough regeneration. Many of our young people's plays are well enough; the more simple and modest dancings are well enough; and the drama might undoubtedly be elevated to something like a Practical Christian standard of purity. But those vulgar and obscene sports to which I refer, those fashionable night balls, those giddy waltzes, the theater as it generally is, and much of the current ballad singing, I denounce as intolerable under my Social System.

5. *Passional bewitchment* is also a dangerous element in many kinds of amusement. It influences the feelings and imagination of ill-constituted persons to such a degree as to disaffect them with all the sober realities of life, and to render them slavish devotees of fiction, exaggeration and exciting pleasure. This must be constantly guarded against by the supervisors of Community recreations. But if the children, youth and adults of our Republic can be so satisfied and contented with the amusements provided for them on their own domains, as not to rove abroad after those of the outside world, this evil will be easily controlled.

It seems to me that there is hardly any limit to the improvements which our people will be able and disposed to make, when once they shall have resolutely taken hold of this work. They will first adopt all the athletic, gymnastic, calisthenic, mirthful, graceful and pleasant physical recreations which may be selected as healthful and innocent. Then all the unexceptionable intellectual ones, of which the world has already a considerable assortment. Then a great number of new intellectual entertainments may be invented. And finally members of our Preceptive Circle will be able to invent an indefinite number of moral, religious and spiritual amusements – a class hitherto almost unthought of by mankind. The *pleasing* and the *useful* may be so combined, as effectually to secure an incalculable amount of good. In order to secure such desirable and glorious results, I recommend the following suggestions:

1. That some competent member or members of the Preceptive Circle devote special attention to this subject with a view to the selection, invention and combination of unexceptionable amusements, and their arrangement into a practical system.

2. That the proposed system be set forth in a Manual, adapted to furnish parents, educators and legislators with all needful information respecting the various series of amusements proper for infants, for juveniles, for older youth and for adults.

3. That parents, educators and all persons concerned, endeavor to concur in the adoption of the system recommended, or at least so much thereof as they can conscientiously approve, and then cordially cooperate in reducing the same to practice.

4. That each Community afford ample patronage, accommodation, encouragement, counsel and guardianship to the system of amusements adopted.

5. That the system be altered, amended and improved progressively, as time and experience shall dictate.

6. That the practical working of the system be always so conducted as to exert a salutary and elevating influence on visitors and outside spectators, as well as home participators.

7. That all excesses, abuses and perversions, which may occasionally develop themselves in spite of preventive vigilance, be promptly corrected.

Chapter 10

Education for Sex, Marriage, and Family Life

Sexual Education

Let the young be trained to behave with propriety in their sexual relations. I name this last, but not because it is *least*. It is the central pivot on which the whole social machinery turns. Right social education respecting the intercourse of the sexes is of vital importance. What is the desideratum on this point? It is to train the young all the way up from childhood to marriage-able years in such a manner as to render them mutually just, truthful, kind, friendly, courteous, agreeable and intimate, without unchastity, without premature development of amativeness, and without any habits adverse to their subsequent happiness. A most desirable but most difficult achievement. In order to such a result I venture to recommend the following precepts:

1. Let both sexes be brought up and educated *together* in the family, and in the places of instruction and association – not artificially kept strangers to each other.

2. Let both sexes be carefully instructed, at the earliest suitable age, concerning their respective sexual constitutions, and made to understand the capabilities, liabilities, susceptibilities, dangers and responsibilities of each. This should be done long before puberty. It should be done by parents and educators whom the young reverence and love. It should be done, degree by degree, in a private and confidential way, and in such a manner as to make the pupil feel that he or she is entrusted with sacred knowledge. Ignorance and mystification are to be utterly laid aside as safeguards to virtue. Knowledge and truthful explanation, judiciously imparted by suitable persons, are to be relied on with confidence. Nothing is to be left to guesswork and greedy surmise. Neither are the pupils to be left to corrupt and clandestine tutors. Everything is to be done wisely, seriously and thoroughly by competent educators.

3. Let both sexes be plainly taught and profoundly impressed from the beginning, that the male was created to be the father, and the female to be the mother of immortal offspring; that this is the central and sacred use of the genital organs; that this cannot innocently take place except in a state of acknowledged marriage; and that true marriage is the most responsible of all human contracts between persons who are fit to be married, and who tenderly love each other.

4. The rightfulness of genital sexual intercourse out of the married state being utterly excluded, let both sexes be carefully trained to avoid all known provocations, incitements and occasions of venereal amativeness – likewise all abuses, perversions and pollutions of the genital organs. Never let the genital organs be touched by the hand, except for purposes of natural incidental necessity. Avoid pollutive fingering and friction. Let them never be spoken of *frivolously,* by lascivious innuendo, or otherwise than in the language of purity. Let them never be thought of impurely; turn away from all unclean imaginations; they are dangerous – the germs of pollution.

5. Keep the mind, the imagination, the affections and the bodily energies well employed in concernments foreign to amative indulgences and abuse.

As many come into the world hereditarily perverted, and others will have already become corrupted by evil practices solitary or social, educators will find themselves involved in a very perplexing and disagreeable task. But they must not shrink nor relax. What cannot be prevented may in time be corrected, or if not corrected, yet greatly restrained. Regard must be had to diet and regimen, to company kept, to books read, to amusements followed, and to all things which tend to precocious or perverse development of amativeness. And to make sure of good results, let the following rules be strictly observed by both sexes.

These rules, scrupulously followed, will *prevent*, and even *cure*, the perversions deprecated. There is no greater misfortune than lascivious, perverted, restless, lustful amativeness. The difference between a young man or woman pure, cool, calm, free from amative inflammations up to the marriageable age, and one corrupted, self-abused, precocious and restless with the fires of lust, is the difference between, I might almost say, an angel and a devil. Besides all its other evils it precipitates even well-disposed persons into the most unsuitable and unhappy marriages. It hurries them forward against all the remonstrances of reason, wisdom and friendship, into connections which their better judgment would have condemned. It also poisons the general intercourse between male and female, which otherwise would be pure, guileless and pleasant.

I would let the intercourse of the sexes be as unrestrained as it can be with perfect chastity, friendship and refined courtesy on all occasions. Let there be no caresses, or fondling familiarities which incite the least lasciviousness, or trench on rudeness, but a refined and genial companionship, such as the best educated brothers and sisters may approvingly maintain in the presence of wise parents; provided always, that the parties are on terms of reciprocal esteem and good understanding. Let every young man and woman equally disdain to infract the laws of chastity, friendship, courtesy and sexual honor. Let each be alike emulous to preserve the other's virtue and reputation uncontaminated and unsuspected. With this noble and refining intercourse, both sexes will at length enter on the adult stage of life well qualified, not only to form happy marriage connections, but to diffuse through every department of society the most genial and salutary influences. It seems to me that with such an education the vices of self-pollution, lewdness, obscenity, lasciviousness, fornication, adultery, seduction, prostitution and their kindred evils would become as rare as they are now common. The two sexes would recognize each other as essentially equal in human rights, would mutually promote each other's happiness, and would be comparatively free from most of the perversions which now debase both.

On Amativeness

The proper control and regulation of amativeness is a radical requisite. Here I tread on delicate ground – not on altogether "holy" ground which requires me to put off my shoes,[1] but ground consecrated by the multitude to the goddess of fastidious mystification. Nevertheless, I shall presume to make myself understood without mincing matters.

What is amativeness? I mean by the term that organic instinct which attracts the sexes toward each other with reciprocal interest, courtesy, kindness, tenderness, love; in other words, the sexual affection which ultimates in conjugal unity.

Now it should be well understood that amativeness, in human beings, is not a self-limited, self-regulating instinct, as in some of the lower orders of creation. The Creator having endowed man with the facilities of imagination, moral sentiment and reason, it became impossible to confine any of his fundamental instincts and propensities within the fixed bounds constitutionally prescribed in lower natures. More range must be given them on this higher plane of creation. Hence they assimilate themselves with the superior facilities of mind, and must be mainly controlled by them. The necessary consequence is, that the instincts are capable of great elevation and great degradation, according to the mind's good or evil state. They may be *angelified*, or *brutified*, to almost any extent. Amativeness may be sublimated and exalted to heaven, or perverted and debased to hell. The perversions and abuses to which it is liable are legion. And unhappily it is now almost universally in a diseased, perverted state, by reason of hereditary, customary and habitual abuse. Were it otherwise, its activities might be regulated with less difficulty. But the best must be done that can be done under existing circumstances.

Amativeness appears to have three spheres of activity. The first may be called its sphere of generality. In this it inspires each sex with a peculiar interest in the opposite one. Hence the reciprocal deference, attention, courtesy and kindness frequently manifested by one sex to the other, with little or no reference to mere personal congenialities. The second may be called its sphere of partiality. In this amativeness grows select, and inspires individuals with a partiality for congenial individuals of the opposite sex. They feel a decided attraction towards those agreeable individuals, pay them particular deference, show them marked attentions, and take peculiar pleasure in their society; yet have no such tender and exclusive love for them as to desire marriage. The third is the sphere of connubiality or strong conjugal love between two individuals exclusively.

In each of these three spheres of activity amativeness manifests itself on three planes: the spiritual, the intellectual, and the sensual. On its spiritual plane, it is refined, unselfish, noble, and swayed by high moral considerations. On its intellectual plane, it is ideal, imaginative, literary; it dotes on intellectual excellences and congenialities. On its sensual plane, it seeks physical conjunction and sensual pleasure as the chief object.

In each of these three planes, amativeness has various degrees of intensity. In its minimum degree, it makes scarcely any external demonstrations; it sees, thinks, feels and acts, but with great moderation and circumspection. In its medium or second degree, it becomes strong and unequivocal, but confines its demonstrations within narrow limits. It is in earnest, yet calm and temperate. In its maximum degree, it becomes the most powerful, determined and uncontrollable of all human affections in this mortal state. And what is most deplorable of all, the great mass of those therefrom suffering do not suspect, and will not be made to believe, that they are the victims, directly or indirectly, of abused, perverted amativeness.

From this analysis, it may be seen how vast the difference must be between normal, healthful, innocent amativeness, and abnormal, perverted, criminal amativeness. The difference is that between heaven and hell. It may also be seen how important and at the same time how difficult it must be to keep amativeness controlled and regulated by the higher faculties of the mind. If it were so controlled and regulated, neither male nor female would ever be guilty of the solitary vice called self-pollution; of lascivious actions, gestures, speech or imagination; of fornication; of adultery; and much less of seduction, or of rape. Neither would the marriage bed ever witness the intemperance, abuse and abomination now so frequently committed. And then a multitude of diseases and infirmities, some of them the worst that afflict humanity, would pass away forever. But if abnormal, perverse, criminal amativeness be allowed to prevail, outside or inside of marriage, the evils thence resulting will render it utterly impossible to regenerate mankind.

Now shall amativeness be an unspeakable curse, or shall it be an unspeakable blessing? I would do all in my power to render it an unspeakable blessing, at least within the new social order I am endeavoring to establish. It is not to be annihilated, nor suppressed, but properly controlled and regulated. This is a cardinal requisite of true marriage. Let those who contemplate matrimony disabuse their minds of the following very common errors:

1. That venereal pleasure is the staple good, and an indispensable object of marriage. It is but a minor incidental one.

2. That marriage gives unbounded license for the indulgence of amativeness on its sensual plane. It gives no license whatever to be intemperate, or disorderly, in such indulgence.

3. That genital orgasm must take place somewhat frequently, especially with the male, in order to relieve the system of seminal repletion which would endanger health. This is an utterly unfounded and most pernicious notion. There is no such natural necessity; but the danger lies in the other direction.

4. That the husband has an absolute right, by marriage, to demand sexual indulgence as an accommodation. Neither party has any such right; and no such thing should ever take place without cordial, mutual spontaneity.

5. That the wife must have her decreed number of children, and as fast as her system will allow of gestation. It is folly, superstition, absurdity. She should never have a child without deliberately consenting and agreeing to it; nor without a just regard to good conditions.

6. That husbands cannot have physical conjunction with their wives without imparting the seminal element, and thereby exposing them to impregnation even against their will. It is a great mistake of ignorance, and a very bad habit. A self-disciplined, decent, kind husband may and *will* completely control that matter. It is only an ignorant, ungovernable, reckless one who will continue to repeat such wrongs.

7. That the husband and wife cannot have satisfactory physical conjunction without genital orgasm. It is not so. If living in true sympathetic companionship and in the proper exercise of intellectual and spiritual amativeness, they will not frequently resort to that which is sensual. But when they do, it will partake of intellectual and spiritual delights. It will be calm, temperate, and controllable. It may thus become incomparably more pleasurable, refined and innocent *without* orgasm than with. Purpose, discipline, habit will render it not only possible but easy. There should very seldom be orgasm, except designedly for the mutually understood purpose of generating offspring. This should be firmly resolved on from the beginning, and studiously persisted in through life. Then would the married pair retain their nervous vitality, their love, cheerfulness, courtesy and caressive agreeableness in perpetual vivacity down to old age; not waste and squander it by frequent exhaustions, as is generally done, to the loss of all that renders connubial life delightful. Marriage ought to be and may be a happy perpetuation of the best phases of sensible courtship. But this is utterly impossible without the proper control and regulation of amativeness.

Persons disposed to profit by these suggestions will accept the following precepts:

1. Endeavor by every possible means to understand the nature, different spheres, planes and degrees, of amativeness, its uses and abuses.

2. Endeavor to determine precisely what are normal, healthful, innocent and God-approved exercises of amativeness, and what not.

3. Endeavor to cast away errors, break off bad practices, and by studious self-discipline to form right habits in this department of human responsibility.

4. Aspire and resolutely labor to elevate amativeness to its highest capabilities of excellence, that its spiritual activity may transcend all lower ones, or at least sanctify them.

5. Be sure and keep it in its proper place, subordinate to conscience and reason, in harmony with all other instincts and sentiments.

6. Be prepared before marriage to act wisely and dutifully after marriage.

7. Unite only with a companion who understands and is willing to act the proper part in controlling and regulating amativeness.

8. Prefer rational, conscientious, useful celibacy always to bad marriage. Celibacy for righteousness' sake is approved of God and bedewed with his eternal benedictions.

What Marriage Is

Marriage, as I define and shall treat of it, is a sacred union of one man with one woman, formed by mutual covenant of the parties to live in exclusive sexual communion with each other, as true husband and wife, till separated by death.

Marriage takes place by covenant of the parties. There must be a deliberate, voluntary covenant or agreement between the man and woman themselves to be husband and wife. I would exclude all dictation and compulsion of parents, guardians, relatives, society and government. Likewise all teasing and over-urging. Marriage should be the free act and deed of the parties themselves.

Others may recommend, advise, dissuade, protest, remonstrate, or approve. They may take acknowledgment of the covenant, witness it, record it. But the parties themselves must make and acknowledge the contract. Such a declaration ought to be made, witnessed and recorded; nor is there any valid objection to forms, ceremonies, customs and laws relative to the transaction. Suitable ones may be very proper. I insist only that the parties shall virtually marry themselves; that marriage shall be the free act and deed of the woman, as well as the man; that it shall not be forced by parents or any outside dictators. The idea of a woman being contracted for and bargained away, without her own choice, is utterly inadmissible in a true order of society. Royal, aristocratic and plutocratic families, or savages, may act upon it, but Practical Christian Republicans never.

Marriage pledges the parties to exclusive sexual intercourse with each other during continuance of the matrimonial bonds. I go squarely and uncompromisingly against polygamy, concubinage, and Free Love promiscuity, as well as old-fashioned adultery. I cannot do otherwise, and adhere to the Christian Religion, one cardinal principle of which is *Purity in all things.*

What then of the Patriarchs of the Old Testament, with their numerous wives and concubines? I accord to them all the reverence due them for their many virtues, and for their fidelity to their own highest religious standard. I leave their imperfections, errors and frailties to molder with their mortal dust, or to the chronicles of their own times. I have no idolatry for their weaknesses or their sins, and no contempt for their excellences on account of accompanying defects.

I am aware that nearly two-thirds of the human race are in favor of polygamy, concubinage and various decrees of sexual promiscuity. The whole Pagan and Mahometan populations of the world, embracing a host of distinguished Prophets, Priests, and Philosophers, are against me. The great Mormon Prophet and his saints are against me; eminent Socialists, physiological doctors, Individual Sovereigns and sinless Perfectionists, go for a Free Love promiscuity of sexual delights. Many of these either claim to have received revelations from heaven in support of their liberalism, or to have drawn it by philosophic research from the profundities of nature, or to have mined it scientifically out of the depths of Anthropology and Physiology, or to have deduced it fairly from the native Sovereignty of the Individual as an inherent prerogative to enjoy pleasure, or to have derived it from the great law of perfect love which abolishes all selfishness. All these claim to be intelligent, pure minded, disinterested Progressives, lovers of humanity, deprecators of vice, patrons of virtue, and seekers after the holiness and happiness of mankind.

It is no terror to me to be in a lean minority, if I can but feel the assurance that I am true to the sovereignty of divine principles. In the present case I have this assurance to the fullest extent. I have no quarrel with nations, nor with men. I deal with principles and their practical consequences. "By their fruits ye shall know them." [2] The fruits of a principle may not be developed in their first teachers, nor in all their disciples. But they will certainly be developed sooner or later, in the few or the many. It is high time that mankind reasoned from cause to effect. It would save them oceans of misery. "Experience keeps a dear school, but fools will learn in no other." [3] When will people take a hint, and spare themselves so much cost? They now regard anything and everything superficially, rather than with reference to solid principle and sure working experience. They are all opposed to gross evil results, and horrified at them when they come; but they cannot trace them back to their causative principles.

The bonds of matrimony are dissolved by death. The great Swedenborg and many noble minds since his time, have maintained that true marriage is for eternity. Many delight in that doctrine, and would give it up with great reluctance. The doctrine is that sex is of the soul, in the interior spiritual constitution of human beings, not of the flesh; that each male has his appropriate female counterpart somewhere in the great world of souls; that the true pair will certainly come together after death if not in this life; and that if good they will enjoy unspeakable bliss with each other to all eternity.

To my mind nothing in the Christian revelation declares what will be the precise relations of male and female in the immortal state. That husbands and wives, parents and children, relatives and friends, who are congenial and true to each other in this life, will sustain endearing intimacies in the future state, I do not doubt. But how exclusive any of those intimacies will be is to me uncertain. All will be right, we may rest assured. If others know or believe with particularity how it will be, I need not dispute them, and shall not. But however it may actually be in the next life, the Christian revelation treats of marriage in this world as confined to this world, so far as concerns the exclusive sexual intimacy of the parties. It leaves the man and the woman free after the death of a companion to marry again. Reason, I think, does the same.

If it be really true that there is marriage in heaven, as Swedenborg saw, and as others teach, it must be different in two most important respects from earthly marriage: 1. The marriage there will be *perfect*; the true pair will come together by instinct without a possible mistake. 2. There will be no procreation of children. This radical difference between earthly and heavenly marriage justifies the Christian position of treating the latter as having no necessary connection with the former. For granting that men and women will be paired together in perfect and eternal marriage in the immortal state, where they are to have no children nor unpleasant care, it would be quite impracticable to adjust earthly marriages to such a theory. Let us look at the difficulties which would arise.

All marriages in which the true pair for eternity did not come together must be false and virtually adulterous. It is so extremely uncertain who *do* belong together for eternity, that with the best of intentions a mistake must be made at least three times out of every four, if not nine out of ten. People would suspect a mistake quite as often as there really was one, and would be looking around to find their true mate; which, whether successful or not, would be sure to increase their discontent at home. In many cases, if they really believed they were living in virtual adultery with the companion they were tied to, they would lug in religion to sanction the greedy demands of insane amativeness in favor of separation and the trial of a new chance in the matrimonial lottery. Others would come to the conclusion, that they were mismated at home, but that they knew who their true companions probably were, and that sexual communion with a clear congenial soul must be innocent in the sight of God. Hence spiritual wives and husbands would become numerous, and proportionate discord would reign among temporal ones. To complicate all these difficulties still more, almost every married pair, however ill-matched, contrive to be blessed with children, all of whom need nourishment, clothing, shelter, education and sundry other comforts of life.

So it is easy to see how impracticable it would be to adjust mortal and immortal marriages, even if we believed in the latter. It is wise therefore, in my judgment, to leave this matter where Christ left it, and to treat of marriage in this world as terminating at death. Whatever of marriage there may be in the angelic world will be regulated wisely by the laws of that world.

The Fallacy of "Free Love"

I have no doubt that all the plausible and specious theories, put forth against the doctrine of exclusive sexual communion between husband and wife, are false and demoralizing. I have acquainted myself with those theories and the arguments by which they are sustained, and reject them all as illusory, presumptive and fallacious.

The two sexes of the human race exist in equal numbers or very nearly so. Therefore so far as polygamy is concerned, it is a plain violation of natural rights. One man has no right to monopolize two or more women, and thus leave others without any. But if it be right for one man to have a plurality of wives or concubines, it must also be right for one woman to have a plurality of husbands or Free Love conveniences. Thus comes promiscuity as a matter of equal rights.

Promiscuity of intimate sexual communion is revolting and degrading to pure minded lovers. It is unnatural. It comes from perverted amativeness, despotism, artificial education, sophistication, or arbitrary custom. What pure minded man could endure the thought of his wife's giving herself to the embrace of other admirers, or of her choosing another man to be the father of a proposed child! Or what pure minded woman ever received the proposition of a beloved husband to conjoin himself with a new wife, concubine or lover, without revulsion and anguish. The natural instincts of true love and purity are against it. There may be submission and conformity, but it is forced, or comes from other sources. And any assertion, that the revulsion thus felt at promiscuity arises from selfishness, is simply contemptible. It is not selfishness, but an instinct implanted by God himself to ensure moral and social order.

Sexual promiscuity inevitably tends to moral and social disorder. It sophisticates, perverts and demoralizes its practitioners. It stimulates and confirms the lust of variety. Amativeness, like all the passional appetites, has no inherent self-government. It grows by indulgence, and becomes both inordinate and capricious by license, till it knows not where to stop. It is the most sinister, serpentine, illusive and infatuating of all our propensities. When in the ascendant, neither reason nor conscience can overrule its freaks, follies and crimes. It may begin in a very nice, select, fastidious and modest way; but it is sure to end in lawless self-indulgence. No sooner has it obtained ample room, broken over its original bounds, and become assured in its license, than it befogs the intellect, sears the conscience and vitiates more or less the whole moral nature. Safety lies in subordinating amativeness strictly to reason and the moral sentiment. And the sooner this is done in every human being the better.

But not only does unduly indulged amativeness demoralize the individuals who obey its lusts; it also vitiates others, and tends to disorder all the elements of society. What would become of the family under the promiscuity practice? It would be abolished, or worse than abolished. Here are six, eight or ten children with half a dozen different pairs of parents, cross-matched in ways most curious to imagine. Who are responsible for the maintenance, the education and government of these children? What unity is there, what affection, what confidence, what responsibility? Will the Community adopt them, and provide them nurses, teachers and all the concomitant necessaries of a good bringing up? Who are to compose such a Community, and how long will its materials cohere, in the absence of those cements which appertain to family chastity and integrity? It is a dream which never can be actualized. Shall each woman be endowed with a mansion and an annual stipend or pension sufficient to rear and educate half a dozen children begotten by half a dozen different fathers? Who are to produce or contribute the means necessary to all this? Or how is this independent mistress to manage her speckled flock single handed? Preposterous and presumptuous proposition at best! Whatever dissolves the bonds of matrimony dissolves the integral family; and whatever does this renders society a chaos, or a wretched despotism.

Sexual promiscuity must degrade and oppress woman. Woman is subjected by nature to disadvantages for which a husband's love, sympathy, fidelity and devotion are the only adequate compensation. In virgin youth she has personal charms which attract man, and make him for the time almost her worshiper. She is wooed, won and wed. She becomes a mother once, twice, thrice etc. It exhausts her strength, preys on her nervous system, impairs her beauty, confines her to the nursery, reduces her health and despoils her of much that was formerly attractive. Love, duty, necessity have rendered her at once more weak, helpless and dependent than in the bloom of her virginity. Now it is that she needs the love, sympathy, and devotion of the man that won her heart and hand with such protestations of devoted love. Is she not entitled to this? Is she just then to be told that her attractions have ceased, that the marriage has faded out of the record, that new charmers have come up, that she may go among the brokers in love and find a new admirer! Where is her husband, where his now indispensable sympathy, where her home, where her subsistence? By whom are her little ones to be directed and protected? What would life be worth under such circumstances? But attraction has ceased, and with it the ties of marriage!

What man would not thank God for the great mercy of creating him free from the curse of womanhood! What affectionate father and mother would not prefer to bury a lovely daughter, rather than to launch her on the turbid waters of sexual promiscuity! And what intelligent, pure maiden would not choose virginity, or death, rather than such an experience? It may be denied that Free Love promiscuity will ever work in this way. Believe no such denials. It *will*, in numberless cases, so surely as water runs and fire burns. The principle cannot fail to bring forth just such bitter fruits. It will degrade and wrong woman outrageously! If any are foolish enough to try the experiment, they will find it so to their sorrow.

Finally, sexual promiscuity, having poisoned the fountainheads of virtue and social order, will send untold mischiefs down their streams into all the relations and concernments of life. Distrust, suspicion, jealousy, contention, hatred, revenge and violence will run to seed in every part of society. It will spring up between pretended lovers, between rivals, between children, between neighbors, between coteries, between Communities. There will be mutual reproach, insult, resentment and conflict. It is proposed, I know, by our theoretic Free Lovites, to have no such troubles. All are to be intelligent, refined, circumspect, loving and harmonious, when promiscuity shall have been once fairly inaugurated! Human nature will then have ascended to the sphere of purity, unselfishness and peace! It will have become completely regenerated! Is there so great a simpleton as to believe that men will "gather grapes of thorns, or figs of thistles"?[4] What must be the credulity of one who believes that sexual promiscuity will legitimately produce purity, harmony, peace, and bliss among mankind! Where is the uniform testimony of history? Where that of observation? Where that of bitter experience? Where is the voice of reason? And where that of God himself? I will not argue, nor declaim. I am as certain that the results I have contemplated will ensue from such causes, as I am that man cannot handle pitch without defilement,[5] nor violate the eternal laws of order without involving himself in sin and misery.

In conclusion on this point, I ask, in the name of God and humanity, what necessity or demand there is for this Free Love promiscuity? Who is suffering for want of this kind of freedom? Not the vicious and the licentious, certainly. They would only abuse it. Not those who have become pre-eminently pure, spiritually minded and perfect in holiness. They must have got beyond dependence on such gratifications. Who then are suffering from restriction and privation in respect to sexual indulgence? Let us know what class of persons need this enlargement of their limits. Whoever they may be, one thing is certain, that the liberty demanded for them will be the liberty of making themselves miserable slaves to their own deluded passions!

The Bonds of Matrimony

The bonds of matrimony are threefold. The husband and wife are under most sacred obligations to each other, to society, and to God.

1. *Obligations to each other.* They are mutually bound to maintain inviolate the sanctity of an exclusive sexual communion with each other during their joint earthly lifetime; and consequently to abstain from all actions, intentions, desires and occasions tending to matrimonial infidelity. They are mutually bound to maintain a devoted sympathetic companionship for life, in which they shall pre-eminently share each other's joys and sorrows, bear each other's burdens and infirmities, and be guardians of each other's welfare. They are mutually bound to seek pre-eminently each other's intellectual, moral and spiritual improvement, and to promote each other's highest good for time and eternity. They are mutually bound properly to provide for, educate and train up the children they may bring into the world. Thus much they solemnly pledge to each other, when they covenant to be husband and wife. No matter whether it be expressed distinctly and promised in words, or not; it is all implied in the union formed.

2. *Obligations to society.* Husbands and wives are solemnly bound to set such an example of conjugal fidelity, sympathetic companionship and family order, as shall purify, elevate, harmonize and strengthen society; as shall occasion society the least amount of burden, and the greatest amount of beneficent support.

3. *Obligations to God.* Husbands and wives are solemnly bound to act conscientiously toward their heavenly Father, in conforming to his laws of conjugal order. He created man male and female. He instituted the marriage relation as indispensable to human happiness. He has prescribed the laws necessary to the realization of connubial felicity and all the complex good of the institution. The married are bound to reverence the author of the institution, to honor him by using it without abuse, and by studiously conforming themselves to all his requirements respecting it.

These are the bonds of matrimony. We cannot trifle with them. They are determined by the eternal laws of divine order, and cannot be subjected to human expediency.

The Principal Objects of Marriage

Every rational, conscientious and enlightened person will enter into marriage with certain important objects in view. Such a person will not rush into it thoughtlessly and presumptuously. The legitimate objects of marriage may all be included in three principal ones:

1. Sympathetic companionship.
2. Mutual improvement and progress.
3. The rearing of good offspring.

No objects radically incompatible with these three are justifiable. Those who enter into marriage must do so with all three of these cardinal objects in view; excepting the third, in cases wherein the age of child-bearing may have passed, wherein the capacity for it may be known not to exist, or wherein ill health, or the peculiar circumstances of one or both the parties, render it improper to attempt rearing offspring. In all other cases the three objects should be deliberately contemplated before actually entering into marriage, and kept distinctly in view.

Sympathetic companionship. I mean by companionship in marriage a mutually respectful, cordial, confidential, coequal intimacy – the relationship of real companions, as distinguished from that of master and slave, ruler and subject, numeral and cipher, proprietor and property, superior and inferior. By sympathetic companionship, I mean a loving, congenial, trustful companionship, in which the husband and wife not only recognize and treat each other as coequal partners, but feel a hearty interest in each other's ruling loves, aims, pursuits and responsibilities.

Sympathetic companionship, as I understand it, does not require perfect similarity. This is neither possible nor desirable. Indeed, there are many dissimilarities of male and female which render them the proper counterparts and complements of each other, like the cup and ball. But if their dissimilarities are of a nature to breed disgusts and antipathies, they will be fatal to high connubial happiness. It is these radical and irreconcilable differences that I deprecate as incompatible with sympathetic companionship. It does not matter how much a husband and wife are unlike each other, if they heartily sympathize and cooperate on all the important points felt by either to be essential to happiness.

Suppose they are sympathetic in only one, two or three particulars, and antipathetic or exceedingly cold in all the remaining important interests of life. Suppose one is very religious, and the other decidedly irreligious; that one is tenderly conscientious, and the other exceedingly unscrupulous; that one is benevolent, and the other very selfish; that one is intellectual, and the other quite unintellectual; that one is social, and the other antisocial; that one is domestic, and the other perpetually agog after pleasure abroad; that one is an inquirer, investigator, reformer and progressive, and the other exactly the reverse; that one finds supreme delight in bettering the condition of humanity, and the other in making money, showing off, or in some way pampering self; that one is devoted to the arts and sciences, or to some active and responsible profession, and the other to frivolous amusements; in fine, that one dislikes and is disgusted with nine things out or ten which are the delight of the other. Or suppose that one is cowered down, domineered over and made a trembling slave by the other. What coldness, alienation, distrust and misery must reign between such ill-matched pairs! We all want sympathetic companions; someone to love and confide in above every other; someone who will love us, confide in us and take pleasure in sharing our joys and sorrows; someone in whose darling pursuits we can cheerfully cooperate; someone who will delight in our delights, and be truly a helpmeet. If we marry and fail of this sympathetic companionship, we may possibly endure it without public complaint, and even without private contention, but we cannot enjoy much real connubial happiness.

And yet how many such marriages there are! What have the generality of people known concerning the cardinal objects and requisites of justifiable marriage? What is ordinary match-making and courtship but a game of hide-and-seek, in which it is almost unbecoming to act soberly and rationally? How few know themselves, or their intended companions, or what each should possess as indispensable qualifications for a happy marriage! Who stops to ascertain and consider whether there is a fair probability of sympathetic companionship between the parties? Somehow and to some extent they are "in love." So they make haste to put on the nuptial yoke, not dreaming that it will ever gall their necks. They pass a few months, or perhaps years, under the magic spell that entranced them, when to their great astonishment they come to themselves and find two beings bound together for life who are sympathetic companions in scarcely two things important to solid happiness. Is it at all strange? They came together ignorantly, without consideration, at random, and in a mere passion. The wonder is that so many matches are tolerable. There is need of a great reform.

Mutual improvement and progress is the second cardinal and indispensable object of justifiable marriage. I mean mutual physical, intellectual, moral and spiritual improvement and progress. The husband and the wife ought both to be gainers by their union: physically, intellectually, morally and spiritually. Neither should use up the other. Neither should make a mere convenience of the other. Neither should thrive at the expense of the other. They are to be mutual helpers.

In all that relates to health and the physical comforts of life they ought to improve each other's condition. But especially ought they to be mutual helpers in intellectual, moral and spiritual progress. In useful knowledge, in genuine goodness, in all that expands, elevates and purifies the soul, marriage should minister to the absolute progress of both husband and wife. And no two persons should ever decide to enter into this sacred union, without considering whether it is probable they can promote each other's improvement and progress, nor without a mutual understanding that this shall be a cardinal object of their intimate relationship. They ought to regard each other as really immortal beings, tabernacled for this life in flesh and blood, but destined to a vast future of progress, which will be greatly advanced or retarded by their conduct here on earth. And in view of all this, both should firmly resolve never to be a hindrance but always a help to the other. With sympathetic companionship and mutual improvement in a good degree realized as the fundamental objects of marriage, how great a blessing would it be to the connubial pair and to all around them! Every such marriage would be a miniature heaven; a general order of society in which such marriages abounded would be a complex social heaven on earth.

The rearing of good offspring is the third grand object of marriage. I mean children of proper physical conformation and health, fair intellect, decent moral sentiment, and tolerable capabilities; such as with good advantages of education will be blessings to themselves, their families and society. This is a laudable, a noble, a sublime object. There cannot be a more important and sacred one. To be the parents and educators of good offspring – of incipient angels and archangels, who are to shine as stars in the spiritual firmament of heaven forever and ever, is an office and a privilege the real dignity and responsibility of which few have yet worthily considered.

God has given married pairs large discretionary power to determine whether they will have children or not, when they will have them, how many and of what general constitution; and they are to be held in a high degree responsible for the number and quality of the offspring they bring into the world. Of course there are qualifications and exceptions to this doctrine; but it is substantially sound. I affirm that no child ought ever to be generated, without a deliberate design, understanding and harmonious agreement of the parents. It may not be in human power to determine that a child shall come into the world, nor to command all the conditions necessary to have a proper and well-constituted one; but it is in human power to refrain from generating children at improper times, and under known unpropitious circumstances. It is our imperative duty to be sure that we can command the requisite conditions for rearing good offspring, or else to refrain from procreation.

Parents who are living in sympathetic companionship, and sincerely endeavoring to promote each other's spiritual as well as intellectual improvement, will find no difficulty in conforming to this doctrine. Actualizing the first two grand objects of marriage, it will be comparatively easy for them to achieve the third. And how glorious an achievement! How beautiful, how admirable the spectacle of a family of healthful, intelligent, affectionate, virtuous, well educated sons and daughters, all generated in love and wisdom by parents who are what they ought to be themselves, and are harmoniously endeavoring to render their offspring such! Blessings ineffable cluster around such parents and such children through all their earthly life, and will be multiplied to them forever in the immortal state; because they live and act in essential harmony with the eternal divine order.

The Cardinal Requisites of Marriage

If the principal objects of marriage are attainable, it can only be done by complying with the requisites of divine order. God allows nothing great and good to be accomplished without proportionate pains. This is especially true of human improvement, and marriage is no exception. Suppose then that a number of men and women are sincerely desirous of knowing the conditions required to ensure successful and happy marriages. To such I should reply substantially as follows:

1. *A good general education.* Without something like the habits, knowledge and moral character aimed at in our educational system, I do not see how marriage could be eminently successful and happy. None of the present generation have been thus thoroughly educated. Still their matches may be very tolerable. It is in the power of those who are greatly deficient in the details of such an education to profit by the study of the system. If they understandingly assent to the principles laid down and the suggestions presented, they will thereby receive solid advantage.

2. *A good knowledge of sexual physiology* and its concomitants. It is a shame for people to enter into such delicate and sacred intimacies as those of marriage in gross ignorance of their sexual constitution and the laws of health. If they have not received an education sufficiently explicit and thorough on these points, there are books and living teachers to be had; and all who are honestly intent on this kind of useful knowledge should seek it. This physiological knowledge is not to be deferred till the last moment before marriage. It should be acquired in season – just before, at, or soon after puberty; at all events before marriage.

3. *A good knowledge of the nature, principal objects, and cardinal requisites of marriage.* Whoever will study and endeavor to profit by this exposition may put him or herself in the way of attaining all the information required. But certainly the knowledge itself, however acquired, is a most important requisite to successful and happy marriage. No person is qualified to be a husband or a wife who is ignorant of these truths.

4. *A good knowledge of one's self.* "Know thyself" is an ancient, truthful, significant and unspeakably important precept. In respect to marriage it is doubly important. Yet how willingly and almost willfully ignorant people in general are of themselves! Nevertheless, I insist that if they mean to be successful and happy in marriage, they must try to know themselves. Let them analyze themselves thoroughly – their predominant appetites, passions,

motives, sentiments, principles, habits, peculiarities and characteristics. If anything ought to be checked, corrected or radically changed, set about it resolutely at once. And whatever is to be adhered to or persisted in, as essential to the happiness of life, let it be laid down in the map of permanent outlines and calculated on accordingly. Then a man or woman has a basis of judgment on which a stand can be made for determining what sort of a person would be a suitable matrimonial companion.

5. *A good knowledge of the person to be wedded.* In order to determine whether a particular person will be a suitable partner, that person must be thoroughly known. And this knowledge should be had before the parties commit themselves to each other as lovers. Fashionable courtship is wholly inadequate to the interchange of such knowledge. It is a silly and deceitful farce in most cases. If the parties are not so circumstanced as to have good opportunities for becoming thoroughly acquainted with each other, I would recommend the employment of competent and responsible mediators, such as are designated in the eighth Article of the Constitution of our Republic. At all events, the marriage should never be contracted until the parties have a good knowledge of themselves and each other. This is too important a requisite of justifiable marriage to be dispensed with.

6. *True connubial love* is indispensable. Though all other matters and things were unexceptionable, the man and the woman should be personally and affectionally congenial, should be mutually attracted to each other, should on close intimacy cordially love each other. Without taking proper opportunities to enjoy close intimacy, and finding to their entire satisfaction that they do thus love each other, they should never pass through the external forms of marriage. Some will say that love is the beginning, middle and end of marriage, and that all the rest of the requisites are necessarily involved in or superseded by it. With such minds conscience, reason, wisdom are mere words, which have no distinct significance apart from love. And love itself is a mysterious something which comes and goes in a manner quite inexplicable to the human understanding. I do not belong to that school, and shall therefore leave them to gyrate undisturbed in the mazy regions of their own incomprehensible limbo.

7. *Sufficient knowledge and ability to preside over the family.* Marriage institutes a family. The husband and wife are the presiding heads, or rather the joint head of the family. Important responsibilities devolve on the husband and wife both severally and jointly. There must be a domicile, furniture,

food, clothing and all the necessaries of life, to say nothing of extra comforts. These should be provided honestly, and managed in a neat, economical and orderly manner. All this costs money, judgment, skill, labor, care and pains. The intellect and moral sentiment must also receive due consideration, and be properly provided for. If the husband and wife both know what is necessary, and are competent to discharge their respective responsibilities creditably, they may begin with comparatively small pecuniary means. But if either of them, or still worse both, are ignorant, incompetent and irresponsible, what right have they to involve themselves and others in all the complicated troubles which are certain to follow if they marry? None at all. It would be a downright sin for such persons to perpetrate matrimony. It may seem cruel to restrain such persons from marriage, but it is even more cruel, all things considered, to encourage them. I would take the middle ground; that is, insist on disciplining the tolerable cases as thoroughly as possible, holding out the hope of marriage when they should be qualified. Perhaps their strong anxiety to reach the matrimonial consummation might reconcile them to a decent preparation.

Divorce and Separation

Article 8, Section 3, of our General Constitution states:

> Divorce from the bonds of matrimony shall never be allowable within the membership of this Republic, except for adultery conclusively proved against the accused party. But separations for other sufficient reasons may be sanctioned; with the distinct understanding, that neither party shall be at liberty to marry again during the natural lifetime of the other.

I have met with some persons who dislike this Section very much. They pronounce it despotic, arbitrary, irrational and incompatible with the progressive spirit of the age. I will endeavor to give satisfaction in these particulars, but I do not promise to satisfy fully the objectors. Many of them are too completely committed to their foregone conclusions, for that. Nothing but time, observation and bitter experience will satisfy them that they are in error.

What do I mean by divorce from the bonds of matrimony? A complete dissolution of the marriage contract, covenant, obligation and connection. The civil law of most countries authorizes two kinds of divorce: divorce from the bonds of matrimony, and divorce from bed and board. Divorce from the bonds of matrimony is a complete discharge of the party obtaining it, and leaves him or her at perfect liberty to marry again. Divorce from bed and board is a personal separation of the parties from matrimonial intimacy, without allowing either of them to contract a new marriage. In our Republic we apply the term divorce only to cases of absolute dissolution of the marriage tie. All other cases are included under the general term, "separations."

From the manner in which some of our Free Marriage, Free Divorce and Free Love Doctors hold forth on this subject, one might suppose that very few people in the married world ever voluntarily obligated themselves to be husband and wife; but were tied together, *nolens volens*, by some priest or magistrate, and then kept in their matrimonial yokes by the penal civil law. These Doctors vehemently denounce priests, magistrates and governments, as chiefly responsible for the miseries of married life; and earnestly contend, that if men and women were universally left at perfect liberty to cohabit or separate according to their attractions and repulsions, most of those miseries would be prevented.

I regard such notions as very silly, extravagant and mischievous. The miseries of married life are great and complicated, no doubt. But we ought not to ascribe them to mistaken causes, nor propose to cure them by mistaken remedies. Low and deplorable as the married world is, the same persons would sink much lower without marriage, and be far more miserable. The grand difficulty is not in marriage, but in the ignorance, imperfection, frailty and perverseness of people themselves. Until they are trained to think, feel, speak and act in accordance with higher principles, it is vain to expect better things of them. Would we remedy the evils complained of, by giving people full license to follow their sexual impulses, inclinations and wills from day to day? Unless their wills were first rendered less carnal and more spiritual, they would only "leap from the frying pan into the fire."

The truth is, that a very large majority of people who are unhappy in their marriage relations were ignorant and full of disorderly passions when they entered into the marriage contract. They knew not themselves, nor their proposed companions, nor the requisites of conjugal happiness. They were wheedled, cajoled and infatuated, either by match-making busybodies, or by unprincipled adventurers, or by their own inordinate lusts, or by a romantic imagination, or by all these together. Then, instead of considering how all this ill luck happened, or how to amend it, many of them foolishly imagine that if they could only select a new companion, they would escape all their misery and secure a matrimonial paradise at once. Little do they dream, that more than half the goblins which torment them have a *hell-nest* within their own bosoms, and that they are likely to carry with them the seeds of wretchedness into the next match. Just in this state of things, our Love Doctors come along and set up a grand denunciation of priests, magistrates, the government and laws, as the principal authors of their conjugal infelicity. These may have great sins to answer for; but I protest against their being accused of sins they never committed. Let those who make bad matches be held responsible for them.

A couple request me to take acknowledgment of their matrimonial contract before witnesses, and to cause proper record to be made of the fact that they take each other as husband and wife. I comply. After a few weeks or months of intemperate amativeness, they get disgusted with each other and repent of their bargain! Am I to be cursed for *their* errors and follies? Did I thrust them into wedlock? Was it not their own free act and deed? But they complain of me for having been the principal agent of society in solemnizing, establishing and perpetuating their marriage contract; and they complain of the civil law and government of the land for holding them so strictly to their bargain. Then the whole controversy concentrates on two points: the right of society to insist on having permanent proof of marriage contracts, and its right to insist on the faithful observance of such contracts. Would the complainants abolish all religious and civil society? They could not if they would, and ought not if they could.

Society – good, bad or indifferent – must exist, wherever human beings exist. Nothing like orderly society can be sustained without orderly marriages, and decently regulated families. Society then has a deep and abiding interest in marriage, an interest almost equal, on the whole, to that of the connubial pair. If so, it has a clear right to insist that the marriage contract shall be publicly acknowledged and recorded. I am equally confident that society has a clear right to insist on its members duly respecting the obligations of their marriage contracts. I will even say that it is the imperative *duty* of society thus to insist. The demand for greater freedom of divorce is, in my judgment, anti-Christian, unwise and unjustifiable.

Society does little now to prevent connubial abuses and miseries. At the same time, it licenses, connives at, or tolerates a host of demoralizing causes which ought to be plucked up root and branch from its midst. I would urge that society abolish all laws which subject wives to injustice, oppression and wrong from their husbands under pretext of the marriage relation. They are essentially equals before God in all natural rights, and should be so treated in every department of society. Neither sex should be tolerated in trespassing on the rights of the other. I would also urge society to provide for the sexual education of the rising generation, that they may be better qualified for marriage.

There are those who boldly and pertinaciously deny that true marriage involves these obligations; who contend that there is no other bond of matrimony than attraction and mutual elective affinity for the time being; that when this affinity ceases, marriage ceases; that society has no rightful business with the matter; that God has so constituted nature that the intercourse of male and female will instinctively regulate itself; and who therefore protest against all interference with marriage by human law, custom or public sentiment. I regard and treat all such persons as moral incendiaries with whom it is useless to reason, and warn the public against them as the enemies of social and moral order.

You can hardly imagine the assurance and zeal with which some of the Free Love apostles press their doctrines. All the time, they solemnly protest that their grand aim is to do away with sexual licentiousness, and to inaugurate the universal reign of immaculate chastity. Another class of them denounce exclusive sexual communion as sheer selfishness, together with all special interest in one's own family; alleging that it is sinful for husbands and wives, parents and children, to do more for *each other* than for *any* human being outside of their family connections.

An ingenious talker may make some of them appear quite specious, but they have no foundation in truth. "Order is heaven's first law." In this order there are many circles of relationships. Each circle has its own particular loves and duties. These devolve on its own inmates more especially than on the inmates of other circles. But there is no conflict between particular and general duties, or particular and general loves. Hence the loves and duties of the connubial circle, and of the consanguinal circle, may all be fulfilled without neglecting those of any wider circle. On the contrary, all loves and duties are *best* fulfilled when they are attended to in their own order and season.

The husband owes certain loves and duties to his wife, which no other man owes her, or can discharge towards her. Likewise, the wife to the husband. Likewise parents to their children. Likewise the associates of every circle to each other, from the family to the nation. What if a man bestow his attentions on another man's wife, leaving his own to receive those of another woman's husband? What if he provide for another man's children, leaving his own to be provided for by some other benevolent adventurer? Or what if a mother bestow her nourishment on her neighbor's babe, expecting some stranger to nurse her own? Or what if a Community furnish homes, employment and education to the needy of a distant Community, leaving its own needy ones to be provided for by some other Association? If this random and miscellaneous course of fulfilling the loves and duties of human nature were adopted, would more good be done, on the whole, or would anybody be happier than by conforming to the divine order? No; "confusion worse confounded" would be the result.[6] Away then with the flippant sophistry which would persuade us that the special loves and duties of the connubial circle, or of the consanguinal circle, are incompatible with the loves and duties of friendship, of neighborhood, or of humanity at large. He who loves his wife and children as he ought, in their place, is none the worse but much better qualified to love his neighbor as himself, to love his country, to love strangers and enemies, to cherish all the loves and discharge all the duties God has required of him.

Having now a clear view of the obligations of marriage, we are prepared to appreciate the importance of divorce; which is a complete dissolution of these bonds. We are also prepared to consider the doctrine of the Christian religion, that divorce should take place only for one capital cause – adultery. Jesus thus taught in the following Scriptures:

> The Pharisees came to him, and asked him, Is it lawful for a man to put away his wife? tempting him. And he answered and said unto them, What did Moses command you? And they said, Moses suffered to write a bill of divorcement, and to put her away. And Jesus answered and said unto them, For the hardness of your heart he wrote you this precept. But from the beginning of the creation God made them male and female. For this cause shall a man leave his father and mother, and cleave to his wife; and they twain shall be one flesh. So then they are no more twain, but one flesh. What therefore God hath joined together, let not man put asunder. Whosoever shall put away his wife, and marry another, committeth adultery against her. And if a woman shall put away her husband, and be married to another, she committeth adultery.[7]

In his Sermon on the Mount Jesus said,

> It hath been said, Whosoever shall put away his wife, let him give a writing of divorcement; but I say unto you, that whosoever shall put away his wife, saving for the cause of fornication, causeth her to commit adultery; and whosoever shall marry her that is divorced committeth adultery.[8]

I think it is plain from these quotations, that the Christian religion permits divorce for one cause only: adultery. Technically the word "fornication" signifies the sexual coition of unmarried persons, and the word "adultery" such coition of a married person with one to whom he or she is not married. But the original Greek term in the passages before us, rendered fornication, evidently signifies that sexual infidelity which we technically designate as adultery. Dr. Adam Clarke renders the original "whoredom." We understand well enough what Jesus meant, and it is not worth while to be over particular about mere verbalism or phraseology.

Taking for granted that Jesus meant the sexual laxity which expresses itself in acts of fornication, whoredom and adultery as circumstances offer occasion, I do not consider such an offense strictly unpardonable. Repentance and forgiveness should have the same scope in respect to adultery as to all other offenses. If the offender repented, the aggrieved party would be bound by the Christian law to forgive, and doubtless in many instances would do so. But the extent of restoration to unity and confidence would be determinable by the party wronged. It would be the right of the husband or wife, against whom the infidelity had been committed, to consider the marriage dissolved, and to extend forgiveness only to the point of that charity which seeks the highest good of all fellow humans as such. Reinstatement of a sinner in the identical position occupied before transgression is not necessarily involved in forgiveness. God does not always forgive to this extent; nor is man required always to do so. But forgiveness always implies an assurance to the forgiven party that the forgiver will be as good a friend as if the offense had never been committed. As to the extent of reinstatement in former position and confidence, other considerations must determine it.

If a man commit adultery, repent, and his wife forgive him, must she not love him as before? And if she love him as before, will she not, as a matter of course, replace him in his former position, to enjoy her confidence as a husband?

She may, or may not. It is her right to determine how far she will replace him in the confidence he has forfeited; and to God alone is she responsible for her decision. She may truly forgive him, without loving and trusting him, as before, with connubial love and confidence. There may be no place or foundation left for connubial love and confidence. Does not God truly forgive millions of penitents, without replacing them exactly in their former peculiar positions, and without doing away *all* the consequences of their sins? Why then may not human beings truly forgive one another, without completely reinstating the offender in former place and confidence? Under the second great commandment, she is bound to love him as herself, just as she is bound to love all other men and women. She was bound to love him thus as a fellow human, before the marriage was thought of. Was she therefore obliged to love and accept him as her husband? Not at all. Neither would she be obliged to re-accept him as her husband after he had forfeited that position, even though he repented and she had forgiven him. The love of benevolence is universal and unchangeable. Conjugal love is select and conditional. These different loves must not be confounded with each other.

The conclusion then is, that the act of adultery is a capital violation of the marriage contract; that it works a forfeiture of conjugal love and confidence; and that it absolves the party aggrieved from the bonds of matrimony; nevertheless, leaving him or her to determine the extent of forgiveness and restoration. Now comes another very important question: Ought adultery to be considered the only sufficient cause of divorce? I affirm that no husband or wife ought to divorce his or her companion for any other cause than adultery conclusively proved.

Sexual fidelity is the grand, central indispensable bond of marriage, solemnly pledged to each other as inviolable by the husband and wife when they become such. Therefore no breach of *other* obligations can justify the injured party in violating *this* all-important bond. But he or she who should divorce a companion for other causes, and should marry again, would be guilty of violating this sacred obligation. In this grand particular, he or she would be the *infidel* party; with no other excuse than that the divorced companion had committed certain other wrongs. One wrong cannot justify another. Hence it is not allowable for husbands or wives to falsify their solemn pledge of sexual fidelity by taking a new companion, under plea that other breaches of faith have been committed against them. This cardinal bond of matrimony was not made contingent on good behavior in other respects. It stands by itself, and is to be held peculiarly inviolable. Many causes might warrant and even necessitate personal separations of husband and wife; but adultery alone justifies absolute divorce.

So long as sexual fidelity remains inviolate, there is a basis of effort and hope for the removal of other causes of disaffection. Errors, follies and sins may be corrected; reformation may be accomplished; the parties may be reconciled; the breaches maybe healed. The parties and all their friends are bound to use their best endeavors to this end. It would be wicked in them to throw away the great advantages afforded them by this unbroken bond of sexual fidelity. The aggrieved party owes it, by solemn pledge to the delinquent one, to bear with and try to correct all infirmities, frailties and offenses possible. This too is the dictate of pure love.

Marriage is an institution so sacred in its nature, so essential to the welfare of human society, and so indispensable to moral order, that all who enter into it are in duty bound to make great sacrifices of personal feeling and convenience for its sake. They ought not to treat it lightly. They ought not to contract or dissolve its bonds wantonly. They ought not to profane and desecrate it. They ought not to set an evil example of recklessness, either in forming, or dissolving its peculiar relationship. If they have formed an unhappy connection, it is their duty to endure it, if possible, so long as their companion is guiltless of conjugal infidelity; and if they are obliged to separate for other causes, then to bear their discomforts patiently in voluntary abstinence from all sexual indulgence. Thus would they honor and strengthen the marriage institution. And thus would they admonish mankind to avoid bad marriages by precaution and self-discipline, rather than hope to escape from them by divorce.

If divorce be allowed for other causes than that of adultery, it may be allowed for any and every cause pleaded by the disaffected party. There will be no stopping place short of sheer caprice. So it was under the Old Testament. Moses permitted husbands to divorce their wives, by a written discharge or bill of divorcement. This precept was abused more and more till the facile Jewish lawyers of our Savior's time construed it into a warrant for divorce on the most frivolous grounds. And in our own country many of the States have lowered down the standard of divorce till marriage has become a contract dissoluble almost at pleasure. Still the latitudinarian Love Doctors cry aloud for more liberty. There is no bottom to this pit. Divorce for other causes must have an inevitable tendency to undermine the sanctity and stability of the marriage institution, to render it a thing of little importance in the estimation of thousands predisposed to reckless self-indulgence, and to encourage the formation of transient unions with the intention, of at least one of the parties, to quit the partnership at pleasure. This demoralizing influence will send pestilence through all the ramifications of society, and result in incalculable evils. Pleasure, convenience and passional self-gratification, will become the highest law. I must deprecate all these evil tendencies and results. Such are my principal reasons for adhering to the doctrine of Christ relative to divorce. I walk by my highest light; and as I understand the teachings of inspiration, history, observation, experience and reason, they all confirm me in the same conclusion.

Separation

When the Practical Christian Republic shall have become so far established as to give its rising generation the education I have endeavored to recommend, and to discipline its people in accordance with their declared Constitutional Polity, cases of divorce will be exceedingly rare. So will cases of separation. Nevertheless, they are contemplated and provided for as sometimes unavoidable in the nature of things. They will probably be frequent during the early stages of the Republic, on account of the continual transitions from the old order of society into ours, and the cross connections of our families with outsiders.

There are many causes of disaffection, alienation and antagonism, which render it quite difficult, if not impossible, for some husbands and wives to dwell together in any tolerable peace or comfort. Many of them can be done away with, where there is a will in the principal parties and a judicious concurrence of friends. Others are of so gross and outrageous a nature that a separation of the parties more or less widely from each other, is the only tolerable alternative. In such cases a separation should take place.

Personal outrage, violence, cruelty, wickedness, quarrelsomeness, intemperance, etc., are frequently carried to such a pitch as to be absolutely intolerable. In all such cases the suffering party must seek safety and peace in separation; and friends must assist in bringing it about. Doubtless there are also cases of uncongeniality and mutual repugnance without anything like outrage of conduct, which become so unendurable that the parties ought to separate, at least till they are confident they can live together comfortably. Let them separate. But in no case where sexual fidelity remains inviolate, may either party consider him or herself at liberty to marry again during the natural lifetime of the other. Let each be considered in duty bound to do the other all the good that can be judiciously done under the circumstances.

I can easily bring up cases of drunkenness, brutality and wickedness, far more insufferable than ordinary cases of adultery. Why should not the injured party be entitled to divorce in these cases, as well as in the sometimes less afflictive one of adultery? For the reasons already assigned. Evils are not to be measured by their immediate local and external insufferability, but by their internal and ultimate general malignancy. Thus adultery, all things considered, is more intolerable than any of these dreadful kinds of conduct. Besides, if men and women are placed on a footing of equal rights, as I insist they should be, and if those who cannot live peaceably together shall go into quiet separation, each with what justly belongs to him or her, what more would you have? It must be the liberty to contract a new sexual connection.

I do not see that the people of our Republic are in much danger of hard cases in the matrimonial line, unless they bring their troubles with them out of the old social state. Our sovereign divine principles, Non-Resistance, Teetotalism, Women's rights, our religious discipline, our educational system, our views of marriage, our whole social polity and moral order, are in the highest degree preventive of the causes which render divorce and separations necessary in existing society.

As to the world in general, its bad matches and connubial miseries are undoubtedly deplorable. I have no faith that freedom of divorce is the remedy for these evils. I am sure that it will only render a bad matter worse. In this I am at irreconcilable issue with the whole Free Love school. I insist on precaution, prevention, enlightenment, education, reformation, forbearance, self-discipline and the utmost endurance of hard experience, as the principal means to be relied on for diminishing and overcoming matrimonial mischiefs.

In closing, I offer the following advice to the unhappy in married life:

1. Search out and try to understand the real cause or causes of your unhappiness. Otherwise you cannot hope to find relief.

2. Examine yourself conscientiously and thoroughly, to see wherein and how much you are in fault. It may be that the chief defect, or the main offense is in yourself. Or if in your companion, it may be that you are too impatient, resentful and retaliatory, or too neglectful of the means necessary to correct the evil.

3. Put forth your best endeavors first to correct and reform yourself; then your companion.

4. Pray earnestly without ceasing for divine assistance, wisdom and grace to prosecute the work of reformation; and especially for patience to bear with what remains unreformed.

5. Crucify petty willfulness and pride of self-infallibility. Be not sullen, obstinate or pertinacious. Acknowledge your wrongs. Confess your faults. Be frank and truthful. Yield your own will, taste and convenience to those

of your companion, in all cases not contrary to the dictates of conscience. Herein is great wisdom.

6. Magnify not your companion's offenses, faults or defects. Proclaim them not to others. Overlook, bear with, forgive and overcome them to the utmost extent of justice and charity. Abstain from taunt and reproach. Rake not open smoldering embers.

7. Be exceedingly slow to confide your connubial difficulties to third persons. Not one in fifty of them can do you any good, but many will certainly help on your troubles. Call in arbitrators only in the last extremity, and then the best you can find.

8. Govern your passions, your temper, your tongue, your tastes and your imagination. Be moderate, calm and self-controllable.

9. Be true to the sovereignty of divine principles, according to your highest light. Be firm in doing your plain duty. Never consent to neglect an imperative duty, nor to commit a known sin, for the sake of pleasing your companion. Never exact any such sacrifice of principle. You have no right to demand, or to make such a sacrifice. This is a sacred point. Beware how you trifle with it.

10. Spare no pains to acquire knowledge respecting the nature, objects and requisites of true marriage; and then use that knowledge to the best advantage possible in obviating the difficulties of your own case.

11. If, after all, you find it impossible to remove the causes of your unhappiness, endure them as long and as well as you can. But if worst come to worst, quit yourself of them with dignity and heroic decision.

12. Above all things, govern your amativeness. Shun excess. Correct bad habits of indulgence. Look not abroad lustfully. Beware of seductive intimacies and fond partialities away from home. Imagine not another fitted to make you happier than your own. Poison, disappointment, wretchedness and death will be the fruit of such dreams. Become temperate, chaste, circumspect, and you will be surprised to find health, cheerfulness, courteousness and family sunshine returning to you. Then a little *innocent* pleasure will be incomparably greater than the lawless abundance which ends in death. Be wise in this thing, and you shall rejoice in a safe escape from one of the most prolific scourges of conjugal life.

Let these precepts be seriously pondered, in connection with what I have before said on the subject of marriage, and I am confident they will prove to thousands a far "more excellent way" out of connubial misery, than divorce.

Afterword

Advice to Practical Christians

For Persons Desirous of Entering the Practical Christian Republic
I have nearly completed this Exposition. I have fully unfolded to you my Social System. I hope I have fulfilled my original promises, and realized the expectations I raised in your mind. I propose now to condense into precepts the best advice my experience and reflection enable me to offer to the principal classes of persons who may become interested in our grand movement.

1. Read, inquire and reflect till you thoroughly understand the fundamental objects, principles, polity and peculiarities of Practical Christian Socialism.

2. Consider the whole matter well. Look before you leap. Count the cost of espousing such a cause. Do not be in haste. We want soldiers, like Gideon's of old, willing to lap up water from the running stream, each with pitcher and lamp invincible.

3. Let each examine him or herself by such questions as these: Is it my ruling desire and supreme motive to do RIGHT, according to my highest knowledge and ability? Am I fully convinced that Practical Christian Socialism enjoins what *is really right* toward God, neighbors, friends, enemies, strangers, and myself? Am I willing to use my talents, skill, acquirements, property, industrial energies, and entire personal influence as required by such a standard of righteousness? Am I prepared to relinquish all the advantages, honors, conveniences and pleasures of the old social state that are radically incompatible with this standard? Have I faith that, all things considered, it would be best for me, my friends and the human race to do so? How much of a martyr am I willing, by God's help, to be for the sake of this cause? Have I religion and reason enough in harmonious cooperation to be a decent member of the Practical Christian Republic?

229

4. Having been admitted to membership, do not, like too many who join the nominal Christian Church, imagine your principal work done, but consider it merely begun. Consider yourself an *enterer*, not a *graduate*, of the Practical Christian school; and that you have committed yourself to a life's work of religious, moral and social progress. Henceforth you are a reformer of all that needs reformation, and a conservative of all that is worthy of conservation.

5. Study to be useful. Be diligent and persistent in rational endeavors to enlighten, purify and elevate yourself, your family, your friends, your neighborhood, society and the world.

6. In due time, become a member of some Integral Community, if the way shall fairly open and duty not forbid. But be not in haste. There may be good reasons why you should remain in comparative isolation. Yet do not therefore conclude that you cannot be useful to the cause. You can do much for it where you are.

7. Live the right life at home and among your neighbors. This will exert the most powerful of influences in the right direction.

8. Be punctilious in attending those regular religious and business meetings of the Republic with which you are immediately connected. Slackness in this particular will lead to slackness in everything else.

9. Encourage every instrumentality of the Republic for improvement. Contribute liberally of your time, talents and means to the maintenance of such instrumentalities. Stinginess in these respects will infallibly prove the insincerity of your high professions.

10. Look well to the matter of education at home, and throughout the sphere of your influence. Make no truce with ignorance.

11. Supply yourself and family dependents liberally with the periodicals, books, pamphlets and tracts of the new social order. Induce as many of your neighbors as you can to read such publications, either at your expense, or their own. Be not an obtrusive proselyter, and yet a faithful commender of truth and righteousness.

12. Employ, patronize and cooperate with your fellow members in all their laudable pursuits, in preference to outsiders, whenever you can do so without injustice or unkindness to the latter. If it be possible, live peaceably with all mankind, but be sure that you compromise no essential divine principle.

For Those Desirous of Entering the Unitive Circle

All the foregoing, and the following in addition:

1. Remember that the better people are, the nearer they can live comfortably together, and the worse they are, the farther must they be kept apart.

2. Remember that a bad neighbor always carries one with him, and never finds a good neighborhood.

3. Be sure therefore, that you carry no bad neighbor along with you into a Rural or Joint Stock Community, either in your own person or in your family. You will there come in close contact with your fellow members, and every considerable defect of character will ere long come to light. The best test of personal worth is close intimacy in acquaintance, counsel, business and the every day affairs of life. But this is a severe test, before which the gold of many superficial fair-seemers turns into dross. The *substantially good* can be lived with *comfortably,* in spite of weak spots and incidental imperfections. And they with whom we cannot be intimate in the every day affairs of life, without getting frequently stung, thorned and tormented, are not to be recognized as Practical Christians. Let such become further regenerated before they enter the Unitive Circle of our Republic. These are strong but salutary hints. Remember that fair *talkers* and *writers* often turn out to be very *un*fair *doers.*

4. Before you offer yourself for membership in any Community, be careful to understand its Constitution, Covenants, Enactments and peculiar social arrangements. Thus you will know your rights, duties and responsibilities, and also those of your associates. There is a great proneness to slide over these things superficially, and to remain in ignorance of numerous facts which require only a few hours of reading and inquiry to be well understood. This is utterly inexcusable under a social system which vests the supreme sovereignty in plainly declared divine principles, requires everything to be done openly, and excludes all capricious management of leaders.

5. On being admitted to membership, resolve to occupy your proper position, discharge your duties, and exercise your rights conscientiously.

6. Be modest, unassuming, conciliatory, reasonable and accommodating.

7. Be just, truthful, frank and reliable. Whatever you promise or undertake, execute with punctilious fidelity, if within the bounds of possibility.

8. Be yielding to the last degree in mere non-essentials; but firm, uncompromising and inflexible on all points of absolute principle. Take care not to mistake your own will or self-interest for principle.

9. Take care to exemplify the glorious Christian axiom, "It is more blessed to give than to receive." Resolve to impose few burdens on others, and to bear many.

10. Do not sponge, plunder and prey upon the Community. Consider all its corporate property as inviolable as that of the most orderly individual. Have a conscience void of offense toward the Community, as well as toward God and each neighbor.

11. Resolve that the Community shall never be made poorer or weaker by your connection with it.

12. Be not a grumbler, croaker or panic maker.

13. Bear patiently with and excuse all mere weaknesses and imperfections; but rebuke unmistakable sins without respect of persons. Obvious falsehood, dishonesty, injustice, cruelty, ugliness, selfishness, quarrelsomeness, arrogance, tyranny, etc., if you should be so unfortunate as to witness them in any of your associates, must be reproved and discountenanced promptly without fear or favor. Your own good, the wrongdoer's good, and the common good imperatively demand this.

14. Cheerfully conform to all laws, rules and regulations of the Community for the time being, unless repugnant to your conscientious scruples. If they are thus repugnant, declare it publicly, and request to be excused, or move a repeal. If you cannot succeed in obtaining either, withdraw honorably and peaceably.

15. Cultivate common sense and plain good nature as indispensable staples of Community happiness. Where these are sadly lacking, or either of them, expect trouble.

16. Govern your animal appetites, your passions and your tongue.

17. Preserve your individuality, without magnifying it. True individuality and sociality are perfectly consonant with each other.

18. Be prompt and firm in upholding Community order and discipline.

19. Confess frankly and amend honorably your own faults.

20. Stickle not for your own rights and dues in little matters; but be very careful to respect those of others.

21. Execute all your work, and transact all business committed to your charge, with such thoroughness and fidelity that neither friend nor foe can reasonably complain.

22. Be no office-seeker, and never allow yourself to complain that you are not appreciated. Deserve well, and leave the rest to God. If elected to office and there be no good reason to decline, accept modestly and perform its duties in the most orderly and faithful manner of which you are capable. If *over* others, make your leadership pleasant to them. If *under* others, make their leadership pleasant to *them*. In every station and relation study to be *agreeable*, and at the same time to be truly respected.

23. Walk humbly with God. Give a portion of every day to secret prayer, meditation and self-examination. Do not neglect this; it will enable you to do everything else better, and to bear every trial with more patience.

24. Finally, do all things and bear all things *conscientiously,* to the glory of God, and thus to the highest good of yourself, your family, your friends, your Community, your Republic and the human race. Be what you profess, and you will have nothing to fear.

The Communitive Circle

Most of the foregoing, and somewhat additional:

1. You are aspiring to a very high and difficult position. It requires virtues and excellences which few have hitherto possessed. Consider well whether you are unselfish and wise enough to assume such close relations, and to sustain them without friction. Your ambition is laudable, but fearful.

2. Try it, if you have faith and full persuasion. But do not put it on the ground of absolute duty. Regard it as a privilege, which you are to honor or dishonor by assuming, and which will prove a blessing or a curse to you, according as you shall make a good or ill use of it. If you succeed well, you are not to be inflated with self-righteousness, nor to look down on others with contempt. If you fail, as two chances to one you will, you need not despair. Fall back into the Unitive Circle, and there do your duty cheerfully. You have a safe retreat. Nevertheless, try it, if you choose. Success will be glorious.

3. Remember that you are not to build up a Community of autocrats and serfs, masters and slaves, where the few are to become giants by making all the rest pigmies; but a Community of equality and fraternity, liberty and law, congeniality and order, where the sovereignty of divine principles, not persons, must govern, and where nothing must be required or done without a valid reason. This is a difficult problem to solve.

4. Do not take for granted that the serpent of human selfishness has but one *head* – *love of money* – *lust of property*. It is a hydra with an hundred heads. Too many communists think that if individual property can be abolished, all goods held in common, and trade superseded, selfishness will have been annihilated, and a paradise established at once. But they greatly mistake. There are numerous causes of human misery. Selfishness manifests itself through many lusts. Among these are the following: The lust of power, authority, leadership, management, dictation, usurpation, tyranny; the lust of preeminence, distinction, display, self-exhibition; the lust of talking, speechifying, babbling, tattling; the lust of antagonism, debate, rivalry, mastery, triumph; the lust of cabal, faction, machination, underhand conspiracy; the lust of envy, contempt, vexation, teasing, thwarting, depreciation of others' merit, detraction, and leveling down betters; the lust of revenge, punishment, censure, denunciation, crushing and humiliating offenders; the lust of willfulness, obstinacy, doggedness, stiff-neckedness; the lust of ease, indolence, carelessness, idleness, laziness; the lust of novelty, frivolity, trifling, sporting, jesting, changing; the lust of Paul Pryism, impertinence, improper interference, meddling with other people's business; the lust of secretiveness, slyness, cunning, craftiness, guile, deceit, under-working and over-reaching; the lust of eating, drinking, dressing, using and consuming whatever gratifies the palate, the taste, the eye, the fancy – undue liberality to self, often at the expense of others; and finally the "lust of the flesh," amative self-indulgence of every kind, from wanton kissing to lecherous coition – from *self* pollution to gross *social* pollution. All these lusts must be mortified to a greater or less extent. Whether agreeable or disagreeable, they must all be subjected to the dictates of divine principles. Then selfishness will be thoroughly subdued. So you see that scotching the *lust of property* is not the cure-all for social evils, and that selfishness is a serpent with many heads – a HYDRA.

5. Remember that you are proposing to enter into a Community which preserves the integrality of the family, and holds its rights sacred. Therefore your family, if you have one, must be congenial and united. Husband and wife, parents and children must be in harmony and order within their own circle. If there be antagonism and discord there, do not think of joining a Common Stock Community.

6. Remember that, in order to happiness in such a closely associated Community, the inmates must not only possess an inexhaustible fund of pure

principle, benevolence and reason, but nicely balanced minds and excellent self-discipline. They must be rationally agreeable and pleasant associates. Otherwise intimacy will be living misery. Reciprocal disgust, vexation and contempt are not the ingredients of social happiness. In such Communities, little things become great, in proportion to proximity of persons and unity of interests. Manners will grow into importance. To say, do and be just the proper thing at all times will be more necessary, yet no less difficult, there than elsewhere. To be truly agreeable associates you must keep the happy medium between extremes. You must go far enough and not too far. You must have religion without superstition, inflexible devotion to principle without bigotry, liberality without licentiousness, dignity without pride, frankness without offensive bluntness, personal independence without defiance, courtesy without finesse, caution without timidity, positiveness without arrogance, gentleness without effeminacy, accommodation without servility, humility without degradation, familiarity without indecorum or impertinence, freedom of speech without garrulity, communicability without imprudent leakiness, industriousness without slavish drudgery, frugality without parsimony, economy without sordidness, generosity without lavishness, mirth without rudeness, order without fussiness, neatness without fastidiousness, boldness without impudence, courage without rashness, moderation without slackness, responsibleness without over-anxiety, and scrupulous conscientiousness in all things without overstrained nicety.

7. Before you enter a Community, have your reserved rights, as well as your obligations, unmistakably understood by all parties concerned. Then endeavor faithfully to fulfill your part of the common covenant so long as you remain a member. If you find yourself congenially and usefully situated, you will not desire to withdraw. If otherwise, retire peaceably and honorably.

Precepts for Members of the Preceptive Circle
Only a few brief injunctions additional to the foregoing.

1. Presume not to teach what you do not understand.

2. Presume not to preach what you are either unable or unwilling to practice.

3. Study and labor earnestly through life to show yourselves approved of God and good men.

4. Consecrate yourselves and all your resources to the cause of Practical Christian Socialism.

5. Be just and charitable to all, but turn neither to the right hand nor to the left from your great work.[2] Unswerved by allurement, neglect, denunciation, fear or discouragement, in God's strength move steadily, perseveringly and invincibly forward. Lead on the gradually increasing hosts of our new social order to a peaceful, beneficent and glorious victory. Halt not till the Practical Christian Republic shall have lived down contempt and triumphed over all opposition.

6. Jesus Christ is your Lord and Master. Adhere faithfully to him. In him God is with us. Without him we can do nothing. With him and through the power of his cross, we shall prove more than conquerors. Be not ashamed nor distrustful of the Christian Religion. "It is the power of God unto salvation."[3]

7. Be the zealous promoters of every righteous instrumentality, agency, measure and expedient for increasing the intelligence, wisdom, strength, order and harmony of our beloved Republic. Make it, under God, self-subsisting, self-expansive and self-triumphant. Be faithful unto death, and yours shall be the crown of life.

Precepts for Communal Officers and Managers
In addition to the foregoing, I will briefly say to all official servants:

1. Thoroughly acquaint yourselves with your duties.

2. Perform them promptly, faithfully and cheerfully; otherwise, resign and give place to those who will.

3. Be orderly, accurate, judicious and careful in all your transactions. Consider it inexcusable to be negligent, slovenly and careless in respect to any thing under your official oversight.

4. Be resolute and firm in the discharge of all your duties, whoever may complain or find fault.

5. Be humble, modest and obliging towards all persons under your direction and with whom you have to deal, but never to the violation of any sovereign divine principle.

6. Never be mean or small in pecuniary matters, with insiders or outsiders, for the sake of the Community. The Community will only be injured and disgraced by such transactions. On the other hand, do not allow the Community to be sponged and plundered by conscienceless persons, under pretext that corporation property is less sacred than that of individuals. Under our social system, corporations and individuals stand on the same level, as to rights and obligations.

7. Look well to your records, papers and all written evidence of transactions.

8. Be prompt and inflexible, yet kind and judicious, in the execution of laws, and the administration of discipline.

9. Insist on the thorough, neat, orderly and seasonable execution of all industry.

10. You are the immediate representatives of your Community among outsiders. Take care that neither your actions, words nor tempers ever disgrace the Republic. Give no human being just cause of complaint.

11. Be able and willing always to render good reasons for your requirements and proceedings.

12. Be truly official *servants,* not *lordlings.* Seek not your own interest, advantage, convenience, ease or *will,* but the public good and the glory of God. Govern and be governed always by the sovereignty of divine principles.

Formation and Establishment of New Integral Communities

1. Find suitable persons to lead in the enterprise. There should be at least one religious and moral teacher, one legislator and social constructor, one financier and commercialist, one mechanical genius, one agricultural manager, one educator, and one general counselor. These seven functional capabilities are indispensable. Possibly some two of them might be combined in the same person. If not, seven such persons must be found; and they ought to be decidedly competent persons; the more so, the better. They should be devoted to the movement and well united. Then let as many other useful persons of various capabilities be enlisted as can be conveniently associated, and let the Community be organized.

2. Make sure of funds, by subscription or otherwise, for the purchase of a Community Domain. This matter must not be left at loose ends. Windy promises must not be trusted. The means that can be commanded at a specified period must not be over-estimated. There must be some financial certainty as to what can be depended on.

3. A suitable Domain must be sought and selected. An unhealthy one would not be suitable. A very costly one, beyond the Community's means, would not be suitable. One of difficult access to a decent market would be unsuitable. One in an intolerant country, where wrong and violence were prevalent, would be unsuitable. One situated in the midst of a general population decidedly unsympathetic and hopelessly irreformable for a long period would not be suitable. One not tolerably adapted to the leading pursuits of

the contemplated Community would be unsuitable. Every Community should combine agricultural, mechanical and manufacturing pursuits, to a greater or less extent. A decent water power, or some equivalent, would therefore always be desirable. But when Communities become numerous, some will lead off in one general pursuit, and some in another; trusting to equitable exchanges with each other for all necessaries not produced at home. A suitable Domain for one might therefore not be equally so for another. Let competent delegates of the Community examine and report; and then let a decision be made.

4. Much caution, circumspection and prudence must be used in purchasing a Domain, arranging payments and securing a good title.

5. Next the Domain is to be settled. Sound judgment and practical common sense will be indispensable in this process. The Village Site, public grounds, cemetery etc., are to be laid off. Proceed deliberately, and do everything in order.

6. Gradually the whole circle of Community interests and operations must be organically arranged. Let the officers avail themselves of all the knowledge that can be derived from books, and especially from documents, published and unpublished, which set forth the experience of already established Communities. Let them also take counsel with the most intelligent members of such Communities on difficult points. Then let all possible improvements be superadded.

7. Let great allowance be made for drawbacks and disappointments. Make an average discount of fifty per cent on the professions, promises and representations of persons not absolutely *known* to be reliable. Put little confidence in letters, written recommendations, or fine talk. Prove candidates for membership well before admitting them. Almost everything you calculate on will more or less disappoint sanguine expectations.

8. Do not run too fast, nor undertake too much. People desirous of joining you will be impatient to do so before you are ready for them. They will profess a perfect willingness to suffer all manner of inconvenience, if you will receive them at once. Do no such thing; unless you can house and employ them comfortably. They will embarrass you, and soon grow sick of their situation. It is your business to know how far you can go and how much you can comfortably accomplish in these matters. Be cool; do right; and all parties will be better pleased in the end.

9. Beware of giving and of receiving *much credit* in pecuniary matters. It is very dangerous. Make your Community a self-subsisting one from the

very beginning, if possible. Live within your means. Do not seek thrift by begging, nor by getting trusted without solid security.

10. Take care not to over-appraise Community property in making up your annual account. You will be strongly tempted to do so. But it will prove bad policy in the end. Better not make yourselves richer on *paper* than you really are in *pocket*.

11. Take great pains with all your industrial productions and fabrications, especially those intended for sale, to establish a good reputation. Your work and your commerce will preach you *up* or *down* more effectually than a dozen public talkers. Deserve well of your neighbors.

12. Form good habits from the beginning in respect to all your social and organic, as well as your individual conduct. Insist unitedly and resolutely on having everything done as it ought to be. Then fear not a failure.

13. Institute regular religious and disciplinary meetings, and the best educational instrumentalities you can, at the very outset of your settlement. It may be a little inconvenient, but "it will pay." It will give character, strength and success to your infant Community. The genius of Practical Christian Socialism forbids you to dispense with these institutions. In our movement, everything depends on the proper cultivation of the religious sentiment, social affections, intellect and reason.

14. Take all reasonable pains to enlighten, reform and elevate the people of your general vicinity. To this end, let a friendly general intercourse be maintained with such of them as are disposed to reciprocate it. Let them have the benefit of lectures, preaching, social conferences, books, papers and conversation. Only be careful not to lose moral purity and power by compromise of principle.

A Few Words to Practical Christian Socialists as a People

Your declared objects, principles and social polity are the best, the noblest and the worthiest that human nature can embrace, live for, or die for. Try to appreciate their sublime excellency. Hold the glorious cause in which they are combined *first* and *dearest* of all others. Be ardently and indissolubly attached to it. Never be ashamed of it, however contemned by "the wise and prudent."[4] It has a destiny of triumphant success recorded among the decrees of Heaven. Though its beginning was as a little leaven hid in many measures of meal, it will leaven the whole lump.[5]

Have faith. "Fear not little flock; it is your Father's good pleasure to give you the kingdom."[6]

Be faithful. Be persevering. Keep steadily at work like the industrious ants and bees, each in his or her own best way. The world will give little heed to you at present. Some will notice you with a sneer. Others will bid you leave your *little* cause and join their *great* one. "Many will say, lo here, or lo there" is the all-important work to be done.[7] Be not moved. Work on. Plant one Community after another and consolidate it. Step by step, slowly but surely, advance toward your distant goal.

Ask not for applause. Demand not that the world appreciate your enterprise. Depend not on popular smiles, nor the favor of the great. Court not the old Church; neither fawn before the old State. You are to build up your own Church and your own State on the solid foundation of Practical Christianity. You are to solve your own problem, and work out your own destiny. Therefore walk on your own feet; use your own hands; eat your own bread; sit under your own vines and fig trees.[8] Make your Republic religiously, morally, intellectually, socially, pecuniarily, peacefully and benevolently independent. In process of time the dimmest eyes will see its actualities; the dullest ears will hear of its fame; and the most inveterate skeptics will confess that you have succeeded.

Be hopeful. Be united. Stand by each other in every emergency. Trust in God. Be indomitable. Be what you profess. So shall your banner of truth, love and peace finally wave in serene majesty over every temple turret of regenerated humanity. And then shall the will of our Universal Father "be done in earth as it is done in heaven." For "of him, and through him, and to him are all things; to whom be glory forever, Amen."[9] And may the approbation of God our Father, the inspiring unction of the Holy Christ-Spirit, the ministrations of heavenly angels, the sympathies of all true souls, and the solaces of a good conscience be with us and our beloved associates forevermore.

THE END

Appendixes

Appendix A

Standard of Practical Christianity

Humbly desirous of promoting Christian piety and morality in their primitive purity, the undersigned do solemnly acknowledge the Principles, Sentiments, and Duties declared in the following Standard, viz.:

We are Christians. Our creed is the New Testament. Our religion is love. Our only law is the will of God. Our grand object is the restoration of man, especially the most fallen and friendless. Our immediate concern is the promotion of useful knowledge, moral improvement, and Christian perfection. We recognize no Spiritual Father but God; no master but Christ. We belong to that kingdom of "righteousness, peace, and joy" which is "not of this world"; whose throne is holiness, whose scepter is truth, whose greatness is humility, whose preeminence is service, whose patriotism is love of enemies, whose heroism is forbearance, whose glory is self-sacrifice, whose wealth is charity, whose triumphs are salvation. Therefore, we can make no earthly object our chief good, nor be governed by any motive but the love of *Right*, nor compromise duty with worldly convenience, nor seek the preservation of our property, our reputation, our personal liberty, or our life, by the sacrifice of Conscience. We cannot live merely to eat, drink, sleep, gratify our sensual appetites, dress, display ourselves, acquire property, and be accounted great in this world; but to do good.

All that we are and have, with all that God shall ever bestow upon us, we unreservedly dedicate to the cause of universal righteousness, expecting for ourselves in the order of divine providence only a comfortable subsistence until death, and in the world to come eternal life.

Placing unlimited confidence in our Heavenly Father, we distrust all other guidance. We cannot be governed by the will of man, however solemnly and formally declared, nor put our trust in an arm of flesh. Hence we voluntarily withdraw from all interference with the governments of this world. We can take no part in the politics, the administration, or the defense of those governments, either by voting at their polls, holding their offices, aiding in the execution of their legal vengeance, fighting under their banners, claiming their protection against violence, seeking redress in their courts, petitioning their legislatures to enact laws, or obeying their unrighteous requirements. Neither can we participate in any rebellion, insurrection, sedition, riot, conspiracy, or plot against any of these governments, nor resist any of their ordinances by physical force, nor do anything unbecoming a peaceable submission to the existing powers; but will quietly pay the taxes levied upon us, conform to all innocent laws and usages, enjoy all righteous privileges, abstain from all civil commotions, freely express our opinions of governmental acts, and patiently endure whatever penalties we may for conscience' sake incur.

We cannot employ carnal weapons nor any physical violence whatsoever to compel moral agents to do right, or to prevent their doing wrong – not even for the preservation of our lives. We cannot render evil for evil, railing for railing, wrath for wrath, nor revenge insults and injuries, nor lay up grudges, nor be overcome of evil, nor do otherwise than "love our enemies, bless them that curse us, do good to them that hate us, and pray for them that despitefully use us and persecute us."

We cannot indulge the lust of dominion, nor exercise arbitrary authority, nor cherish bigotry, nor be egotistical, nor receive honorary titles, nor accept flattery, nor seek human applause, nor assume the place of dignity. We cannot be pharisaical, self-righteous, nor dogmatical. We cannot do evil that good may come. We cannot resent reproof, nor justify our faults, nor persist in wrong-doing.

We cannot excommunicate, anathematize, or execrate an apostate, heretic, or reprobate person otherwise than withdrawing our fellowship, refusing our confidence, and declining familiar intercourse.

We cannot be cruel, even to the beasts of the earth. We cann ot be inhuman, unmerciful, unjust, unkind, abusive, or injurious to any being of our race. We cannot be indifferent to the sufferings of distressed humanity, nor treat the unfortunate with contempt. But we hold ourselves bound to do good, as we have opportunity, unto all mankind; to feed the hungry, clothe the naked, minister to the sick, visit the imprisoned, entertain the stranger, protect the helpless, comfort the afflicted, plead for the oppressed, seek the lost, lift up the fallen, rescue the ensnared, reclaim the wandering, reform the vicious, enlighten the benighted, instruct the young, admonish the wayward, rebuke the scornful, encourage the penitent, confirm the upright, and diffuse a universal charity.

We cannot go with a multitude to do evil, nor take part with the mighty against the feeble, nor excite enmity between the rich and the poor, nor stand aloof from the friendless, nor abandon them that take refuge with us, nor court the great, nor despise the small, nor be afraid of the terrible, nor take advantage of the timid, nor show respect of persons, nor side with a friend in what is wrong, nor oppose an enemy in what is right, nor forbid others to do good because they follow not us, nor set up names and forms above personal holiness, nor refuse to cooperate with any man, class, or association of men on our own principles in favor of righteousness, nor contemn any new light, improvement, excellence, which may be commended to our attention from any direction whatsoever.

We cannot make a trade or emolument of preaching the gospel, nor be supported therein by unwilling contributions, nor keep back any truth thereof which ought to be declared, nor consent to preach anything more or less than God directs us, nor encourage religious devotion in mere worldly show, nor pursue any course of conduct whereby the *money*, the *smiles*, or the *frowns* of corrupt men may overrule the divine law and testimony. We cannot surrender the right of serving God according to the dictates of our own conscience, nor interfere with others in their exercise of the same liberty.

We hold it impossible to cherish a holy love for mankind without abhorring sin. Therefore, we can give no countenance, express or implied, to any iniquity, vice, wrong, or evil, on the ground that the same is established by law, or is a source of pecuniary profit to any class of men, or is fashionable in high life, or is popular with the multitude; but we hold ourselves bound so much the more to testify plainly, faithfully, and fearlessly against such sins. Hence, we declare our utter abhorrence of war, slavery, intemperance, licentiousness, covetousness, and worldly ambitions in all their forms. We cannot partake in these sins nor apologize for them, nor remain neutral concerning them, nor refrain from rebuking their various manifestations; but must forever abstain from and oppose them.

We cannot promote our own advantage at the expense of others by deceiving, defrauding, corrupting, degrading, overbearing, or impoverishing them. We cannot take away their good name by defamation, nor by retailing the scandal of their enemies, nor by spreading abroad evil reports on mere hearsay authority, nor by wantonly publishing their failings. We cannot be busybodies in other people's affairs, nor tale-bearers of domestic privacy, nor proclaimers of matters unsuitable for the public ear. We cannot rashly judge men's motives, nor raise evil suspicions against them, nor join in condemning the accused without a hearing, nor delay reparation to the injured, nor make any one's necessity our advantage, nor willingly render ourselves burdensome to others, nor cause any one a single unnecessary step for our mere gratification; but we will always deem it "more blessed to give than to receive," to serve than to be served – sacrificing *nothing* of *holy principle*, though, if need be, everything of personal convenience.

We cannot live in idleness, nor be careless or extravagant, nor on the other hand avaricious, parsimonious, or niggardly. We cannot indulge a feverish anxiety in any of our temporal concerns, nor fret ourselves under disappointment, nor repine at anything that marks our lot. We cannot be austere, morose, or rude; nor capricious, ungrateful, or treacherous. We cannot practice dissimulation, nor offer fulsome compliments, nor use a flattering courtesy. We cannot follow pernicious fashions, nor encourage theatrical exhibitions, nor join in frivolous amusements, nor countenance games of chance, nor array ourselves in costly apparel, nor wear useless ornaments, nor put on badges of mourning, nor distinguish ourselves by any peculiar formalities of raiment or language.

We cannot indulge to excess in eating, drinking, sleeping, recreation, labor, study, joy, or sorrow, nor permit our passions to tyrannize over our reason. We cannot harbor pride, envy, anger, malice, wrath, ill-will, sullenness, or peevishness; nor cherish any unholy lusts, imaginations, or tempers.

We cannot swear by any matter of oath, nor make any rash vows, nor offer any extraordinary protestations of our innocence, sincerity, or veracity; nor utter any blasphemy, imprecation, falsehood, obscene expression, foolish jest, or profane exclamation.

We cannot enter into the state of matrimony without grave deliberation and an assurance of divine approbation. We cannot neglect or abuse our families, nor evince any want of natural affection towards our bosom companion, our aged parents, or our helpless offspring. We cannot imbrute our children by disregarding their education, nor by setting them an evil example, nor by over-fondness, nor by harshness and severity, nor by corporeal punishment, nor by petulance and scolding.

We cannot neglect our brethren in their adversity, nor call anything our own when their necessities demand relief, nor be silent when they are unjustly accused or reproached. We cannot speak of their faults in their absence without first having conferred with and admonished them; nor then if they have promised amendment.

We cannot over-urge any person to unite with us, nor resort to undignified artifices of proselytism, nor seek debate with unreasonable men, nor protract a controversy for the sake of the last word, nor introduce sacred subjects for discussion in a company of scorners. Yet we will hold ourselves ready to give an answer to everyone that asketh of us a reason for our faith, opinion, or conduct, with meekness, frankness, and patience.

Finally, as disciples of Jesus Christ, before whose judgment seat all must appear, we acknowledge ourselves bound by the most sublime, solemn, and indispensable obligations to be perfect as our Father in heaven is perfect, in all possible respects; and whereinsoever we come short thereof to take shame to ourselves, confess our sins, seek divine pardon, repair to the utmost our delinquencies, and bring forth fruits meet for repentance. And for all this, our sufficiency is of God, to whom be glory, world without end. Amen.

ADIN BALLOU, DAVID R. LAMSON, DANIEL S. WHITNEY, WM. H. FISH, *Ministers.*
CHARLES GLADDING, WM. W. COOK, *Laymen concurring.*

Constitution of a
Parochial Community

We the undersigned, members of the Practical Christian Republic, belonging chiefly to its Adoptive Circle, do hereby associate ourselves, in conformity with the 5th Article of the General Constitution, as a Parochial Community, to be called

The ——— Parochial Community;

which shall be organized and regulated in accordance with the following articles of compact, viz.:

ARTICLE 1.

Section 1. This Community, being a constituent body of the Practical Christian Republic, shall be in perpetual confederation with all other constituent bodies thereof wheresoever existing.

Section 2. No act or proceeding of this Community shall designedly conflict in any respect with the General Constitution of the Practical Christian Republic; nor shall any person be admitted or retained a member of this Community who does not declaratively approve said Constitution.

Section 3. Any person declaratively approving and adopting the General Constitution of the Practical Christian Republic, and recommended by three members thereof as sponsors, may be admitted into the membership of this Community, at any regular meeting subsequent to the one at which he or she shall have been proposed, by a two-thirds vote of the members then present and acting; provided, that the candidate shall thereupon in open meeting subscribe this Compact.

Section 4. Every member, with his or her family dependents, shall be entitled to the guarantees specified in Article 1, Object 4 of the General Constitution, viz.: "a comfortable home, suitable employment, adequate subsistence, congenial associates, a good education, proper stimulants to personal righteousness, sympathetic aid in distress, and due protection in the exercise of all natural rights," so far as it may be in the power of this Community by reasonable exertions to fulfill the said guarantees.

Section 5. All the members shall be subject to Christian discipline, as indicated in the eighteenth Chapter of Matthew's Gospel, and shall be responsible for the orderly conduct of their respective family dependents.

Section 6. Any person may resign or withdraw membership at discretion by giving written notice to that effect. Any person having united with a Society of people, radically opposed in principle, practice or spirit to the Practical Christian Republic, shall be deemed to have relinquished membership; also, any person not having attended meeting, nor corresponded by letter, with this Community for a period of two years.

Section 7. This Community shall prescribe by standing rule a uniform mode of notifying its meetings. Nine members shall constitute a quorum for the transaction of business; and a two-thirds vote of the members present and acting shall be necessary to the determination of all questions, excepting the election of officers, the process of which shall be prescribed by standing rule.

ARTICLE 2.

Section 1. This Community, being established to promote religious, mental and social improvement, so far as may be found practicable in a promiscuously inhabited neighborhood, the members shall endeavor to sustain at least one meeting on the first day of the week for public instruction, devotion and exhortation, a Sabbath School and suitable library for the benefit of their rising generation, a regular Monthly Meeting for Christian discipline and the transaction of Community business, and such other social arrangements as experience shall demonstrate to be useful.

Section 2. All members and dependents of the Community, not prevented by conscientious scruples, indispensable duties, sickness or other justifying necessity, shall be expected to attend regularly and punctually the public Sabbath meetings. Also, to abstain from all uses of the day not obviously promotive of physical health, social order, humane sympathies, moral improvement, spiritual progress and the regeneration of mankind.

Section 3. The funds necessary to sustain the Community's authorized instrumentalities of improvement shall be raised by such fraternal and equitable methods as may from time to time be prescribed by the members in regular meeting assembled.

Section 4. Whenever this Community shall possess public buildings, or other real estate, for any of its purposes, the same shall be held and supervised for its sole use and benefit by five Trustees elected to serve during mutual satisfaction, any three of whom, but never a less number, shall be competent to receive and execute title deeds of all such estate. And the said Trustees shall execute and enter for record in the Registry of Deeds for the County of ––– a Declaration of Trust explicitly setting forth their prerogatives and responsibilities; to the end that all controversy both at law and in equity may be effectually prevented.

Section 5. This Community shall have power, if at any time deemed expedient, to purchase and make such real and movable estate in joint stock proprietorship, or otherwise, as may be necessary to the convenient fulfillment or the guarantees specified in Article 1, Section 4, of this Compact.

ARTICLE 3.
Section 1. This Community shall annually elect the following designated officers, viz.: a President and not less than three Directors, a Recorder, a Treasurer, a Steward and such others as may be found necessary.

Section 2. The duties of these officers, not clearly indicated by their titles, shall be prescribed from time to time by general regulation, rule or special instruction.

ARTICLE 4.
Section 1. This Community shall have power to enact any rules and regulations, not inconsistent with this Compact, which may from time to time be deemed requisite.

Section 2. This Compact may be altered, amended or revised, at any regular meeting of the Community duly notified for that purpose subsequent to the one at which such change shall have been proposed.

Constitution of a Rural Community

We the undersigned, members of the Practical Christian Republic, do hereby associate ourselves, in conformity with the 5th Article of the General Constitution, as a Rural Community, to be called

The --- Rural Community;

which shall be organized and regulated in accordance with the following articles of compact, viz.:

ARTICLE 1.

Section 1. This Community, being a constituent body of the Practical Christian Republic, shall be in perpetual confederation with all other constituent bodies thereof wheresoever existing.

Section 2. No act or proceeding of this Community shall designedly conflict in any respect with the General Constitution of the Practical Christian Republic; nor shall any person be admitted or retained a member of this Community who does not declaratively approve said Constitution.

Section 3. Any person declaratively approving and adopting the General Constitution of the Practical Christian Republic, and recommended by three members thereof as sponsors, may be admitted into the membership of this Community, at any regular meeting subsequent to the one at which he or she shall have been proposed, by a two-thirds vote of the members then present and acting; provided, that the candidate shall thereupon in open meeting subscribe this Compact.

Section 4. Every member, with his or her family dependents, shall be entitled to the guarantees specified in Article 1, Object 4 of the General Constitution, viz.: "a comfortable home, suitable employment, adequate subsistence, congenial associates, a good education, proper stimulants to personal righteousness, sympathetic aid in distress, and due protection in the exercise of all natural

251

rights," so far as it may be in the power of this Community by reasonable exertions to fulfill the said guarantees.

Section 5. All the members shall be subject to Christian discipline, as indicated in the eighteenth Chapter of Matthew's Gospel, and shall be responsible for the orderly conduct of their respective family dependents.

Section 6. Any person may resign or withdraw membership at discretion by giving written notice to that effect. Any person having united with a Society of people, radically opposed in principle, practice or spirit to the Practical Christian Republic, shall be deemed to have relinquished membership; also, any person not having attended meeting, nor corresponded by letter, with this Community for a period of two years.

Section 7. This Community shall prescribe by standing rule a uniform mode of notifying its meetings. Nine members shall constitute a quorum for the transaction of business; and a two-thirds vote of the members present and acting shall be necessary to the determination of all questions, excepting the election of officers, the process of which shall be prescribed by standing rule.

ARTICLE 2.

Section 1. This Community shall own and control an integral territorial Domain, to be inhabited exclusively by members of the Practical Christian Republic, their family dependents, and such other persons as may receive permission of residence thereon for limited periods of time. And the absolute ownership and control of such Domain within the said membership is hereby solemnly guaranteed forever.

Section 2. The entire territorial Domain of this Community shall primarily be purchased and held in legal possession by five Trustees, elected to serve during mutual satisfaction and pledged to act always in conformity with this Constitution, with the Enactments made under the same, and with the specific instructions of their constituents. Three of these Trustees, but never a less number, shall be competent to receive and execute conveyances of real estate in behalf of the Community. They shall take the utmost care that all titles to real estate conveyed to or from them shall be so expressed, executed and recorded as effectually to preclude all ulterior controversy either at law or in equity. And for the security of all parties concerned in these transactions, they shall execute and cause to be recorded in the Registry of Deeds for the County of ––– a Declaration of Trust explicitly setting forth their powers, prerogatives and responsibilities.

Section 3. The pecuniary capital necessary to the primary purchase of all Domain real estate shall be raised by a Subscription Loan, in sums of not less than -- dollars, payable to the subscribers in appraised homesteads, house lots or cash, according to stipulated terms.

Section 4. After the Trustees shall have come into legal possession of real estate sufficient for a territorial Domain on which to commence a Community settlement, they shall proceed, under the specific instructions of their constituents to select an eligible Village Site, and also a parcel of ground suitable for a Community Cemetery. They shall then lay off the Village Site by accurate survey into streets, commons and house lots; reserving liberal plats of ground for public buildings of every kind likely to be needed by the Community. In like manner they shall lay off a sufficient portion of the Cemetery into burial lots, reserving convenient common grounds. They shall also lay off the remaining lands of the Domain, according to their instructions, into homesteads of various size suited to the wants of families and small associations. They shall cause properly drafted Plans to be made of all these layings off, one copy thereof to be entered for record in the County Registry of Deeds, and two copies to be kept for the convenience of the Community. They shall appraise equitably all the house lots and homesteads, at sums sufficient in the aggregate to cover the then actual cost of the Domain, and to leave a clear surplus equal to -- per cent. on the said cost. This surplus shall be devoted to such common religious, educational and social uses as the Community may determine.

Section 5. House lots in the Village Site, and homesteads on the Domain may be sold to any members of the Practical Christian Republic, whether belonging to this particular Community or not, who in purchasing the same will come under obligations that the premises with all their buildings and betterments shall revert to the Trustees of this Community whenever they shall cease to be owned within the membership of said Republic. And whenever any house lot or homestead shall be sold, on the conditions aforesaid, the Trustees shall execute a legal title deed thereof to the purchaser, substantially in a form to be carefully devised by some eminent conveyancer, and adopted by the Community for that purpose.

Section 6. In order to insure the prompt redemption of all real estate which may revert to the Trustees of this Community, as contemplated in the preceding Section, a Redemption Fund shall be created and sustained, in the manner herein after prescribed, to wit: Every member of this Community, possessing property clear of debt to the value of three hundred dollars, shall be required to make a promissory note equal in amount to ten per cent of the property so possessed, running to the Trustees, and payable on demand with interest at three per cent per annum. The Trustees shall have a right from year to year to require of new members such promissory notes, to renew any notes which may need revision, and to call for the interest annually due on all the notes comprising the Fund. They shall credit all moneys received on said notes to the Redemption Fund, and shall charge the same with their services and all moneys expended on account thereof. They shall also report their official transactions, and the standing of the Redemption Fund, to the Community at least once a year.

Section 7. When any real estate on the Community Domain shall cease to be owned within the membership of the Practical Christian Republic, the Trustees shall immediately take measures to provide for its redemption from the legal claimant or claimants. They shall first endeavor to find some member of the Practical Christian Republic to purchase the reverted property. If unsuccessful in this, they shall next endeavor to find one who will loan them the requisite sum of money. If unsuccessful in obtaining such a loan within the membership of the Republic, they shall seek one wherever it may be obtained on reasonable terms. But if unsuccessful in all such attempts, they shall demand payment of the promissory notes constituting the Redemption Fund, or such portion of said notes as will meet the necessities of the case. In this last contingency, they shall return to such of the payers as may desire it the moneys received from them respectively, so soon as a fresh sale of the redeemed estate will enable them to do so. And when any person shall cease to be a member of this Community, against whom the Trustees shall hold one of the said promissory notes, they shall surrender such note to the rightful claimant, together with any unexpended balance which may be due for moneys paid to them on the principal thereof. But no claim for interest paid to the Trustees on such notes shall ever be allowed.

ARTICLE 3.

Section 1. This Community shall sustain all the institutions and instrumentalities for religious, mental and social improvement which its available resources will warrant. Public religious meetings shall be held regularly on the first day of the week, at which such devotional exercises, and ministrations of divine truth, shall be encouraged as the Community may from time to time approve. All members, dependents and residents of the Community, not prevented by conscientious scruples, indispensable duties, sickness or other justifying necessity, shall be expected punctually and regularly to attend these meetings. Also to abstain from all uses of the day not obviously promotive of physical health, social order, humane sympathies, moral improvement, spiritual progress and the regeneration of mankind. A Sabbath school and library, or some equivalent therefor, shall be sustained for the religious and moral culture of the young; together with such other inductive methods for the formation of character as may be found practicable. The Community shall also hold a regular Monthly Meeting for discipline and the transaction of pending business.

Section 2. This Community shall promote the education of its rising generation, and the mental improvement of its entire population, by devoted exertions to sustain good schools, a good library, a good lyceum and all similar instrumentalities. It shall aim also to elevate and genialize social intercourse among its inhabitants by all commendable devices and customs. Also, to encourage all the industrial, commercial, domestic and other economies possible in a Community of individual proprietorship.

Section 3. The funds necessary to promote and sustain the various instrumentalities of improvement contemplated in this Article shall be provided in such ways as the Community may from time to time determine.

ARTICLE 4.

Section 1. This Community shall annually elect the following designated officers, viz.: a President and not less than three Directors, a Recorder, a Treasurer, a Steward and such others as may be found necessary.

Section 2. The duties of these officers, not clearly indicated by their titles, shall be prescribed from time to time by general regulation, rule or special instruction.

ARTICLE 5.

Section 1. This Community shall have power to enact any rules and regulations, not inconsistent with this Compact, which may from time to time be deemed requisite.

Section 2. This Compact may be altered, amended or revised, at any regular meeting of the Community duly notified for that purpose subsequent to the one at which such change shall have been proposed.

Constitution of a Common Stock Community

We whose names are hereunto subscribed, being members of the Practical Christian Republic, and aspiring to exemplify the virtues justly expected of its Communitive Circle, do hereby enter into sacred compact with each other, as a Common Stock Community, to be called

The ——— Community

And we do make with each other .and establish the following *Covenant,* to wit:

That this Community shall be in perpetual confederation with all the constituent bodies of the Practical Christian Republic wheresoever existing.

That all the property of its members, for the time being, shall be held in Common Stock, by five Trustees to be chosen, qualified and instructed by the Community for that purpose.

That all the members shall be treated as coequal brethren and sisters, under a common unitary system of arrangements.

That each member, originally investing property in the Common Stock, shall be credited by the Trustees for the same on the Financial Books of the Community, and also, shall be credited from year to year with his or her equal share of the net increase of the common property, if on a fair annual appraisal there shall be any such increase.

That every person who shall have resigned membership, or been discharged by the Community, shall be paid ninety per cent of the amount credited to him or her as investments in the Common Stock without interest, and shall give a written receipt therefor to the Trustees in full of all demands; all which payments shall be made within one year after cessation of membership.

That every member shall have the right to bequeath or devise, by last Will and Testament, ninety per cent of the amount credited to him or her on the

256

Community Books as investments in the Common Stock; which shall be paid within one year after the Testator's decease without interest. But if any member die intestate the Community shall inherit all his or her property, and the same shall be reckoned as a part of its current income.

That the whole Community shall be arranged into Families, varying from nine to twenty-five persons, at least one third of whom shall be *members*, as distinguished from *probationers* and *dependents*.

That each family shall be formed on the principle of elective affinity, with due regard to the common convenience, shall be provided with domiciliary and all other accommodations suited to the reasonable wants of its inmates on a footing of equality with all the other families, shall choose its domestic Father and Mother as occasion may require, and shall manage its own internal affairs in all respects not contrary to positive Community regulations.

That the Fathers and Mothers of the several Families, for the time being, shall constitute a Community Legislative Council; and that two-thirds of said Council acting in concurrence with three of the Trustees shall have power to enact any regulation, appoint any official servant, authorize, any measure, and determine any question, deemed necessary to the general welfare of the Community. Provided nevertheless, that if the minority of said Council, or of the Trustees, shall deem the decision of the majority in any case a violation of this Covenant, or of the Constitution of the Practical Christian Republic, they may make an appeal to the Community at large, and the decision thereof, by a two-thirds vote of the members present and acting in regular meeting, shall be final.

That the five Trustees of this Community shall be elected by the members at large by a two-thirds vote of all present and acting in a regular meeting duly notified for that purpose, to serve during mutual satisfaction; that they shall be required to execute and enter for record in the Registry of Deeds for the County of ———, and also in the Community archives, a Declaration of Trust explicitly setting forth their powers, obligations and liabilities; and that any three of them, but never a less number, shall be competent to receive and to execute conveyances of real estate in behalf of the Community.

That the Trustees shall be required to keep reliable records of their official transactions, accurate Book Accounts exhibiting plain statements of the Community Finances from month to month, and well arranged Files of all papers worthy of preservation. Also, that their Records and Accounts shall always be subject to the inspection of any member desirous of examining them, that they themselves shall at all times be subject to Community instructions, and that they shall make an explicit financial report to their constituents at least once every year.

That the Legislative Council shall be required to keep ample and explicit records of their proceedings; and that all proceeding of the Community in commons assembled shall be recorded by a Scribe annually elected for that purpose.

That all the members, probationers and dependents of this Community capable of industrial exertion shall cheerfully render their services in some useful occupation during such a number of hours per day, week, month, quarter or year, not exceeding an average of more than – hours per week, as the constituted authorities of the Community may from time to time determine.

That requisitions for industrial services shall be equitably made on Families as such, according to their respective aggregate ability to render the same, leaving each to fulfill its obligations according to internal adjustments most convenient to its own operatives.

That supplies of every description, intended for domestic consumption or use, shall be equitably furnished to families *as such*, according to their respective aggregate wants, leaving each to distribute the same in detail among its inmates, as the official heads or responsible members thereof may determine.

That all rights, privileges and advantages guarantied or afforded by the Community shall always be dispensed as justly, seasonably and satisfactorily as circumstances and the nature of the case will possibly admit.

That the best provisions shall be made for religious, moral, intellectual and social improvement, which the Trustees, Legislative Council and Community at large, may be able to institute.

That no person shall be admitted a member of this Community without having resided on its Domain at least one year, nor without being recommended by some Family declaratively willing to adopt him or her into the same, nor without personally subscribing this Covenant in the presence of at least three Trustees.

That no person shall be retained a member of this Community against his or her declared will, nor after an absence of two years without just cause, nor after persistently setting at naught any fundamental principle or requirement of this Covenant, nor after having proved so uncongenial that no Family in the Community is willing to have him or her an inmate thereof.

That this Community shall contract no debt out of the membership of the Practical Christian Republic, nor within the same except for *temporary* necessity or convenience.

That this Community shall steadily aim to Christianize the production, distribution and consumption of property, by conscientiously subjecting every process thereof to the test of acknowledged divine principles, and eschewing all customs and practices obviously incompatible with those principles.

Finally, we severally and solemnly declare that we are conscious of no selfish motive in entering into this Communal Covenant. That we seek no exemption from toils, cares or burdens, by imposing them wrongfully on others. That we desire no domination over the persons, consciences or affairs of our associates. That we deem it more blessed to give than to receive, and to serve than be served. That we are willing to be reproved, and to reprove others, for all wrong, frankly in the spirit of meekness. That according to our ability, we are determined to do more towards producing the necessaries of life than towards consuming them. That we are resolved to be content with plain wholesome food, raiment and personal accommodations; and to stand on a level with each other in respect to all the advantages and disadvantages of this Community. That we pledge ourselves during our membership never to demand interest or profits on capital invested in its Common Stock, nor wages for labor performed. Also, to resign our membership therein when we cannot cheerfully conform to all our Covenant engagements. Also, in case we shall ever leave this Community for any cause, to accept ninety per cent of the capital credited to us individually on the Financial Books thereof, at any time within one year after cessation of membership, and thereupon to receipt the Community authorities in full of all demands.

Now therefore, in full confirmation of this our Communal Covenant in all its articles, stipulations and clauses, as imperatively us individually, with our respective heirs, executors, administrators, assigns and legal representatives of every description, to the Community, and mutually to each other, we have hereunto severally subscribed our names, at the place and time designated opposite the same.

Notes

Table

Practical Christianity and Practical Christian Socialism

Practical Christianity	Practical Christian Socialism
I: Fundamental Principles	*I: Fundamental Principles*
1. Christianity and Socialism	Conversations 1 and 4
2. Principles of Theological Truth	Conversations 2-8
3. Principles of Personal Righteousness	Conversations 8-10
4. Principles of Social Order	Conversations 11-12
II: The Practical Christian Republic	*II: Constitutional Polity*
5. Objects, Principles, and Policies	Conversations 1, 2, and 6 (articles 1, 2, and 11)
6. Rights and Property	Conversations 2 and 5 (articles 3 and 10)
7. Membership, Organization, and Government	Conversations 3, 4, and 6 (articles 4-7 and 12)
III: Education for Practical Christianity	*II: Constitutional Polity (cont'd.)*
8. Education for Health of Body, Mind, and Spirit	Conversations 7-8 (article 9)
9. Education for Community Life	Conversations 9-11 (article 9)
10. Education for Sex, Marriage, and Family Life	Conversations 9 and 12-14 (articles 8-9)
Afterword	*III: Superiority to Other Systems*
Advice to Practical Christians	Conversation 9

Notes

Preface
[1] Isa. 40:30.
[2] Isa. 60:17.
[3] 1 Cor. 15:28.

Chapter 1: Christianity and Socialism
[1] John 21:25.
[2] John 16:12-15.
[3] 2 Cor. 3:6, 1 Cor. 4:20.
[4] Col. 1:15, Eph. 1:21, Phil. 2:9, Song of Sol. 5:16.
[5] John 14:6, 3:16, 3:36, 15:23, Prov. 8:36.
[6] John 14:23.

Chapter 2: Principles of Theological Truth
[1] 1 Tim. 6:15-16. See also Matt. 5:44-45, Mark 12:28-34, John 4:23-24, Acts 17:24-28, Rom. 9:36, Eph. 4:6, James 1:17, 1 John 1:5-8.
[2] Ps. 139:8-10. See also 1 Kings 8:27.
[3] James Thomson (1700-1748), *Hymn*. A passage from this poem concludes chapter 3.
[4] James 1:17.
[5] Reference to Job 7:17, Ps. 144:3, Heb. 2:6-8.
[6] John 1:1.
[7] See Luke 4:1, 4:18, John 3:34, 20:22, Acts 10:38, Rom. 8:9-10, 1 Cor. 25:45, Eph. 3:16-17.
[8] See the Old Testament prophecies concerning the Anointed One: Ps. 45:2-7, 110:1-4, Isa. 9:6-7, 11:1-9, 61:1-2, Dan. 7:13-14, 9:24-25.
[9] See Matt. 16:13-17, 22:41-46, Luke 4:16-22, John 4:25-26.
[10] John 1:14. See also John 1:18, 5:22-23, 14:9-10, 2 Cor. 5:19, Col. 1:19-20, Phil. 2:9-11.
[11] John 1:1-14.

[12] Prov. 8:22-36.

[13] 2 Cor. 10:13.

[14] John 6:35-38, 8:12, 8:58. See also John 6:32-37, 6:51, 8:38, 14:9-10, 27:5.

[15] Mark 10:18, Matt. 26:38, 27:46. See also John 8:28, 14:10.

[16] Rom. 5:11.

[17] Heb. 2:1-2. See also Eph. 2:20, 2 Tim. 3:16, 1 Pet. 1:11-12, 2 Pet. 1:21.

[18] Luke 20:34-38. See also Matt. 26:52, Luke 2:13-14, 9:30-31, Acts 24:15, Rom. 14:9, 2 Cor. 5:1-9, Heb. 1:6-7, 1:14, 12:22-23, 1 Pet. 3:18-20, 4:5-6.

[19] Luke 24:38-40, John 20:27.

[20] 1 Cor. 15:50; reference to 1 Cor. 15:42-44, 2 Cor. 5:1-8.

[21] John 5:28-29.

[22] 1 Cor. 15:51-52.

[23] 1 Thess. 4:16-17.

[24] 2 Cor. 5:4, Rev. 21:4; reference to Rev. 21:3-5.

[25] 1 Cor. 15:26-28.

[26] Rom. 11:36.

[27] Luke 12:48, Matt. 25:14-29.

[28] Matt. 16:27, 2 Cor. 5:10. See also Matt. 12:36, Luke 12:47-48, Rom. 2:6,11, Gal. 6:7-8, Col. 3:25.

[29] Reference to Matt. 7:16-20.

[30] 1 Cor. 12:31.

[31] John 4:8,16.

[32] Heb. 12:9-10.

[33] Matt. 25:46.

[34] John 3:3, 6. See also John 1:12-13, 1 Cor. 2:14-15, 2 Cor. 5:17, Gal. 6:15, Eph. 2:1-5, Titus 3:5, 1 Pet. 1:23, 1 John 4:7-8.

[35] Mark 4:28.

[36] Rom. 7:14, 18, 22-24. See also Rom. 8:5-9, 2 Cor. 10:4-5, Gal. 5:16-17, Eph. 6:10-13.

[37] 1 Cor. 15:55-58. See also Matt. 3:11-12, 5:17-18, 6:9-10, 12:18-20, 13:31-33, 18:11, 28:18, Luke 2:10-14, John 1:29, 3:17, 3:35, 6:38-39, 12:32, Acts 3:20-21, 10:42, Rom. 5:20-21, 8:19-22, 11:32-36, 14:8-9, 1 Cor. 15:22-28, Eph. 1:8-10, 1:20-23, 4:8-13, Phil. 2:9-11, Col. 1:19-20, 1 Tim. 2:1-6, Heb. 2:9, 2:14-15, 1 John 3:8, 4:8-14, Rev. 21:1-5.

[38] Rom. 3:4, 11:36.

[39] From Alexander Pope, *Essay on Man*, Epistle I.

[40] Closing lines of James Thomson, *Hymn*.

Chapter 3: Principles of Personal Righteousness

[1] Ps. 111:10. See also Prov. 1:7, 9:10, Sirach 1:14.

[2] Reference to Matt. 7:14 and Prov. 3:17.

[3] Luke 9:25. See also Matt. 10:36-38.

[4] Ps. 116:11.

[5] 1 John 4:16.

[6] Reference to Luke 2:14, Matt. 6:10, Rev. 21:4-5.

[7] Matt. 5:43-48.

[8] 1 Cor. 13:2-3.

[9] Opening lines of Matthew Prior (1664-1721), *Charity: a paraphrase on the thirteenth chapter of the first epistle to the Corinthians* (incorrectly attributed by Ballou to Cowper).

[10] Reference to Exod. 28:36, 39:30, 2 Cor. 7:1.

[11] Thomas à Kempis, *Imitation of Christ* 3:21 (incorrectly identified by Ballou as 3:14).

[12] 2 Cor. 8:9, Matt. 5:48. See also John 17:22-23, Phil. 3:12-14, Col. 1:28, Eph. 4:13.

Chapter 4: Principles of Social Order

[1] John 8:42-44.

[2] Luke 6:35, Matt. 23:9, Eph. 4:6. See also Acts 17:24-30, 1 Cor. 8:5-6, Heb. 12:9-10, James 1:17.

[3] 1 John 4:8-19. See also John 3:16-17, Luke 6:35, Rom. 5:8, Eph. 2:4-5.

[4] Mark 12:30-33, also Deut. 6:5, 10:12, Matt. 22:37, Luke 10:27.

[5] Mark 12:31, Matt. 7:12, 1 John 4:20. See also Rom. 13:10, 1 Cor. 13:1-7, 1 John 3:14-17, 4:7-16.

[6] Matt. 5:43-48.

[7] Matt. 18:15-17.

[8] Eph. 5:11. See also Matt. 10:34-38, 15:13, 2 Cor. 6:14-18, 2 Thess. 3:6.

[9] Heb. 12:6.

[10] 1 John 2:6, Luke 23:34.

[11] Matt. 5:38-48.

[12] Rom. 12:14-21.

[13] 1 Thess. 5:15. See also Matt. 10:26, 26:52, Luke 9:54-55, John 18:36, 1 Pet. 2:19-23.

[14] Gen. 4:9.

[15] 1 Cor. 13:1.

[16] Reference to Luke 16:19-21.

[17] Ps. 133:1.

[18] Luke 9:46-48.

[19] John 13:13-17, 13:34-35.

[20] Acts 2: 44-45, 4:32-34.

[21] Rom. 12:4-16.

[22] 1 Cor. 12:12-27. See also Matt. 7: 25-30, 20:25-28, John 10:16, 17:20-22, Acts 20:33-36, Rom. 15:1-2, 6, 11, 1 Cor. 3:3-9, 6:1, 6:5-7, 10:24, Eph. 4:1-16, 1 Pet. 2:9.

The Constitution of the Practical Christian Republic

[1] Matt. 20:27.

Chapter 5: Objects, Principles, and Policies

[1] Ezek. 1:16.

[2] Luke 7:35.

[3] Rom. 13:1.

[4] Gen. 2:23.

[5] Isa. 45:9.

[6] Reference to Matt. 9:17, Mark 2:22, Luke 5:37-39.

[7] Reference to Acts 24-25, Matt. 27:11-14. See also Mark 15:2-5, Luke 23:1-3, John 18:33-38.

Chapter 6: Rights and Property

[1] Luke 16:21.

[2] Matt. 6:34.

[3] Reference to Judges 7:2-7. "And the Lord said unto Gideon, The people are yet too many, bring them down unto the water, and I will try them for thee there ... Every one that lappeth of the water with his tongue, as a dog lappeth, him shalt thou set by himself, likewise every one that boweth down upon his knees to drink ... And the Lord said unto Gideon, By the three hundred men that lapped will I save you, and deliver the Midianites into thine hand."

Chapter 7: Membership, Organization, and Government

[1] Isa. 53:2.

[2] Reference to Micah 5:2; see also Matt. 6:2.

Chapter 8: Education for Health of Body, Mind, and Spirit

[1] Alexander Pope, *Moral Essays*, Epistle I.

[2] Mark 5:9.

[3] 2 Kings 5:13-14.

[4] Attributed to the Dutch physician Herman Boerhaave (1668-1738).

[5] Reference to James 2:26, John 14:15.

Chapter 9: Education for Community Life

[1] Alexander Pope, *Essay on Man*, Epistle IV.

[2] Exod. 20:12.

[3] Paraphrase of Gen. 6:5.

[4] Plato, *Gorgias* 473a-475e.

[5] Paraphrase of Isa. 28:10.

[6] Col 1:12.

[7] Reference to *Hamlet* III.i.

[8] Reference to Matt. 17:20.

[9] Eccles. 3:1-4.

Chapter 10: Education for Sex, Marriage, and Family Life

[1] Reference to Ex. 3:5.

[2] Matt. 7:16-20.

[3] Benjamin Franklin, *Poor Richard's Almanac.*

[4] Matt. 7:16.

[5] Reference to Ecclesiasticus 31:1.

[6] John Milton, *Paradise Lost* 2.996.

[7] Mark 10:1-12.

[8] Matt. 5:31-32.

Afterword

[1] Reference to Judges 7:16. "And he divided the three hundred men into three companies, and he put a trumpet in every man's hand, with empty pitchers, and lamps within the pitchers."

[2] Reference to 2 Chron. 34:2.

[3] Rom. 1:16.

[4] Reference to Matt. 11:25.

[5] Reference to Matt. 13:33. See also 1 Cor. 5:6-7, Gal. 5:9.

[6] Luke 12:32.

[7] Reference to Luke 17:21. "Neither shall they say, Lo here! or, lo there! for, behold, the kingdom of God is within you."

[8] Micah 4:4.

[9] Matt. 6:10, Rom. 11:36.